JESUS IS: THE FIRSTBORN He is the image of the invisible God, the firstborn of all creation (Colossians 1:15) **FORGIVENESS** "For I will be merciful towards their iniquities, and I will remember their sins no more" (Hebrews 8:12) **DELIVERER** "The Spirit of the Lord is upon me, because he has anointed me to proclaim good news to the poor. He has sent me to proclaim liberty to the captives and recovering of sight to the blind, to set at liberty those who are oppressed" (Luke 4:18) **SERVANT** "even as the Son of Man came not to be served but to serve, and to give his life as a ransom for many" (Matthew 20:28) **REWARDER** And without faith it is impossible to please him, for whoever would draw near to God must believe that he exists and that he rewards those who seek him (Hebrews 11:6) **KNOWLEDGE** in whom are hidden all the treasures of wisdom and knowledge (Colossians 2:3) **PEACE** "I have said these things to you, that in me you may have peace. In the world you will have tribulation. But take heart; I have overcome the world" (John 16:33) **RIGHTEOUSNESS** Therefore, as one trespass led to condemnation for all men, so one act of righteousness leads to justification and life for all men (Romans 5:18) **WISDOM** And because of him you are in Christ Jesus, who became to us wisdom from God, righteousness and sanctification and redemption (1 Corinthians 1:30) **GLORY** And the Word became flesh and dwelt among us, and we have seen his glory, glory as of the only Son from the Father, full of grace and truth (John 1:14) **KING OF KINGS AND LORD OF LORDS** On his robe and on his thigh he has a name written, King of kings and Lord of lords (Revelation 19:16) **PROMISE** So when God desired to show more convincingly to the heirs of the promise the unchangeable character of his purpose, he guaranteed it with an oath, so that by two unchangeable things, in which it is impossible for God to lie, we who have fled for refuge might have strong encouragement to hold fast to the hope set before us (Hebrews 6:17-18) **GOODNESS** Oh, how abundant is your goodness, which you have stored up for those who fear you and worked for those who take refuge in you, in the sight of the children of mankind! (Psalm 31:19) **LOVE** nor height nor depth, nor anything else in all creation, will be able to separate us from the love of God in Christ Jesus our Lord (Romans 8:39) **HIS WORD IS ENOUGH** so shall my word be that goes out from my mouth; it shall not return to me empty, but it shall accomplish that which I purpose, and shall succeed in the thing for which I sent it (Isaiah 55:11) **HIS GRACE IS SUFFICIENT** By Silvanus, a faithful brother as I regard him, I have written briefly to you, exhorting and declaring that this is the true grace of God. Stand firm in it (1 Peter 5:12) **INCOMPREHENSIBLE** But, as it is written, "What no eye has seen, nor ear heard, nor the heart of man imagined, what God has prepared for those who love him" (1 Corinthians 2:9) **BEGINNING AND END** "I am the Alpha and the Omega, the first and the last, the beginning and the end" (Revelation 22:13) **YOU CAN'T LIVE WITHOUT HIM** All things were made through him, and without him was not any thing made that was made. In him was life, and the life was the light of men (John 1:3-4) **DEATH COULDN'T HANDLE HIM** We know that Christ, being raised from the dead, will never die again; death no longer has dominion over him (Romans 6:9) **DELIGHT** Your words were found, and I ate them, and your words became to me a joy and the delight of my heart, for I am called by your name, O Lord, God of hosts (Jeremiah 15:16) **PURPOSE** that is, in Christ God was reconciling the world to himself, not counting their trespasses against them, and entrusting to us the message of reconciliation (2 Corinthians 5:19) **HEALER** He himself bore our sins in his body on the tree, that we might die to sin and live to righteousness. By his wounds you have been healed (1 Peter 2:24) **SAVIOUR** And we have seen and testify that the Father has sent his Son to be the Saviour of the world (1 John 4:14) **BRIGHT AND MORNING STAR** "I, Jesus, have sent my angel to testify to you about these things for the churches. I am the root and the descendant of David, the bright morning star" (Revelation 22:16) **THE GOOD SHEPHERD** "I am the good shepherd. The good shepherd lays down his life for the sheep" (John 10:11) **THE WAY, THE TRUTH, THE LIFE** Jesus said to him, "I am the way, and the truth, and the life. No one comes to the Father except through me" (John 14:6) **ABOVE EVERY NAME** far above all rule and authority and power and dominion, and above every name that is named, not only in this age but also in the one to come (Ephesians 1:21) **WONDERFUL** For to us a child is born, to us a son is given; and the government shall be upon his shoulder, and his name shall be called Wonderful Counsellor, Mighty God, Everlasting Father, Prince of Peace (Isaiah 9:6) **UNCHANGING** Jesus Christ is the same yesterday and today and for ever (Hebrews 13:8) **HE IS GOD** In the beginning was the Word, and the Word was with God, and the Word was God (John 1:1) **CREATOR OF ALL THINGS** For by him all things were created, in heaven and on earth, visible and invisible, whether thrones or dominions or rulers or authorities—all things were created through him and for him (Colossians 1:16) **ALL POWERFUL** And Jesus came and said to them, "All authority in heaven and on earth has been given to me" (Matthew 28:18) **SINLESS** For our sake he made him to be sin who knew no sin, so that in him we might become the righteousness of God (2 Corinthians 5:21) **GENTLE** "Take my yoke upon you, and learn from me, for I am gentle and lowly in heart, and you will find rest for your souls" (Matthew 11:29) **HIGH PRIEST** Therefore he had to be made like his brothers in every respect, so that he might become a merciful and faithful high priest in the service of God, to make propitiation for the sins of the people (Hebrews 2:17) **HUMAN/GOD** For there is one God, and there is one mediator between God and men, the man Christ Jesus (1 Timothy 2:5) **ADVOCATE** My little children, I am writing these things to you so that you may not sin. But if anyone does sin, we have an advocate with the Father, Jesus Christ the righteous. (1 John 2:1) **ETERNAL LIFE** For God so loved the world, that he gave his only Son, that whoever believes in him should not perish but have eternal life (John 3:16) **SON OF GOD** Simon Peter replied, "You are the Christ, the Son of the living God" (Matthew 16:16) **CORNERSTONE** Jesus said to them, "Have you never read in the Scriptures: 'The stone that the builders rejected has become the cornerstone; this was the Lord's doing, and it is marvellous in our eyes'?" (Matthew 21:42) **FAITH-HOPE-LOVE** So now faith, hope, and love abide, these three; but the greatest of these is love (1 Corinthians 13:13)

𝕴nspired by the 𝕳oly 𝕾pirit

THE NEW TESTAMENT EXPERIENCE

THE GOSPELS FOR THE MODERN WORLD

PRESENTED TO

. . . .

BY

. . . .

DATE

. . . .

SCRIPTURE

. . . .

Collins, a division of HarperCollins*Publishers*
1 London Bridge Street, London SE1 9GF

This edition first published in Great Britain in 2019 by HarperCollins*Publishers*

The Holy Bible, English Standard Version® (ESV® © 2001 by Crossway,
a publishing ministry of Good News Publishers. All rights reserved.
Anglicized edition © 2002 HarperCollins*Publishers* ESV Text Edition 2016

The Holy Bible, English Standard Version (ESV) is adapted from the Revised Standard Version
of the Bible, © Division of Christian Education of the National Council of the
Churches of Christ in the USA. All rights reserved.

A catalogue record for this book is available from the British Library

ISBN 978-0-00-831743-0

ISBN 978-0-00-797735-2

1

ABRUPT MEDIA

THE NEW TESTAMENT
EXPERIENCE

THE GOSPELS FOR THE MODERN WORLD

ESV

Collins
SINCE 1819

THE TRUE LIGHT,

which enlightens everyone, was coming into the world. He was in the world, and the world was made through him, yet the world did not know him. He came to his own, and his own people did not receive him. But to all who did receive him, who believed in his name, he gave the right to become children of God, who were born, not of blood nor of the will of the flesh nor of the will of man, but of God. And the Word became flesh and dwelt among us, and we have seen his glory, glory as of the only Son from the Father, full of grace and truth.

John 1:9-14

ESV PREFACE

THE BIBLE

The words of the Bible are the very words of God our Creator speaking to us. They are completely truthful; they are pure; they are powerful; and they are wise and righteous. We should read these words with reverence and awe, and with joy and delight. Through these words God gives us eternal life and daily nourishes our spiritual lives.

THE ESV TRANSLATION

The English Standard Version® (ESV®) stands in the classic stream of English Bible translations that goes back nearly five centuries. In this stream, accurate faithfulness to the original text is combined with simplicity, beauty, and dignity of expression. Our goal has been to carry forward this legacy for a new century.

The ESV is an "essentially literal" translation that seeks as far as possible to capture the meaning and structure of the original text and the personal style of each Bible writer. We have sought to be "as literal as possible" while maintaining clear expression and literary excellence. Therefore the ESV is well suited for both personal reading and church ministry, for devotional reflection and serious study, and for Scripture memorization.

THE ESV PUBLISHING TEAM

The ESV publishing team includes more than a hundred people. The fourteen-member Translation Oversight Committee has benefited from the work of fifty biblical experts serving as Translation Review Scholars and from the comments of the more than fifty members of the Advisory Council. This international team from many denominations shares a common commitment to the truth of God's Word and to historic Christian orthodoxy.

TO GOD'S HONOUR AND PRAISE

We know that no Bible translation is perfect or final; but we also know that God uses imperfect and inadequate things to his honour and praise. So to God the Father, Son, and Holy Spirit—and to his people—we offer what we have done, with our prayers that it may prove useful, with gratitude for much help given, and with ongoing wonder that our God should ever have entrusted to us so momentous a task.

To God alone be the glory!
The Translation Oversight Committee

Inspired by the Holy Spirit

CONTENTS

MATTHEW ✝ MARK ✝ LUKE ✝ JOHN

THE TRUE LIGHT, WHICH GIVES LIGHT TO EVERYONE, WAS COMING INTO THE WORLD.
John 1:9

MATTHEW
THE KINGDOM OF HEAVEN
LONDON, GB
P16

MARK
SERVANT KING
NEW YORK, USA
P96

LUKE
SAVIOUR FOR ALL
SYDNEY, AUS
P156

JOHN
JESUS IS GOD
BOGOTÁ, COL
P234

The Gospels

CONTENTS

MATTHEW / MARK / LUKE / JOHN

Welcome
PAGE 8

The Life of Jesus
PAGE 12

Prayer
PAGE 34

The Church
PAGE 58

The Holy Spirit
PAGE 104

The Gospel
PAGE 170

The Bible
PAGE 246

Grace
PAGE 296

Jesus Is
PAGE 309

Salvation Prayer
PAGE 315

JESUS SAID TO THEM, "I AM THE BREAD OF LIFE; WHOEVER COMES TO ME SHALL NOT HUNGER,
AND WHOEVER BELIEVES IN ME SHALL NEVER THIRST."
John 6:35

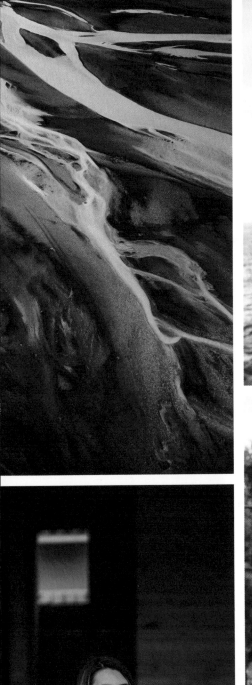

THE NEW TESTAMENT EXPERIENCE: THE GOSPELS FOR THE MODERN WORLD

Welcome to *The New Testament Experience : The Gospels for the Modern World*. This visual representation of the Gospels was created with your relationship to Jesus and his Church at its heart.

We don't just read the Bible, we experience it because the Bible is living and breathing. In the Gospel of John, we are told Jesus is the word of God and in the book of Hebrews it says, *"For the word of God is living and active, sharper than any two-edged sword, piercing to the division of soul and of spirit, of joints and of marrow, and discerning the thoughts and intentions of the heart"* (4:12-13). What you're holding is God's thoughts and intents towards us. Jesus reveals himself through the words, they transform us as we put our faith and our confidence in him and what he has said. God says that if we align our thinking and lives with his word, that we'll be transformed from the inside out. His word reveals the truth about who we are in Jesus Christ and his redeeming love towards us.

God worked through an array of authors to get his message to us, that we are known and called by name to be reconciled to him through his Son, Jesus Christ. We can therefore live a life that reflects his grace and the gift of righteousness. He is the one bringing the whole story of scripture together and completing the promise of reconciliation that we read of in the Gospels.

THE MISSION OF JESUS

The final three-and-a-half years of Jesus' life changed the trajectory of the human race for ever. As the Redeemer and Saviour of humanity, he immersed himself by becoming human so that he could take away the sins of the world and bridge the gap between us and God the Father. The revelation of how we could be reconciled to God is detailed in the Gospels through the life of Jesus and what he shared about his Father, himself and the ways of his kingdom. His life ignited the disciples who followed him. Inspired by the Holy Spirit, they went on to start the early church and write the letters we now know as the Gospels.

The church, which is also referred to as his body, is the community in which we as believers grow in our relationship with Jesus. It's the very thing that Jesus said he would build in Matthew 16:18. The message of Jesus is about his relationship with you and the relationships you have within his church.

Regardless of the circumstances we face, or the narrative of the people around us,

THE FINAL THREE-AND-A-HALF YEARS OF
JESUS' LIFE CHANGED THE TRAJECTORY OF THE
HUMAN RACE FOR EVER. AS THE REDEEMER AND
SAVIOUR OF HUMANITY, HE IMMERSED HIMSELF BY
BECOMING HUMAN SO THAT HE COULD TAKE AWAY
THE SINS OF THE WORLD AND BRIDGE THE GAP
BETWEEN US AND GOD THE FATHER.

we can go to the word and find the truth of God for our everyday lives. God gave us his word so that we could learn how to navigate life, where we can find God's thoughts on all aspects of life, such as relationships, finances and health. In an age when individualism is promoted, and loneliness is an epidemic, the Bible directs us to God's plan for humanity. God's word goes beyond the surface of today's culture and reveals the truth of God's eternal kingdom through the life of Jesus.

MAGAZINE FORMAT

So here you are, thousands of years after the words were first written down, holding what looks like a magazine, full of images of everyday people from all over the world. These are the same scriptures, communicated in a language that makes you see Jesus' life and love for you from a new perspective, from the perspective of your own personal, daily life.

So, why create such a book? Aren't the scriptures holy and not to be touched? Well, they are holy: in John it says that Jesus is the Word in flesh and blood. This visual book isn't looking to replace his holy Scripture or water it down any more that the painters of biblical artwork or makers of stained glass windows in churches hundreds of years ago were trying to. The scriptures, the photography, the illustration, everything is about pointing to and visually illustrating the life of Jesus and the lives he impacted.

Jesus himself taught using parables, stories with a deeper meaning, designed to teach the listener and introduce them to the ways of God's kingdom. They create a mental picture the listener can relate, understand and respond to. The purpose of this book is to bring the characters to life, to help you visualize, remember and connect with the stories and key scriptures. The Gospels give us a better understanding of the true nature of Jesus, his character, why he came, what he accomplished, and what it means to our lives today.

This book was created by the church, for the church. The desire of the team is to present the truth of God and his kingdom in a way that is beautiful, relevant, and authentic. God is raising up a generation of people passionate about communicating the truth in a way that will inspire people and point them to Jesus. We are honoured to play our part and hope this Bible helps you in your walk with Jesus and his church.

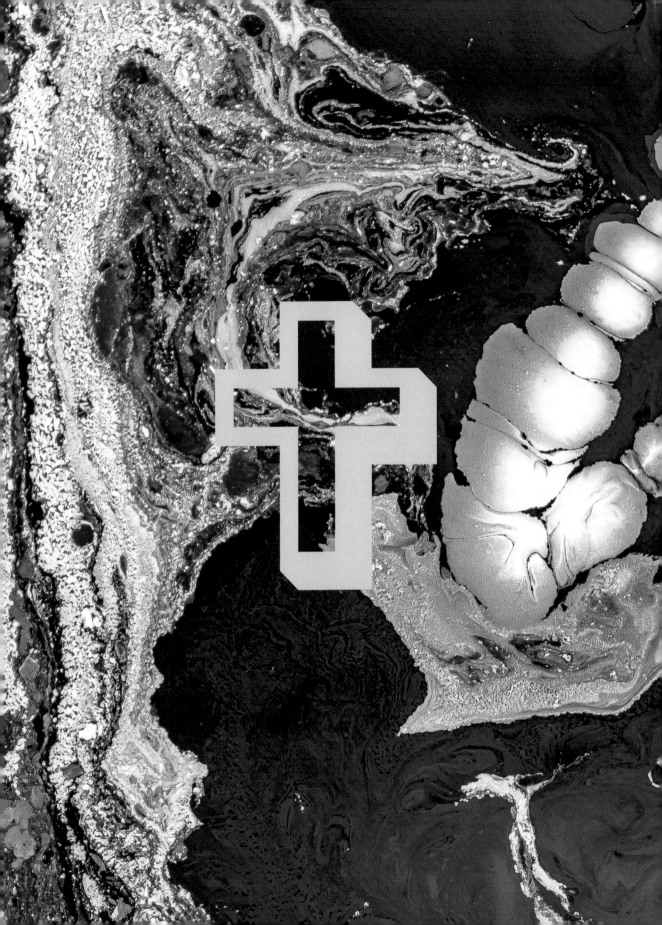

God himself became a person: he walked with us, talked with us and shared his daily life with us.

THE LIFE OF JESUS

The four Gospels (literally, "good news") of the New Testament are memoirs to the most exceptional event in human history: God himself stepping down from heaven and walking the earth he created. The writers of each letter—Matthew, Mark, Luke and John—were ordinary men who witnessed an extraordinary life, and were compelled by the Holy Spirit to record their experiences so others could understand the magnitude of the life of Jesus Christ.

When John ventured to introduce us to the life of Jesus, he penned a prologue of such simple clarity that it was not beyond the grasp of a young child, yet of such endless intricacy that it has tested the mettle of the most learned intellects of the last two thousand years of human history:

And the Word became flesh and dwelt among us, and we have seen his glory, glory as of the only Son from the Father, full of grace and truth.
John 1:14

Pause and consider that for just a moment.

God himself became a person: he walked with us, talked with us and shared his daily life with us. At the same time, God himself experienced the full range of joys and sorrows that are common to all of humanity. The four Gospels are the profound record of time when God himself came and lived amongst us.

If these historical records are accurate (and there's significant, detailed and widely-available research to show that they are), then the Gospels are our primary way of understanding the nature and character of God. If what these four letters report of Jesus are true, then they transcend all other writings, elevate us into the realm of the Divine and provide us with an intimate insight into our Creator. So let's not underestimate the magnitude of these four books in front of us: having access to these letters is akin to Hamlet reading a biography of Shakespeare, Mona Lisa understanding the musings of Da Vinci, or the statue of David being able to comprehend the plans of Michelangelo. It is the created looking into the very mind of the Creator.

As we read through the Gospels, we are struck with two powerful thoughts. One: God knows us. Two: God can be known. As Jesus went about his daily activities, he intentionally intertwined his life with a broad array of people. In doing so, he demonstrated the kind of intimate knowledge of each person that can only come from an all-knowing God. Upon first meeting a young man called Nathanael, Jesus told him that he had seen him sitting alone under a fig tree, and that he knew he was a trustworthy person (John 1:47-48). When he first met a woman from the neighbouring region of Samaria, Jesus surprised her by describing her chequered marital history (John 4:18). He even knew the hearts of people who would betray him (Matthew 26:23, 34; Mark 2:6-8).

In the Gospels,
Jesus shows us that
each one of us is fully
known, and deeply
important to God.

These are but a few examples of God's close and intimate knowledge of every one of us. He knows our hopes and our fears, our joys and our shame. He knows us more than we know ourselves. Like a consummate parent, he knows what brings out the best in us, and what drives our insecurities: yet he still loves us perfectly. In the Gospels, Jesus shows us that each one of us is fully known, and deeply important to God.

Additionally, the Gospels show us that God knows us not only individually but collectively. By "putting on flesh", the infinite and all-powerful God astonishingly chose to confine himself to a finite, frail and vulnerable human body. We read in the Gospels that Jesus showed the full range of human emotions: he hungered and thirsted and became tired, but he also knew what it was like to share a meal with a friend and to be revitalized by genuine human connection. He celebrated when those around him experienced success, but he was moved with compassion when he saw injustice. He openly wept at the loss of a friend, but he fondly told stories of the joy experienced when a friend returned; he marvelled at loyalty, was patient with disbelief, and scorned hypocrisy. Most importantly, he loved deeply — and he was deeply hurt when that love was betrayed. By incarcerating himself in human vulnerability, Jesus made a way for God to understand our weaknesses and empathize with our collective, delicate humanity. Through the Gospels, Jesus shows us that God "gets" us, on our good days and our bad.

Not only does God know us, but the Gospels testify that God can be known. More tellingly, God desires to be known, and was purposeful in revealing himself to us through Jesus. Throughout the four letters, we see that Jesus was unapologetic in declaring that to see and know him was equivalent to seeing and knowing God himself (John 10:30, 14:9). If it is true that this first-century Nazarene arrived to reveal the God of the universe, what kind of God do we see revealed? The first revelation that becomes obvious through the life of Jesus is God's unmatched greatness. From God's ability to create biological human life outside of the typical parameters of conception, to Jesus' ability to calm storms, walk on water, bring sight to the blind, defy illness, subdue demons and call the dead to return to life, we are reminded God must be known as the Almighty and Sovereign God. His power is unlimited and unrivalled in all of creation.

A second observation from the life of Jesus is God's unmerited goodness. Both Jesus' words and his actions indicate God's intention to use his power to set things right. Pain, oppression, lack and rebellion are affronts to God's care and compassion for his creation, and stain the beauty of life lived under God's reign and Kingdom. Jesus' teaching encourages his followers to give attention and preference to others, and to seek the good of others first. All of Jesus' miracles are indications of this goodness in action and give a hint of a future to come: that day when God finally abolishes sickness, drives away injustice and wipes every tear from every eye.

It is the meeting of God's greatness with his goodness, as seen explicitly through the life of Jesus as recorded in the Gospels, that gives us hope. We see that God did not just set the world in motion and then abandon us to our own fate. He broke into our world through Jesus, revealing himself as a God who knows and wants to be known, and he slowly but surely began to set things right again. This is the story of the Gospels, and as you will see as you read, it is the story that you are invited to play a part in.

MATTHEW

THE NEW TESTAMENT EXPERIENCE

Inspired by the Holy Spirit

THE KINGDOM OF HEAVEN

WRITTEN BY MATTHEW THE EVANGELIST

ALL THIS TOOK PLACE TO FULFIL WHAT THE LORD HAD SPOKEN BY THE PROPHET:
"BEHOLD, THE VIRGIN SHALL CONCEIVE AND BEAR A SON, AND THEY SHALL CALL HIS NAME
IMMANUEL" (WHICH MEANS, GOD WITH US). Matthew 1:22-23

IMPORTANT STORIES IN MATTHEW

The Visit of the Wise Men: Matthew 2:1-12 **Baptism of Jesus:** Matthew 3:13-17 **Temptation of Jesus:** Matthew 4:1-11
Blessing of Christ's People: Matthew 5:1-12 **The Lord's Prayer:** Matthew 6:9-13 **Jesus Feeds a Large Crowd:** Matthew 14:13-21
Parable of the Lost Sheep: Matthew 18:10-14 **The Triumphal Entry:** Matthew 21:1-11 **Jesus Suffers and Dies:** Matthew 27:32-56
Jesus Is Alive Again: Matthew 28:1-10 **Jesus Gives Instruction:** Matthew 28:16-20

𝔍𝔫𝔰𝔭𝔦𝔯𝔢𝔡 𝔟𝔶 𝔱𝔥𝔢 𝔥𝔬𝔩𝔶 𝔖𝔭𝔦𝔯𝔦𝔱

INTRODUCTION TO MATTHEW

LONDON, GREAT BRITAIN

AUTHOR, DATE AND AUDIENCE

Matthew was probably written in the late 50s or early 60s AD. Matthew
(also called Levi), the former tax collector who became Jesus' disciple, is the author.
The original audience may have been the church in Antioch of Syria. Its members
included non-Jewish and Christians.

THEME AND PURPOSE

Matthew tells the story of Jesus of Nazareth, the long-expected Messiah
who brought the kingdom of heaven to earth.

Matthew writes his Gospel to demonstrate that Jesus is the Messiah, that he has
the right to the throne of David as Israel's true king, and that he is the ultimate fulfilment
of God's promise to Abraham that his descendant would be a blessing to all the world
(Matthew 1:1; Genesis 12:1-3). Matthew seeks to encourage Jewish Christians (and all future
disciples) to stand strong despite opposition. They should feel secure in the knowledge
of their citizenship in God's kingdom. Matthew shows that Gentiles can also
find salvation through Jesus the Messiah.

AND JESUS ANSWERED HIM,
"BLESSED ARE YOU, SIMON BAR-JONAH!
FOR FLESH AND BLOOD HAS NOT REVEALED THIS
TO YOU, BUT MY FATHER WHO IS IN HEAVEN. AND
I TELL YOU, YOU ARE PETER, AND ON THIS ROCK I
WILL BUILD MY CHURCH, AND THE GATES OF
HELL SHALL NOT PREVAIL AGAINST IT."

Matthew 16:17-18

✝

Chapter One
The Genealogy of Jesus Christ

The book of the genealogy of Jesus Christ, the son of David, the son of Abraham. ²Abraham was the father of Isaac, and Isaac the father of Jacob, and Jacob the father of Judah and his brothers, ³and Judah the father of Perez and Zerah by Tamar, and Perez the father of Hezron, and Hezron the father of Ram, ⁴and Ram the father of Amminadab, and Amminadab the father of Nahshon, and Nahshon the father of Salmon, ⁵and Salmon the father of Boaz by Rahab, and Boaz the father of Obed by Ruth, and Obed the father of Jesse, ⁶and Jesse the father of David the king.

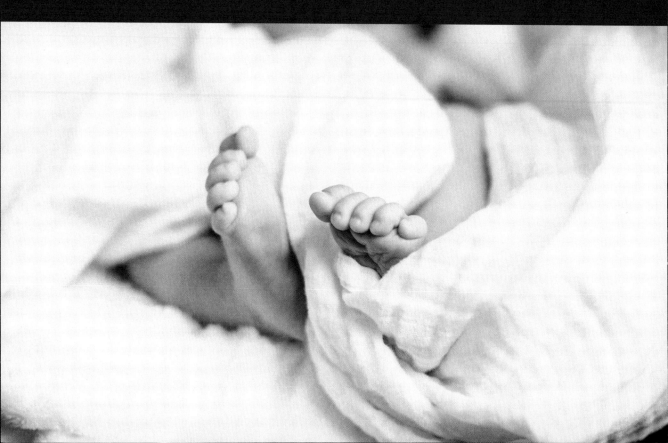

And David was the father of Solomon by the wife of Uriah, ⁷and Solomon the father of Rehoboam, and Rehoboam the father of Abijah, and Abijah the father of Asaph, ⁸and Asaph the father of Jehoshaphat, and Jehoshaphat the father of Joram, and Joram the father of Uzziah, ⁹and Uzziah the father of Jotham, and Jotham the father of Ahaz, and Ahaz the father of Hezekiah, ¹⁰and Hezekiah the father of Manasseh, and Manasseh the father of Amos, and Amos the father of Josiah, ¹¹and Josiah the father of Jechoniah and his brothers, at the time of the deportation to Babylon.

¹²And after the deportation to Babylon: Jechoniah was the father of Shealtiel, and Shealtiel the father of Zerubbabel, ¹³and Zerubbabel the father of Abiud, and Abiud the father of Eliakim, and Eliakim the father of Azor, ¹⁴and Azor the father of Zadok, and Zadok the father of Achim, and Achim the father of Eliud, ¹⁵and Eliud the father of Eleazar, and Eleazar the father of Matthan, and Matthan the father of Jacob, ¹⁶and Jacob the father of Joseph the husband of Mary, of whom Jesus was born, who is called Christ.

¹⁷So all the generations from Abraham to David were fourteen generations, and from David to the deportation to Babylon fourteen generations, and from the deportation to Babylon to the Christ fourteen generations.

The Birth of Jesus Christ

¹⁸Now the birth of Jesus Christ took place in this way. When his mother Mary had been betrothed to Joseph, before they came together she was found to be with child from the Holy Spirit. ¹⁹And her husband Joseph, being a just man and unwilling to put her to shame, resolved to divorce her quietly. ²⁰But as he considered these things, behold, an angel of the Lord appeared to him in a dream, saying, "Joseph, son of David, do not fear to take Mary as your wife, for that which is conceived in her is from the Holy Spirit. ²¹She will bear a son, and you shall call his name Jesus, for he will save his people from their sins." ²²All this took place to fulfil what the Lord had spoken by the prophet:

²³ "Behold, the virgin shall conceive
and bear a son,
and they shall call his name
Immanuel"

(which means, God with us). ²⁴When Joseph woke from sleep, he did as the angel of the Lord commanded him: he took his wife, ²⁵but knew her not until she had given birth to a son. And he called his name Jesus.

Chapter Two
The Visit of the Wise Men

Now after Jesus was born in Bethlehem of Judea in the days of Herod the king, behold, wise men from the east came to Jerusalem, ² saying, "Where is he who has been born king of the Jews? For we saw his star when it rose and have come to worship him." ³ When Herod the king heard this, he was troubled, and all Jerusalem with him; ⁴ and assembling all the chief priests and scribes of the people, he enquired of them where the Christ was to be born. ⁵ They told him, "In Bethlehem of Judea, for so it is written by the prophet:

⁶ "'And you, O Bethlehem, in the
    land of Judah,
    are by no means least among
        the rulers of Judah;
    for from you shall come a ruler
        who will shepherd my people
        Israel.'"

⁷ Then Herod summoned the wise men secretly and ascertained from them what time the star had appeared. ⁸ And he sent them to Bethlehem, saying, "Go and search diligently for the child, and when you have found him, bring me word, that I too may come and worship him." ⁹ After listening to the king, they went on their way. And behold, the star that they had seen when it rose went before them until it came to rest over the place where the child was. ¹⁰ When they saw the star, they rejoiced exceedingly with great joy. ¹¹ And going into the house, they saw the child with Mary his mother, and they fell down and worshipped him. Then, opening their treasures, they offered him gifts, gold and frankincense and myrrh. ¹² And being warned in a dream not to return to Herod, they departed to their own country by another way.

AN ANGEL OF THE
LORD APPEARED IN A
DREAM TO JOSEPH IN
EGYPT, SAYING, "RISE,
TAKE THE CHILD AND
HIS MOTHER AND GO TO
THE LAND OF ISRAEL,
FOR THOSE WHO
SOUGHT THE CHILD'S
LIFE ARE DEAD."

Matthew 2:19-20

The Flight to Egypt

¹³ Now when they had departed, behold, an angel of the Lord appeared to Joseph in a dream and said, "Rise, take the child and his mother, and flee to Egypt, and remain there until I tell you, for Herod is about to search for the child, to destroy him." ¹⁴ And he rose and took the child and his mother by night and departed to Egypt ¹⁵ and remained there until the death of Herod. This was to fulfil what the Lord had spoken by the prophet, "Out of Egypt I called my son."

Herod Kills the Children

¹⁶ Then Herod, when he saw that he had been tricked by the wise men, became furious, and he sent and killed all the male children in Bethlehem and in all that region who were two years old or under, according to the time that he had ascertained from the wise men. ¹⁷ Then was fulfilled what was spoken by the prophet Jeremiah:

¹⁸ "A voice was heard in Ramah,
    weeping and loud lamentation,
 Rachel weeping for her children;
    she refused to be comforted,
        because they are no more."

The Return to Nazareth

¹⁹ But when Herod died, behold, an angel of the Lord appeared in a dream to Joseph in Egypt, ²⁰ saying, "Rise, take the child and his mother and go to the land of Israel, for those who sought the child's life are dead." ²¹ And he rose and took the child and his mother and went to the land of Israel. ²² But when he heard that Archelaus was reigning over Judea in place of his father Herod, he was afraid to go there, and being warned in a dream he withdrew to the district of Galilee. ²³ And he went and lived in a city called Nazareth, so that what was spoken by the prophets might be fulfilled, that he would be called a Nazarene.

Chapter Three
John the Baptist Prepares the Way

In those days John the Baptist came preaching in the wilderness of Judea, ²"Repent, for the kingdom of heaven is at hand." ³For this is he who was spoken of by the prophet Isaiah when he said,

> "The voice of one crying in the
>   wilderness:
> 'Prepare the way of the Lord;
>   make his paths straight.'"

⁴Now John wore a garment of camel's hair and a leather belt round his waist, and his food was locusts and wild honey. ⁵Then Jerusalem and all Judea and all the region about the Jordan were going out to him, ⁶and they were baptized by him in the river Jordan, confessing their sins.

⁷But when he saw many of the Pharisees and Sadducees coming to his baptism, he said to them, "You brood of vipers! Who warned you to flee from the wrath to come? ⁸Bear fruit in keeping with repentance. ⁹And do not presume to say to yourselves, 'We have Abraham as our father', for I tell

AND WHEN JESUS WAS BAPTIZED, IMMEDIATELY HE WENT UP FROM THE WATER, AND BEHOLD, THE HEAVENS WERE OPENED TO HIM, AND HE SAW THE SPIRIT OF GOD DESCENDING LIKE A DOVE AND COMING TO REST ON HIM; AND BEHOLD, A VOICE FROM HEAVEN SAID, "THIS IS MY BELOVED SON, WITH WHOM I AM WELL PLEASED." Matthew 3:16-17

you, God is able from these stones to raise up children for Abraham. ¹⁰ Even now the axe is laid to the root of the trees. Every tree therefore that does not bear good fruit is cut down and thrown into the fire.

¹¹ "I baptize you with water for repentance, but he who is coming after me is mightier than I, whose sandals I am not worthy to carry. He will baptize you with the Holy Spirit and fire. ¹² His winnowing fork is in his hand, and he will clear his threshing floor and gather his wheat into the barn, but the chaff he will burn with unquenchable fire."

The Baptism of Jesus

¹³ Then Jesus came from Galilee to the Jordan to John, to be baptized by him. ¹⁴ John would have prevented him, saying, "I need to be baptized by you, and do you come to me?" ¹⁵ But Jesus answered him, "Let it be so now, for thus it is fitting for us to fulfil all righteousness." Then he consented. ¹⁶ And when Jesus was baptized, immediately he went up from the water, and behold, the heavens were opened to him, and he saw the Spirit of God descending like a dove and coming to rest on him; ¹⁷ and behold, a voice from heaven said, "This is my beloved Son, with whom I am well pleased."

Chapter Four
The Temptation of Jesus

Then Jesus was led up by the Spirit into the wilderness to be tempted by the devil. ² And after fasting forty days and forty nights, he was hungry. ³ And the tempter came and said to him, "If you are the Son of God, command these stones to become loaves of bread." ⁴ But he answered, "It is written,

"'Man shall not live by bread alone,
    but by every word that comes
        from the mouth of God.'"

⁵ Then the devil took him to the holy city and set him on the pinnacle of the temple ⁶ and said to him, "If you are the Son of God, throw yourself down, for it is written,

"'He will command his angels
        concerning you',
    and

"'On their hands they will bear
        you up,
    lest you strike your foot against
        a stone.'"

THE TEMPTER

AND THE TEMPTER CAME AND SAID TO HIM,
"IF YOU ARE THE SON OF GOD,
COMMAND THESE STONES TO BECOME
LOAVES OF BREAD."

JESUS

BUT HE ANSWERED, "IT IS WRITTEN,
'MAN SHALL NOT LIVE BY BREAD ALONE,
BUT BY EVERY WORD THAT COMES
FROM THE MOUTH OF GOD.'"

Matthew 4:3-4

AGAIN, THE DEVIL TOOK HIM TO A VERY HIGH MOUNTAIN AND SHOWED HIM ALL THE KINGDOMS OF THE WORLD AND THEIR GLORY. AND HE SAID TO HIM, "ALL THESE I WILL GIVE YOU, IF YOU WILL FALL DOWN AND WORSHIP ME."

Matthew 4:8-9

7 Jesus said to him, "Again it is written, 'You shall not put the Lord your God to the test.'" 8 Again, the devil took him to a very high mountain and showed him all the kingdoms of the world and their glory. 9 And he said to him, "All these I will give you, if you will fall down and worship me." 10 Then Jesus said to him, "Be gone, Satan! For it is written,

"'You shall worship the Lord
    your God
    and him only shall you serve.'"

11 Then the devil left him, and behold, angels came and were ministering to him.

Jesus Begins His Ministry

12 Now when he heard that John had been arrested, he withdrew into Galilee. 13 And leaving Nazareth he went and lived in Capernaum by the sea, in the territory of Zebulun and Naphtali, 14 so that what was spoken by the prophet Isaiah might be fulfilled:

15   "The land of Zebulun and the land
        of Naphtali,
            the way of the sea, beyond the
            Jordan, Galilee of the
                Gentiles—
16   the people dwelling in darkness
            have seen a great light,
    and for those dwelling in the
            region and shadow of death,
            on them a light has dawned."

17 From that time Jesus began to preach, saying, "Repent, for the kingdom of heaven is at hand."

Jesus Calls the First Disciples

18 While walking by the Sea of Galilee, he saw two brothers, Simon (who is called Peter) and Andrew his brother, casting a net into the sea, for they were fishermen. 19 And he said to them, "Follow me, and I will make you fishers of men." 20 Immediately they left their nets and followed him. 21 And going on from there he saw two other brothers, James the son of Zebedee and John his brother, in the boat with Zebedee their father, mending their nets, and he called them. 22 Immediately they left the boat and their father and followed him.

Jesus Ministers to Great Crowds

23 And he went throughout all Galilee, teaching in their synagogues and proclaiming the gospel of the kingdom and healing every disease and every affliction among the people. 24 So his fame spread throughout all Syria, and they brought him all the sick, those afflicted with various diseases and pains, those oppressed by demons, those having seizures, and paralytics, and he healed them. 25 And great crowds followed him from Galilee and the Decapolis, and from Jerusalem and Judea, and from beyond the Jordan.

Chapter Five
The Sermon on the Mount

Seeing the crowds, he went up on the mountain, and when he sat down, his disciples came to him.

The Beatitudes

² And he opened his mouth and taught them, saying:

"Blessed are the poor in spirit, for theirs is the kingdom of heaven.

⁴"Blessed are those who mourn, for they shall be comforted.

⁵"Blessed are the meek, for they shall inherit the earth.

⁶"Blessed are those who hunger and thirst for righteousness, for they shall be satisfied.

⁷"Blessed are the merciful, for they shall receive mercy.

⁸"Blessed are the pure in heart, for they shall see God.

⁹"Blessed are the peacemakers, for they shall be called sons of God.

¹⁰"Blessed are those who are persecuted for righteousness' sake, for theirs is the kingdom of heaven.

¹¹"Blessed are you when others revile you and persecute you and utter all kinds of evil against you falsely on my account. ¹²Rejoice and be glad, for your reward is great in heaven, for so they persecuted the prophets who were before you.

Salt and Light

¹³"You are the salt of the earth, but if salt has lost its taste, how shall its saltiness be restored? It is no longer good for anything except to be thrown out and trampled under people's feet.

¹⁴"You are the light of the world. A city set on a hill cannot be hidden. ¹⁵Nor do people light a lamp and put it under a basket, but on a stand, and it gives light to all in the house. ¹⁶In the

"YOU ARE THE LIGHT OF THE WORLD. A CITY SET ON A HILL CANNOT BE HIDDEN."

Matthew 5:14

same way, let your light shine before others, so that they may see your good works and give glory to your Father who is in heaven.

Christ Came to Fulfil the Law

[17]"Do not think that I have come to abolish the Law or the Prophets; I have not come to abolish them but to fulfil them. [18]For truly, I say to you, until heaven and earth pass away, not an iota, not a dot, will pass from the Law until all is accomplished. [19]Therefore whoever relaxes one of the least of these commandments and teaches others to do the same will be called least in the kingdom of heaven, but whoever does them and teaches them will be called great in the kingdom of heaven. [20]For I tell you, unless your righteousness exceeds that of the scribes and Pharisees, you will never enter the kingdom of heaven.

Anger

[21]"You have heard that it was said to those of old, 'You shall not murder; and whoever murders will be liable to judgement.' [22]But I say to you that everyone who is angry with his brother will be liable to judgement; whoever insults his brother will be liable to the council; and whoever says, 'You fool!' will be liable to the hell of fire. [23]So if you are offering your gift at the altar and there remember that your brother has something against you, [24]leave your gift there before the altar and go. First be reconciled to your brother, and then come and offer your gift. [25]Come to terms quickly with your accuser while you are going with him to court, lest your accuser hand you over to the judge, and the judge to the guard, and

"BUT I SAY TO YOU, LOVE YOUR ENEMIES AND PRAY FOR THOSE WHO PERSECUTE YOU, SO THAT YOU MAY BE SONS OF YOUR FATHER WHO IS IN HEAVEN. FOR HE MAKES HIS SUN RISE ON THE EVIL AND ON THE GOOD, AND SENDS RAIN ON THE JUST AND ON THE UNJUST."

Matthew 5:44-45

you be put in prison. ²⁶Truly, I say to you, you will never get out until you have paid the last penny.

Lust

²⁷"You have heard that it was said, 'You shall not commit adultery.' ²⁸But I say to you that everyone who looks at a woman with lustful intent has already committed adultery with her in his heart. ²⁹If your right eye causes you to sin, tear it out and throw it away. For it is better that you lose one of your members than that your whole body be thrown into hell. ³⁰And if your right hand causes you to sin, cut it off and throw it away. For it is better that you lose one of your members than that your whole body go into hell.

Divorce

³¹"It was also said, 'Whoever divorces his wife, let him give her a certificate of divorce.' ³²But I say to you that everyone who divorces his wife, except on the ground of sexual immorality, makes her commit adultery, and whoever marries a divorced woman commits adultery.

Oaths

³³"Again you have heard that it was said to those of old, 'You shall not swear falsely, but shall perform to the Lord what you have sworn.' ³⁴But I say to you, Do not take an oath at all, either by heaven, for it is the throne of God, ³⁵or by the earth, for it is his footstool, or by Jerusalem, for it is the city of the great King. ³⁶And do not take an oath by your head, for you cannot make one hair white or black. ³⁷Let what you say be simply 'Yes' or 'No'; anything more than this comes from evil.

Retaliation

³⁸"You have heard that it was said, 'An eye for an eye and a tooth for a tooth.' ³⁹But I say to you, Do not resist the one who is evil. But if anyone slaps you on the right cheek, turn to him the other also. ⁴⁰And if anyone would sue you and take your tunic, let him have your cloak as well. ⁴¹And if anyone forces you to go one mile, go with him two miles. ⁴²Give to the one who begs from you, and do not refuse the one who would borrow from you.

Love Your Enemies

⁴³"You have heard that it was said, 'You shall love your neighbour and hate your enemy.' ⁴⁴But I say to you, Love your enemies and pray for those who persecute you, ⁴⁵so that you may be sons of your Father who is in heaven. For he makes his sun rise on the evil and on the good, and sends rain on the just and on the unjust. ⁴⁶For if you love those who love you, what reward do you have? Do not even the tax collectors do the same? ⁴⁷And if you greet only your brothers, what more are you doing than others? Do not even the Gentiles do the same? ⁴⁸You therefore must be perfect, as your heavenly Father is perfect.

"The eye is the lamp of the body. So, if your eye is healthy, your whole body will be full of light"
Matthew 6:22

Beware of practising your righteousness before other people in order to be seen by them, for then you will have no reward from your Father who is in heaven. ²"Thus, when you give to the needy, sound no trumpet before you, as the hypocrites do in the synagogues and in the streets, that they may be praised by others. Truly, I say to you, they have received their reward. ³But when you give to the needy, do not let your left hand know what your right hand is doing, ⁴so that your giving may be in secret. And your Father who sees in secret will reward you.

The Lord's Prayer
⁵"And when you pray, you must not be like the hypocrites. For they love to stand and pray in the synagogues and at the street corners, that they may be seen by others. Truly, I say to you, they have received their reward. ⁶But when you pray, go into your room and shut the door and pray to your Father who is in secret. And your Father who sees in secret will reward you.

⁷"And when you pray, do not heap up empty phrases as the Gentiles do, for they think that they will be heard for their many words. ⁸Do not be like them, for your Father knows what you need before you ask him. ⁹Pray then like this:

"Our Father in heaven,
hallowed be your name.
¹⁰ Your kingdom come,
your will be done,
on earth as it is in heaven.
¹¹ Give us this day our daily bread,

¹² and forgive us our debts,
as we also have forgiven
our debtors.
¹³ And lead us not into temptation,
but deliver us from evil.

¹⁴ For if you forgive others their trespasses, your heavenly Father will also forgive you, ¹⁵but if you do not forgive others their trespasses, neither will your Father forgive your trespasses.

Fasting
¹⁶ "And when you fast, do not look gloomy like the hypocrites, for they disfigure their faces that their fasting may be seen by others. Truly, I say to you, they have received their reward. ¹⁷But when you fast, anoint your head and wash your face, ¹⁸that your fasting may not be seen by others but by your Father who is in secret. And your Father who sees in secret will reward you.

Lay Up Treasures in Heaven
¹⁹ "Do not lay up for yourselves treasures on earth, where moth and rust destroy and where thieves break in and steal, ²⁰but lay up for yourselves treasures in heaven, where neither moth nor rust destroys and where thieves do not break in and steal. ²¹ For where your treasure is, there your heart will be also.

²² "The eye is the lamp of the body. So, if your eye is healthy, your whole body will be full of light, ²³but if your eye is bad, your whole body will be full of darkness. If then the light in you is darkness, how great is the darkness!

²⁴"No one can serve two masters, for either he will hate the one and love the other, or he will be devoted to the one and despise the other. You cannot serve God and money.

Do Not Be Anxious
²⁵ "Therefore I tell you, do not be anxious about your life, what you will eat or what you will drink, nor about your body, what you will put on. Is not life more than food, and the body more than clothing? ²⁶Look at the birds of the air: they neither sow nor reap nor gather into barns, and yet your heavenly Father feeds them. Are you not of more value than they? ²⁷ And which of you by being anxious can add a single hour to his span of life?²⁸ And why are you anxious about clothing? Consider the lilies of the field, how they grow: they neither toil nor spin, ²⁹yet I tell you, even Solomon in all his glory was not arrayed like one of these. ³⁰But if God so clothes the grass of the field, which today is alive and tomorrow is thrown into the oven, will he not much more clothe you, O you of little faith? ³¹ Therefore do not be anxious, saying, 'What shall we eat?' or 'What shall we drink?' or 'What shall we wear?' ³² For the Gentiles seek after all these things, and your heavenly Father knows that you need them all. ³³But seek first the kingdom of God and his righteousness, and all these things will be added to you.

³⁴"Therefore do not be anxious about tomorrow, for tomorrow will be anxious for itself. Sufficient for the day is its own trouble.

THE ORGANIC NATURE OF

PRAYER

Prayer is one of the great mysteries of life. Over the course of history, it has been a stumbling block for many, even for some of the greatest minds. The truth is that most of us will have questions about prayer at some point in life — questions like "does prayer work?", "does it need to be done in a certain way?" and, ultimately, "what even is prayer??

Prayer is a common practice in the world we live in. Of course,

it is a religious practice, but many agnostics and atheists also admit to praying, especially in times of crisis or hardship. A 2014 survey found that the vast majority (76%) of Americans pray regularly, even if they don't affiliate themselves with an organized religion. So, given that prayer is something that is shared by the vast majority of people, it's crucial that we work out what it actually is, and the best place to go for that is

the Bible.

In Matthew 6 we read about Jesus teaching a crowd of people how to pray during his famous Sermon on the Mount. While speaking to the crowd, he says "pray then like this..." and then continues to instruct them in how best to pray. He gives them some tips on how to pray, to help to shape their view of what prayer is and how prayer should be done. Prayer would have been a part of the culture of the time, as it is today, which suggests that, like us, the people Jesus was speaking to just needed some guidance to get the most out of prayer.

In this passage, Jesus demonstrates that prayer is no more complicated than talking and listening to God. Prayer can be simply defined as being in communication with God—it is a way for us to grow in our relationship with God. It is by talking with God that we grow in our knowledge of who God is and what he has done for us. We can talk to God just as we talk to other people we interact with on a daily basis, knowing that God calls us friends and welcomes us to himself.

Many people think prayer is just about getting things from God, but prayer is not about listing off our demands, as if God was a cosmic Santa Claus who is just there to receive our requests. God's plan for prayer is way bigger than that; he desires us in our entirety, not just our needs and wants. Through prayer we can enter into an intimate relationship with the God of the universe. He desires to be in a relationship with us, and he has opened up a way for us to know him at a personal level! Although

we can pray at any time, it is often beneficial to set aside time in the day to talk to God, and one way of doing this is by starting your day in prayer. Perhaps aim to start your morning in prayer, and then try and pray during the day as you deal with whatever circumstances come your way. Like any relationship in life, the more you talk to the other person, the more your relationship will grow. This is the same for our relationship with God—the more we pray to him, the more we will grow in our knowledge of him. The great thing is that God is always there and is always ready for us to talk to him!

It really is incredible how much our lives can change when we realize that we can have a relationship with God here on earth! Through Jesus' death and resurrection, we can know God at a personal level and grow in our knowledge of him. Jesus modelled what this looked like when he was on earth; he had a relationship with his Father, and he regularly spent time in his presence speaking with him.

You might be wondering how to practically get around to praying, and a useful framework is the 'TSP' prayer

format, which can help you to structure how you pray to God. 'TSP' stands for 'thanks, sorry, please'; three aspects of prayer that you can incorporate into your time with God:

THANKS
Begin your time of prayer by thanking God for who he is and what he has done in your life. This will help you to remain grateful for what God has done for you and how he has provided for your needs.

SORRY
After thanking God, you can say sorry for whatever is going on in your life that you need God's forgiveness for. We know that at the cross Jesus forgave all our sins, so we live from forgiveness and not for it. But as Christians we will still sin and go our own way, and often it's helpful to come back to God in repentance.

PLEASE
As you finish your time with God, make requests to God for what you need. He desires to bless us and provide for our needs, and we can boldly approach him with whatever needs we have on our hearts.

HOWEVER YOU CHOOSE TO PRAY, MAKE A DECISION TO MAKE PRAYER A PART OF YOUR LIFE, AS COMMUNICATION WITH GOD CAN UNLOCK AN INTIMACY IN YOUR RELATIONSHIP WITH GOD THAT YOU CAN'T GET ELSEWHERE. GOD IS ALWAYS THERE FOR YOU, AND THROUGH PRAYER YOU CAN TALK TO HIM AS YOUR LORD, SAVIOUR AND FRIEND.

Chapter Seven
Judging Others

Judge not, that you be not judged. ²For with the judgement you pronounce you will be judged, and with the measure you use it will be measured to you. ³Why do you see the speck that is in your brother's eye, but do not notice the log that is in your own eye? ⁴Or how can you say to your brother, 'Let me take the speck out of your eye', when there is the log in your own eye? ⁵You hypocrite, first take the log out of your own eye, and then you will see clearly to take the speck out of your brother's eye.

⁶"Do not give dogs what is holy, and do not throw your pearls before pigs, lest they trample them underfoot and turn to attack you.

Ask, and It Will Be Given

⁷"Ask, and it will be given to you; seek, and you will find; knock, and it will be opened to you. ⁸For everyone who asks receives, and the one who seeks finds, and to the one who knocks it will be opened. ⁹Or which one of you, if his son asks him for bread, will give him a stone? ¹⁰Or if he asks for a fish, will give him a serpent? ¹¹If you then, who are evil, know how to give good gifts to your children, how much more will your Father who is in heaven give good things to those who ask him!

The Golden Rule

¹²"So whatever you wish that others would do to you, do also to them, for this is the Law and the Prophets.

¹³"Enter by the narrow gate. For the gate is wide and the way is easy that leads to destruction, and those who enter by it are many. ¹⁴For the gate is narrow and the way is hard that leads to life, and those who find it are few.

A Tree and Its Fruit

¹⁵"Beware of false prophets, who come to you in sheep's clothing but inwardly are ravenous wolves. ¹⁶You will recognize them by their fruits.

> "EVERYONE THEN WHO
> HEARS THESE WORDS OF MINE
> AND DOES THEM WILL BE LIKE A WISE
> MAN WHO BUILT HIS HOUSE ON THE
> ROCK. AND THE RAIN FELL, AND THE
> FLOODS CAME, AND THE WINDS BLEW
> AND BEAT ON THAT HOUSE, BUT IT DID
> NOT FALL, BECAUSE IT HAD BEEN
> FOUNDED ON THE ROCK."
>
> Matthew 7:24-25

Are grapes gathered from thorn bushes, or figs from thorn bushes? ¹⁷So, every healthy tree bears good fruit, but the diseased tree bears bad fruit. ¹⁸A healthy tree cannot bear bad fruit, nor can a diseased tree bear good fruit. ¹⁹Every tree that does not bear good fruit is cut down and thrown into the fire. ²⁰Thus you will recognize them by their fruits.

I Never Knew You

²¹"Not everyone who says to me, 'Lord, Lord', will enter the kingdom of heaven, but the one who does the will of my Father who is in heaven. ²²On that day many will say to me, 'Lord, Lord, did we not prophesy in your name, and cast out demons in your name, and do many mighty works in your name?' ²³And then will I declare to them, 'I never knew you; depart from me, you workers of lawlessness.'

Build Your House on the Rock

²⁴"Everyone then who hears these words of mine and does them will be like a wise man who built his house on the rock. ²⁵And the rain fell, and the floods came, and the winds blew and beat on that house, but it did not fall, because it had been founded on the rock. ²⁶And everyone who hears these words of mine and does not do them will be like a foolish man who built his house on the sand. ²⁷And the rain fell, and the floods came, and the winds blew and beat against that house, and it fell, and great was the fall of it."

The Authority of Jesus

²⁸And when Jesus finished these sayings, the crowds were astonished at his teaching, ²⁹for he was teaching them as one who had authority, and not as their scribes.

Chapter Eight
Jesus Cleanses a Leper

hen he came down from the mountain, great crowds followed him. ² And behold, a leper came to him and knelt before him, saying, "Lord, if you will, you can make me clean." ³ And Jesus stretched out his hand and touched him, saying, "I will; be clean." And immediately his leprosy was cleansed. ⁴ And Jesus said to him, "See that you say nothing to anyone, but go, show yourself to the priest and offer the gift that Moses commanded, for a proof to them."

The Faith of a Centurion
⁵ When he had entered Capernaum, a centurion came forward to him, appealing to him, ⁶ "Lord, my servant is lying paralysed at home, suffering terribly." ⁷ And he said to him, "I will come and heal him." ⁸ But the centurion replied, "Lord, I am not worthy to have you come under my roof, but only say the word, and my servant will be healed. ⁹ For I too am a man under authority, with soldiers under me. And I say to one, 'Go', and he goes, and to another, 'Come', and he comes, and to my servant, 'Do this', and he

does it." ¹⁰ When Jesus heard this, he marvelled and said to those who followed him, "Truly, I tell you, with no one in Israel have I found such faith. ¹¹ I tell you, many will come from east and west and recline at table with Abraham, Isaac, and Jacob in the kingdom of heaven, ¹² while the sons of the kingdom will be thrown into the outer darkness. In that place there will be weeping and gnashing of teeth." ¹³ And to the centurion Jesus said, "Go; let it be done for you as you have believed." And the servant was healed at that very moment.

Jesus Heals Many
¹⁴ And when Jesus entered Peter's house, he saw his mother-in-law lying sick with a fever. ¹⁵ He touched her hand, and the fever left her, and she rose and began to serve him. ¹⁶ That evening they brought to him many who were oppressed by demons, and he cast out the spirits with a word and healed all who were sick. ¹⁷ This was to fulfil what was spoken by the prophet Isaiah: "He took our illnesses and bore our diseases."

The Cost of Following Jesus

[18] Now when Jesus saw a crowd around him, he gave orders to go over to the other side. [19] And a scribe came up and said to him, "Teacher, I will follow you wherever you go." [20] And Jesus said to him, "Foxes have holes, and birds of the air have nests, but the Son of Man has nowhere to lay his head." [21] Another of the disciples said to him, "Lord, let me first go and bury my father." [22] And Jesus said to him, "Follow me, and leave the dead to bury their own dead."

Jesus Calms a Storm

[23] And when he got into the boat, his disciples followed him. [24] And behold, there arose a great storm on the sea, so that the boat was being swamped by the waves; but he was asleep. [25] And they went and woke him, saying, "Save us, Lord; we are perishing." [26] And he said to them, "Why are you afraid, O you of little faith?" Then he rose and rebuked the winds and the sea, and there was a great calm. [27] And the men marvelled, saying, "What sort of man is this, that even winds and sea obey him?"

Jesus Heals Two Men with Demons

[28] And when he came to the other side, to the country of the Gadarenes, two demon-possessed men met him, coming out of the tombs, so fierce that no one could pass that way. [29] And behold, they cried out, "What have you to do with us, O Son of God? Have you come here to torment us before the time?" [30] Now a herd of many pigs was feeding at some distance from them. [31] And the demons begged him, saying, "If you cast us out, send us away into the herd of pigs." [32] And he said to them, "Go." So they came out and went into

the pigs, and behold, the whole herd rushed down the steep bank into the sea and drowned in the waters. ³³ The herdsmen fled, and going into the city they told everything, especially what had happened to the demon-possessed men. ³⁴ And behold, all the city came out to meet Jesus, and when they saw him, they begged him to leave their region.

Chapter Nine

Jesus Heals a Paralytic

And getting into a boat he crossed over and came to his own city. ² And behold, some people brought to him a paralytic, lying on a bed. And when Jesus saw their faith, he said to the paralytic, "Take heart, my son; your sins are forgiven." ³ And behold, some of the scribes said to themselves, "This man is blaspheming." ⁴ But Jesus, knowing their thoughts, said, "Why do you think evil in your hearts? ⁵ For which is easier, to say, 'Your sins are forgiven,' or to say, 'Rise and walk'? ⁶ But that you may know that the Son of Man has authority on earth to forgive sins"—he then said to the paralytic—"Rise, pick up your bed and go home." ⁷ And he rose and went home. ⁸ When the crowds saw it, they were afraid, and they glorified God, who had given such authority to men.

Jesus Calls Matthew

⁹ As Jesus passed on from there, he saw a man called Matthew sitting at the tax booth, and he said to him, "Follow me." And he rose and followed him.

¹⁰ And as Jesus reclined at table in the house, behold, many tax collectors and sinners came and were reclining with Jesus and his disciples. ¹¹ And when the Pharisees saw this, they said to his disciples, "Why does your teacher eat with tax collectors and sinners?" ¹² But when he heard it, he said, "Those who are well have no need of a physician, but those who are sick. ¹³ Go and learn what this means: 'I desire mercy, and not sacrifice.' For I came not to call the righteous, but sinners."

A Question About Fasting

¹⁴ Then the disciples of John came to him, saying, "Why do we and the Pharisees fast, but your disciples do not fast?" ¹⁵ And Jesus said to them, "Can the wedding guests mourn as long as the bridegroom is with them? The days will come when the bridegroom is taken away from them, and then they will fast. ¹⁶ No one puts a piece of unshrunk cloth on an old garment, for the patch tears away from the garment, and a worse tear is made. ¹⁷ Neither is new wine put into old wineskins. If it is, the skins burst and the wine is spilled and the skins are destroyed. But new wine is put into fresh wineskins, and so both are preserved."

A Girl Restored to Life and a Woman Healed

¹⁸ While he was saying these things to them, behold, a ruler came in and knelt before him, saying, "My daughter has just died, but come and lay your hand on her, and she will live." ¹⁹ And Jesus rose and followed him, with his disciples. ²⁰ And behold, a woman who had suffered from a discharge of blood for twelve years came up behind him and touched the fringe of his garment, ²¹ for she said to herself, "If I only touch his garment, I will be made well." ²² Jesus turned, and seeing her he said, "Take heart, daughter; your faith has made you well." And instantly the woman was made well. ²³ And when Jesus came to the ruler's house and saw the flute players and the crowd making a commotion, ²⁴ he said, "Go away, for the girl is not dead but sleeping." And they laughed at him. ²⁵ But when the crowd had been put outside, he went in and took her by the hand, and the girl arose.

BUT WHEN HE HEARD IT, HE SAID, "THOSE WHO
ARE WELL HAVE NO NEED OF A PHYSICIAN, BUT THOSE
WHO ARE SICK. GO AND LEARN WHAT THIS MEANS:
'I DESIRE MERCY, AND NOT SACRIFICE.' FOR I CAME
NOT TO CALL THE RIGHTEOUS, BUT SINNERS."

Matthew 9:12-13

"IF I ONLY TOUCH HIS GARMENT, I WILL BE MADE WELL." JESUS TURNED, AND SEEING HER HE SAID, "TAKE HEART, DAUGHTER; YOUR FAITH HAS MADE YOU WELL." AND INSTANTLY THE WOMAN WAS MADE WELL.

Matthew 9:21-22

26 And the report of this went through all that district.

Jesus Heals Two Blind Men

27 And as Jesus passed on from there, two blind men followed him, crying aloud, "Have mercy on us, Son of David." 28 When he entered the house, the blind men came to him, and Jesus said to them, "Do you believe that I am able to do this?" They said to him, "Yes, Lord." 29 Then he touched their eyes, saying, "According to your faith be it done to you." 30 And their eyes were opened. And Jesus sternly warned them, "See that no one knows about it." 31 But they went away and spread his fame through all that district.

Jesus Heals a Man Unable to Speak

32 As they were going away, behold, a demon-oppressed man who was mute was brought to him. 33 And when the demon had been cast out, the mute man spoke. And the crowds marvelled, saying, "Never was anything like this seen in Israel." 34 But the Pharisees said, "He casts out demons by the prince of demons."

The Harvest Is Plentiful, the Labourers Few

35 And Jesus went throughout all the cities and villages, teaching in their synagogues and proclaiming the gospel of the kingdom and healing every disease and every affliction. 36 When he saw the crowds, he had compassion for them, because they were harassed and helpless, like sheep without a shepherd. 37 Then he said to his disciples, "The harvest is plentiful, but the labourers are few; 38 therefore pray earnestly to the Lord of the harvest to send out labourers into his harvest."

Chapter Ten
The Twelve Apostles

And he called to him his twelve disciples and gave them authority over unclean spirits, to cast them out, and to heal every disease and every affliction. ² The names of the twelve apostles are these: first, Simon, who is called Peter, and Andrew his brother; James the son of Zebedee, and John his brother; ³ Philip and Bartholomew; Thomas and Matthew the tax collector; James the son of Alphaeus, and Thaddaeus; ⁴ Simon the Zealot, and Judas Iscariot, who betrayed him.

Jesus Sends Out the Twelve Apostles

⁵ These twelve Jesus sent out, instructing them, "Go nowhere among the Gentiles and enter no town of the Samaritans, ⁶but go rather to the lost sheep of the house of Israel. ⁷And proclaim as you go, saying, 'The kingdom of heaven is at hand.' ⁸Heal the sick, raise the dead, cleanse lepers, cast out demons. You received without paying; give without pay. ⁹Acquire no gold or silver or copper for your belts, ¹⁰no bag for your journey, or two tunics or sandals or a staff, for the labourer

"BEHOLD, I AM SENDING YOU OUT AS SHEEP IN THE MIDST OF WOLVES, SO BE WISE AS SERPENTS AND INNOCENT AS DOVES."

Matthew 10:16

deserves his food. [11]And whatever town or village you enter, find out who is worthy in it and stay there until you depart. [12]As you enter the house, greet it. [13]And if the house is worthy, let your peace come upon it, but if it is not worthy, let your peace return to you. [14]And if anyone will not receive you or listen to your words, shake off the dust from your feet when you leave that house or town. [15]Truly, I say to you, it will be more bearable on the day of judgement for the land of Sodom and Gomorrah than for that town.

Persecution Will Come

[16]"Behold, I am sending you out as sheep in the midst of wolves, so be wise as serpents and innocent as doves. [17]Beware of men, for they will deliver you over to courts and flog you in their synagogues, [18]and you will be dragged before governors and kings for my sake, to bear witness before them and the Gentiles. [19]When they deliver you over, do not be anxious how you are to speak or what you are to say, for what you are to say will be given to you in that hour. [20]For it is not you who speak, but the Spirit of your Father speaking through you. [21]Brother will deliver brother over to death, and the father his child, and children will rise against parents and have them put to death, [22]and you will be hated by all for my name's sake. But the one who endures to the end will be saved. [23]When they persecute you in one town, flee to the next, for truly, I say to you, you will not have gone through all the towns of Israel before the Son of Man comes.

[24]"A disciple is not above his teacher, nor a servant above his master. [25]It is enough for the disciple to be like his teacher, and the servant like his master. If they have called the master of the house Beelzebul, how much more will they malign those of his household.

Have No Fear

[26]"So have no fear of them, for nothing is covered that will not be revealed, or hidden that will not be known. [27]What I tell you in the dark, say in the light, and what you hear whispered, proclaim on the housetops. [28]And do not fear those who kill the body but cannot kill the soul. Rather fear him who can destroy both soul and body in hell. [29]Are not two sparrows sold for a penny? And not one of them will fall to the ground apart from your Father. [30]But even the hairs of your head are all numbered. [31]Fear not, therefore; you are of more value than many sparrows. [32]So everyone who acknowledges me before men, I also will acknowledge before my Father who is in heaven, [33]but whoever denies me before men, I also will deny before my Father who is in heaven.

Not Peace, but a Sword

[34]"Do not think that I have come to bring peace to the earth. I have not come to bring peace, but a sword. [35]For I have come to set a man against his father, and a daughter against her mother, and a daughter-in-law against her mother-in-law. [36]And a person's enemies will be those of his own household. [37]Whoever loves father or mother more than me is not worthy of me, and whoever loves son or daughter more than me is not worthy of me. [38]And whoever does not take his cross and follow me is not worthy of me. [39]Whoever finds his life will lose it, and whoever loses his life for my sake will find it.

Rewards

[40]"Whoever receives you receives me, and whoever receives me receives him who sent me. [41]The one who receives a prophet because he is a prophet will receive a prophet's reward, and the one who receives a righteous person because he is a righteous person will receive a righteous person's reward. [42]And whoever gives one of these little ones even a cup of cold water because he is a disciple, truly, I say to you, he will by no means lose his reward."

THE
KINGDOM
OF HEAVEN
IS AT HAND

THESE TWELVE JESUS
SENT OUT, INSTRUCTING THEM,
"GO NOWHERE AMONG THE
GENTILES AND ENTER NO TOWN
OF THE SAMARITANS, BUT GO
RATHER TO THE LOST SHEEP OF
THE HOUSE OF ISRAEL. AND
PROCLAIM AS YOU GO, SAYING,
'THE KINGDOM OF HEAVEN IS AT
HAND.' HEAL THE SICK, RAISE
THE DEAD, CLEANSE LEPERS,
CAST OUT DEMONS. YOU
RECEIVED WITHOUT PAYING;
GIVE WITHOUT PAY."

Matthew 10:5-8

Chapter Eleven

Messengers from John the Baptist

When Jesus had finished instructing his twelve disciples, he went on from there to teach and preach in their cities.

² Now when John heard in prison about the deeds of the Christ, he sent word by his disciples ³ and said to him, "Are you the one who is to come, or shall we look for another?" ⁴ And Jesus answered them, "Go and tell John what you hear and see: ⁵the blind receive their sight and the lame walk, lepers are cleansed and the deaf hear, and the dead are raised up, and the poor have good news preached to them. ⁶And blessed is the one who is not offended by me."

⁷ As they went away, Jesus began to speak to the crowds concerning John: "What did you go out into the wilderness to see? A reed shaken by the wind? ⁸What then did you go out to see? A man dressed in soft clothing? Behold, those who wear soft clothing are in kings' houses. ⁹What then did you go out to see? A prophet? Yes, I tell you, and more than a prophet. ¹⁰This is he of whom it is written,

"'Behold, I send my messenger
    before your face,
who will prepare your way
    before you.'

¹¹Truly, I say to you, among those born of women there has arisen no one greater than John the Baptist. Yet the one who is least in the kingdom of heaven is greater than he. ¹²From the days of John the Baptist until now the kingdom of heaven has suffered violence, and the violent take it by force. ¹³For all the Prophets and the Law prophesied until John, ¹⁴and if you are willing to accept it, he is Elijah who is to come. ¹⁵He who has ears to hear, let him hear.

¹⁶"But to what shall I compare this generation? It is like children sitting in the market-places and calling to their playmates,

¹⁷   "'We played the flute for you, and
        you did not dance;
    we sang a dirge, and you did not
        mourn.'

¹⁸For John came neither eating nor drinking, and they say, 'He has a demon.' ¹⁹The Son of Man came eating and drinking, and they say, 'Look at him! A glutton and a drunkard, a friend of tax collectors and sinners!' Yet wisdom is justified by her deeds."

Woe to Unrepentant Cities

²⁰Then he began to denounce the cities where most of his mighty works had been done, because they did not repent. ²¹"Woe to you, Chorazin! Woe to you, Bethsaida! For if the mighty works done in you had been done in Tyre and Sidon, they would have repented long ago in sackcloth and ashes. ²²But I tell you, it will be more bearable on the day of judgement for Tyre and Sidon than for you. ²³And you, Capernaum, will you be exalted to heaven? You will be brought down to Hades. For if the mighty works done in you had been done in Sodom, it would have remained until this day. ²⁴But I tell you that it will be more tolerable on the day of judgement for the land of Sodom than for you."

Come to Me, and I Will Give You Rest

²⁵At that time Jesus declared, "I thank you, Father, Lord of heaven and earth, that you have hidden these things from the wise and understanding and revealed them to little children; ²⁶yes, Father, for such was your gracious will. ²⁷All things have been handed over to me by my Father, and no one knows the Son except the Father, and no one knows the Father except the Son and anyone to whom the Son chooses to reveal him. ²⁸Come to me, all who labour and are heavy laden, and I will give you rest. ²⁹Take my yoke upon you, and learn from me, for I am gentle and lowly in heart, and you will find rest for your souls. ³⁰For my yoke is easy, and my burden is light."

Chapter Twelve
Jesus is Lord of the Sabbath

At that time Jesus went through the cornfields on the Sabbath. His disciples were hungry, and they began to pluck ears of corn and to eat. ²But when the Pharisees saw it, they said to him, "Look, your disciples are doing what is not lawful to do on the Sabbath." ³He said to them, "Have you not read what David did when he was hungry, and those who were with him: ⁴how he entered the house of God and ate the bread of the Presence, which it was not lawful for him to eat nor for those who were with him, but only for the priests? ⁵Or have you not read in the Law how on the Sabbath the priests in the temple profane the Sabbath and are guiltless? ⁶I tell you, something greater than the temple is here. ⁷And if you had known what this means, 'I desire mercy, and not sacrifice', you would not have condemned the guiltless. ⁸For the Son of Man is lord of the Sabbath."

A Man with a Withered Hand

⁹He went on from there and entered their synagogue. ¹⁰And a man was there with a withered hand. And they asked him, "Is it lawful to heal on the Sabbath?"—so that they might accuse him. ¹¹He said to them, "Which one of you who has a sheep, if it falls into a pit on the Sabbath, will not take hold of it and lift it out? ¹²Of how much more value is a man than a sheep! So it is lawful to do good on the Sabbath." ¹³Then he said to the man, "Stretch out your hand." And the man stretched it out, and it was

restored, healthy like the other. ¹⁴ But the Pharisees went out and conspired against him, how to destroy him.

God's Chosen Servant

¹⁵ Jesus, aware of this, withdrew from there. And many followed him, and he healed them all ¹⁶ and ordered them not to make him known. ¹⁷ This was to fulfil what was spoken by the prophet Isaiah:

¹⁸   "Behold, my servant whom I have chosen,
            my beloved with whom my soul is well pleased.
        I will put my Spirit upon him,
            and he will proclaim justice to the Gentiles.
¹⁹   He will not quarrel or cry aloud,
            nor will anyone hear his voice in the streets;
²⁰   a bruised reed he will not break,
            and a smouldering wick he will not quench,
        until he brings justice to victory;
²¹   and in his name the Gentiles will hope."

Blasphemy Against the Holy Spirit

²² Then a demon-oppressed man who was blind and mute was brought to him, and he healed him, so that the man spoke and saw. ²³ And all the people were amazed, and said, "Can this be the Son of David?" ²⁴ But when the Pharisees heard it, they said, "It is only by Beelzebul, the prince of demons, that this man casts out demons." ²⁵ Knowing their thoughts, he said to them, "Every kingdom divided against itself is laid waste, and no city or house

divided against itself will stand. ²⁶ And if Satan casts out Satan, he is divided against himself. How then will his kingdom stand? ²⁷ And if I cast out demons by Beelzebul, by whom do your sons cast them out? Therefore they will be your judges. ²⁸ But if it is by the Spirit of God that I cast out demons, then the kingdom of God has come upon you. ²⁹ Or how can someone enter a strong man's house and plunder his goods, unless he first binds the strong man? Then indeed he may plunder his house. ³⁰ Whoever is not with me is against me, and whoever does not gather with me scatters. ³¹ Therefore I tell you, every sin and blasphemy will be forgiven people, but the blasphemy against the Spirit will not be forgiven. ³² And whoever speaks a word against the Son of Man will be forgiven, but whoever speaks against the Holy Spirit will not be forgiven, either in this age or in the age to come.

A Tree Is Known by Its Fruit

³³ "Either make the tree good and its fruit good, or make the tree bad and its fruit bad, for the tree is known by its fruit. ³⁴ You brood of vipers! How can you speak good, when you are evil? For out of the abundance of the heart the mouth speaks. ³⁵ The good person out of his good treasure brings forth good, and the evil person out of his evil treasure brings forth evil. ³⁶ I tell you, on the day of judgement people will give account for every careless word they speak, ³⁷ for by your words you will be justified, and by your words you will be condemned."

"BEHOLD, MY SERVANT WHOM I HAVE CHOSEN, MY BELOVED WITH WHOM MY SOUL IS WELL PLEASED. I WILL PUT MY SPIRIT UPON HIM, AND HE WILL PROCLAIM JUSTICE TO THE GENTILES." Matthew 12:18

The Sign of Jonah

³⁸ Then some of the scribes and Pharisees answered him, saying, "Teacher, we wish to see a sign from you." ³⁹ But he answered them, "An evil and adulterous generation seeks for a sign, but no sign will be given to it except the sign of the prophet Jonah. ⁴⁰For just as Jonah was three days and three nights in the belly of the great fish, so will the Son of Man be three days and three nights in the heart of the earth. ⁴¹The men of Nineveh will rise up at the judgement with this generation and condemn it, for they repented at the preaching of Jonah, and behold, something greater than Jonah is here. ⁴²The queen of the South will rise up at the judgement with this generation and condemn it, for she came from the ends of the earth to hear the wisdom of Solomon, and behold, something greater than Solomon is here.

Return of an Unclean Spirit

⁴³"When the unclean spirit has gone out of a person, it passes through waterless places seeking rest, but finds none. ⁴⁴Then it says, 'I will return to my house from which I came.' And when it comes, it finds the house empty, swept, and put in order. ⁴⁵Then it goes and brings with it seven other spirits more evil than itself, and they enter and dwell there, and the last state of that person is worse than the first. So also will it be with this evil generation."

Jesus' Mother and Brothers

⁴⁶ While he was still speaking to the people, behold, his mother and his brothers stood outside, asking to speak to him. ⁴⁸ But he replied to the man who told him, "Who is my mother, and who are my brothers?" ⁴⁹ And stretching out his hand towards his disciples, he said, "Here are my mother and my brothers! ⁵⁰For whoever does the will of my Father in heaven is my brother and sister and mother."

Chapter Thirteen
The Parable of the Sower

"For truly, I say to you, many prophets and righteous people longed to see what you see, and did not see it, and to hear what you hear, and did not hear it."

Matthew 13:17

That same day Jesus went out of the house and sat beside the lake. ² And great crowds gathered about him, so that he got into a boat and sat down. And the whole crowd stood on the beach. ³ And he told them many things in parables, saying: "A sower went out to sow. ⁴ And as he sowed, some seeds fell along the path, and the birds came and devoured them. ⁵ Other seeds fell on rocky ground, where they did not have much soil, and immediately they sprang up, since they had no depth of soil, ⁶ but when the sun rose they were scorched. And since they had no root, they withered away. ⁷ Other seeds fell among thorns, and the thorns grew up and choked them. ⁸ Other seeds fell on good soil and produced grain, some a hundredfold, some sixty, some thirty. ⁹ He who has ears, let him hear."

The Purpose of the Parables

¹⁰ Then the disciples came and said to him, "Why do you speak to them in parables?" ¹¹ And he answered them, "To you it has been given to know the secrets of the kingdom of heaven, but to them it has not been given. ¹² For to the one who has, more will be given, and he will have an abundance, but from the one who has not, even what he has will be taken away. ¹³ This is why I speak to them in parables, because seeing they do not see, and hearing they

do not hear, nor do they understand. ¹⁴ Indeed, in their case the prophecy of Isaiah is fulfilled that says:

"‘"You will indeed hear but never understand,
and you will indeed see but never perceive."
¹⁵ For this people's heart has grown dull,
and with their ears they can barely hear,
and their eyes they have closed,
lest they should see with their eyes
and hear with their ears
and understand with their heart
and turn, and I would heal them.'

¹⁶ But blessed are your eyes, for they see, and your ears, for they hear. ¹⁷ For truly, I say to you, many prophets and righteous people longed to see what you see, and did not see it, and to hear what you hear, and did not hear it.

The Parable of the Sower Explained

¹⁸ "Hear then the parable of the sower: ¹⁹ When anyone hears the word of the kingdom and does not understand it, the evil one comes and snatches away what has been sown in his heart. This is what was sown along the path. ²⁰ As for what was sown on rocky ground,

this is the one who hears the word and immediately receives it with joy, ²¹ yet he has no root in himself, but endures for a while, and when tribulation or persecution arises on account of the word, immediately he falls away. ²² As for what was sown among thorns, this is the one who hears the word, but the cares of the world and the deceitfulness of riches choke the word, and it proves unfruitful. ²³ As for what was sown on good soil, this is the one who hears the word and understands it. He indeed bears fruit and yields, in one case a hundredfold, in another sixty, and in another thirty."

The Parable of the Weeds

²⁴ He put another parable before them, saying, "The kingdom of heaven may be compared to a man who sowed good seed in his field, ²⁵ but while his men were sleeping, his enemy came and sowed weeds among the wheat and went away. ²⁶ So when the plants came up and bore grain, then the weeds appeared also. ²⁷ And the servants of the master of the house came and said to him, 'Master, did you not sow good seed in your field? How then does it have weeds?' ²⁸ He said to them, 'An enemy has done this.' So the servants said to him, 'Then do you want us to go and gather them?' ²⁹ But he said, 'No,

lest in gathering the weeds you root up the wheat along with them. ³⁰Let both grow together until the harvest, and at harvest time I will tell the reapers, "Gather the weeds first and bind them in bundles to be burned, but gather the wheat into my barn."'"

The Mustard Seed and the Leaven

³¹He put another parable before them, saying, "The kingdom of heaven is like a grain of mustard seed that a man took and sowed in his field. ³²It is the smallest of all seeds, but when it has grown it is larger than all the garden plants and becomes a tree, so that the birds of the air come and make nests in its branches."

³³He told them another parable. "The kingdom of heaven is like leaven that a woman took and hid in three measures of flour, till it was all leavened."

Prophecy and Parables

³⁴All these things Jesus said to the crowds in parables; indeed, he said nothing to them without a parable. ³⁵This was to fulfil what was spoken by the prophet:

> "I will open my mouth in
>   parables;
>   I will utter what has been
>   hidden since the foundation
>   of the world."

The Parable of the Weeds Explained

³⁶Then he left the crowds and went into the house. And his disciples came to him, saying, "Explain to us the parable of the weeds of the field." ³⁷He answered, "The one who sows the good seed is the Son of Man. ³⁸The field is the world, and the good seed is the sons of the kingdom. The weeds are the sons of the evil one, ³⁹and the enemy who sowed them is the devil. The harvest is the end of the age, and the reapers are angels. ⁴⁰Just as the weeds are gathered and burned with fire, so will it be at the end of the age. ⁴¹The Son of Man will send his angels, and they will gather out of his kingdom all causes of sin and all law-breakers, ⁴²and throw them into the fiery furnace. In that place there will be weeping and gnashing of teeth. ⁴³Then the righteous will shine like the sun in the kingdom of their Father. He who has ears, let him hear.

The Parable of the Hidden Treasure

⁴⁴"The kingdom of heaven is like treasure hidden in a field, which a man found and covered up. Then in his joy he goes and sells all that he has and buys that field.

The Parable of the Pearl of Great Value

⁴⁵"Again, the kingdom of heaven is like a merchant in search of fine pearls, ⁴⁶who, on finding one pearl of great value, went and sold all that he had and bought it.

The Parable of the Net

⁴⁷"Again, the kingdom of heaven is like a net that was thrown into the sea and gathered fish of every kind. ⁴⁸When it was full, men drew it ashore and sat down and sorted the good into containers but threw away the bad. ⁴⁹So it will be at the end of the age. The angels will come out and separate the evil from the righteous ⁵⁰and throw them into the fiery furnace. In that place there will be weeping and gnashing of teeth.

New and Old Treasures

⁵¹"Have you understood all these things?" They said to him, "Yes." ⁵²And he said to them, "Therefore every scribe who has been trained for the kingdom of heaven is like a master of a house, who brings out of his treasure what is new and what is old."

Jesus Rejected at Nazareth

⁵³And when Jesus had finished these parables, he went away from there, ⁵⁴and coming to his home town he taught them in their synagogue, so that they were astonished, and said, "Where did this man get this wisdom and these mighty works? ⁵⁵Is not this the carpenter's son? Is not his mother called Mary? And are not his brothers James and Joseph and Simon and Judas? ⁵⁶And are not all his sisters with us? Where then did this man get all these things?" ⁵⁷And they took offence at him. But Jesus said to them, "A prophet is not without honour except in his home town and in his own household." ⁵⁸And he did not do many mighty works there, because of their unbelief.

AND THEY TOOK OFFENCE AT HIM. BUT JESUS SAID TO THEM, "A PROPHET IS NOT WITHOUT HONOUR EXCEPT IN HIS HOME TOWN AND IN HIS OWN HOUSHOLD." AND HE DID NOT DO MANY MIGHTY WORKS THERE, BECAUSE OF THEIR UNBELIEF.

Matthew 13:57-58

AND PETER
ANSWERED
HIM, "LORD,
IF IT IS YOU,
COMMAND ME
TO COME TO
YOU ON THE
WATER." HE
SAID, "COME."
SO PETER GOT
OUT OF THE
BOAT AND
WALKED ON
THE WATER
AND CAME
TO JESUS.

Matthew 14:28-29

Chapter Fourteen
The Death of John the Baptist

At that time Herod the tetrarch heard about the fame of Jesus, ²and he said to his servants, "This is John the Baptist. He has been raised from the dead; that is why these miraculous powers are at work in him." ³For Herod had seized John and bound him and put him in prison for the sake of Herodias, his brother Philip's wife, ⁴because John had been saying to him, "It is not lawful for you to have her." ⁵And though he wanted to put him to death, he feared the people, because they held him to be a prophet. ⁶But when Herod's birthday came, the daughter of Herodias danced before the company and pleased Herod, ⁷so that he promised with an oath to give her whatever she might ask. ⁸Prompted by her mother, she said, "Give me the head of John the Baptist here on a platter." ⁹And the king was sorry, but because of his oaths and his guests he commanded it to be given. ¹⁰He sent and had John beheaded in the prison, ¹¹and his head was brought on a platter and given to the girl, and she brought it to her mother. ¹²And his disciples came and took the body and buried it, and they went and told Jesus.

Jesus Feeds the Five Thousand
¹³Now when Jesus heard this, he withdrew from there in a boat to a desolate place by himself. But when the crowds heard it, they followed him on foot from the towns. ¹⁴When he went ashore he saw a great crowd, and he had compassion on them and healed their sick. ¹⁵Now when it was evening, the disciples came to him and said, "This is a desolate place, and the day is now over; send the crowds away to go into the villages and buy food for themselves." ¹⁶But Jesus said, "They need not go away; you give them something to eat." ¹⁷They said to him, "We have only five loaves here and two fish." ¹⁸And he said, "Bring them here to me." ¹⁹Then he ordered the crowds to sit down on the grass, and taking the five loaves and the two fish, he looked up to heaven and said a blessing. Then he broke the loaves and gave them to the disciples, and the disciples gave them to the crowds. ²⁰And they all ate and were satisfied. And they took up twelve baskets full of the broken pieces left over. ²¹And those who ate were about five thousand men, besides women and children.

Jesus Walks on the Water
²²Immediately he made the disciples get into the boat and go before him to the other side, while he dismissed the crowds. ²³And after he had dismissed the crowds, he went up on the mountain by himself to pray. When evening came, he was there alone, ²⁴but the boat by this time was a long way from the

land, beaten by the waves, for the wind was against them. ²⁵ And in the fourth watch of the night he came to them, walking on the sea. ²⁶ But when the disciples saw him walking on the sea, they were terrified, and said, "It is a ghost!" and they cried out in fear. ²⁷ But immediately Jesus spoke to them, saying, "Take heart; it is I. Do not be afraid."

²⁸ And Peter answered him, "Lord, if it is you, command me to come to you on the water." ²⁹ He said, "Come." So Peter got out of the boat and walked on the water and came to Jesus. ³⁰ But when he saw the wind, he was afraid, and beginning to sink he cried out, "Lord, save me." ³¹ Jesus immediately reached out his hand and took hold of him, saying to him, "O you of little faith, why did you doubt?" ³² And when they got into the boat, the wind ceased. ³³ And those in the boat worshipped him, saying, "Truly you are the Son of God."

Jesus Heals the Sick in Gennesaret

³⁴ And when they had crossed over, they came to land at Gennesaret. ³⁵ And when the men of that place recognized him, they sent word around to all that region and brought to him all who were sick ³⁶ and implored him that they might only touch the fringe of his garment. And as many as touched it were made well.

Chapter Fifteen
Traditions and Commandments

Then Pharisees and scribes came to Jesus from Jerusalem and said, ² "Why do your disciples break the tradition of the elders? For they do not wash their hands when they eat." ³ He answered them, "And why do you break the commandment of God for the sake of your tradition? ⁴ For God commanded, 'Honour your father and your mother,' and, 'Whoever reviles father or mother must surely die.' ⁵ But you say, 'If anyone tells his father or his mother, "What you would have gained from me is given to God," ⁶ he need not honour his father.' So for the sake of your tradition you have made void the word of God. ⁷ You hypocrites! Well did Isaiah prophesy of you, when he said:

⁸   "'This people honours me with
        their lips,
           but their heart is far from me;
⁹   in vain do they worship me,
        teaching as doctrines the
           commandments of men.' "

What Defiles a Person

¹⁰ And he called the people to him and said to them, "Hear and understand: ¹¹ it is not what goes into the mouth that defiles a person, but what comes out of the mouth; this defiles a person." ¹² Then the disciples came and said to him, "Do you know that the Pharisees were offended when they heard this saying?" ¹³ He answered, "Every plant that my heavenly Father has not planted will be rooted up. ¹⁴ Let them alone; they are blind guides. And if the blind lead the blind, both will fall into a pit." ¹⁵ But Peter said to him, "Explain the parable to us." ¹⁶ And he said, "Are you also still without understanding? ¹⁷ Do you not see that whatever goes into the mouth passes into the stomach and is expelled? ¹⁸ But what comes out of the mouth proceeds from the heart, and this defiles a person. ¹⁹ For out of the heart come evil thoughts, murder, adultery, sexual immorality, theft, false witness, slander. ²⁰ These are what defile a person. But to eat with unwashed hands does not defile anyone."

The Faith of a Canaanite Woman

²¹ And Jesus went away from there and withdrew to the district of Tyre and Sidon. ²² And behold, a Canaanite woman from that region came out

THEN JESUS
ANSWERED
HER, "O
WOMAN,
GREAT IS
YOUR FAITH!
BE IT DONE
FOR YOU AS
YOU DESIRE."
AND HER
DAUGHTER
WAS HEALED
INSTANTLY.

Matthew 15:28

and was crying, "Have mercy on me, O Lord, Son of David; my daughter is severely oppressed by a demon." [23] But he did not answer her a word. And his disciples came and begged him, saying, "Send her away, for she is crying out after us." [24] He answered, "I was sent only to the lost sheep of the house of Israel." [25] But she came and knelt before him, saying, "Lord, help me." [26] And he answered, "It is not right to take the children's bread and throw it to the dogs." [27] She said, "Yes, Lord, yet even the dogs eat the crumbs that fall from their masters' table." [28] Then Jesus answered her, "O woman, great is your faith! Be it done for you as you desire." And her daughter was healed instantly.

Jesus Heals Many

[29] Jesus went on from there and walked beside the Sea of Galilee. And he went up on the mountain and sat down there. [30] And great crowds came to him, bringing with them the lame, the blind, the crippled, the mute, and many others, and they put them at his feet, and he healed them, [31] so that the crowd wondered, when they saw the mute speaking, the crippled healthy, the lame walking, and the blind seeing. And they glorified the God of Israel.

Jesus Feeds the Four Thousand

[32] Then Jesus called his disciples to him and said, "I have compassion on the crowd because they have been with me now three days and have nothing to eat. And I am unwilling to send them away hungry, lest they faint on the way." [33] And the disciples said to him, "Where are we to get enough bread in such a desolate place to feed so great a crowd?" [34] And Jesus said to them, "How many loaves do you have?" They said, "Seven, and a few small fish." [35] And directing the crowd to sit down on the ground, [36] he took the seven loaves and the fish, and having given thanks he broke them and gave them to the disciples, and the disciples gave them to the crowds. [37] And they all ate and were satisfied. And they took up seven baskets full of the broken pieces left over. [38] Those who ate were four thousand men, besides women and children. [39] And after sending away the crowds, he got into the boat and went to the region of Magadan.

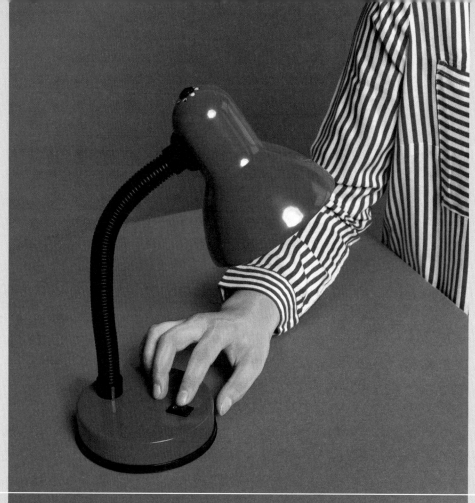

THE CHURCH

GOD'S PLAN FOR HUMANITY

What comes to mind when you hear the word 'church'? Perhaps it is a building you are familiar with from where you live or a denomination that impacted your childhood. Perhaps you immediately think of the community work that the church does around the globe or a memory of an early church experience. Whatever it is, whether positive or negative, there is always something that we first think of when someone mentions the church, and that first instinct often influences our opinion of what the church actually is.

All of us have varying opinions of what church is, and these opinions are often rooted in our differing experiences of interacting with the church. The challenge, though, is not to let our experiences dictate our view of what the church is, but rather let what the Bible says about the church dictate our opinion.

The Bible provides a clear picture of what the church actually is, and what it should be, and so regardless of our own personal experiences, we should start first with the biblical picture of the church.

Here in Matthew 16 we read of the Bible's first reference to the church, in which Jesus tells one of his disciples, Peter, "I will build my church, and the gates of hell shall not prevail against it." This one statement set in motion the global movement that we call the church, which to this day has spread all around the world, into an innumerable number of cultures and countries.

The New Testament tells us about churches being planted all over the Roman Empire, and today we see that the church has spread around the world, even to countries where Christians are persecuted and where it is illegal to even go to church. Despite all the attempts to defeat the church of Jesus Christ, history has proven what Jesus said to be true: if Jesus builds the church not even the gates of hell will be able to stop it.

The word 'church' is a translation of the Greek word *ecclesia*, which refers to an assembly or a gathering of people. *Ecclesia* was originally a secular word which was adopted by the early Christians to refer to their community. So, when Jesus says that he is going to build his church, he is not talking about a specific building, an institution or a denomination, but rather about a community of people who will embody his message of grace, love and truth.

So the church is you and me; the called-out people of God who have entered into a relationship with God and who come together to build a community to demonstrate God's love. It's really not about a church service on a Sunday, but rather about a life shared with people who believe in God and want to encourage you in your God-given potential. That's an incredibly liberating truth because it means that God's plans for humanity are not confined to a particular building, but are actually outworked through the lives of you and me.

God desires to see every human being brought into relationship with him, and his chosen mechanism of doing this is the church! The church is God's rescue plan for humanity, and so we shouldn't be surprised when he uses us to share his message of grace, love and truth to the people around us.

Often people will ask why the church even exists, and one of the reasons is that as humans we were created for community. There is a desire for relationship and social connection intrinsic to each of us, and it's clear that life was never meant to be done alone. God's answer to that desire for social connection is the church; it's the ideal habitat for humans to flourish and to truly be who we were created to be.

In Acts 2:42-47 we read a description of what the church looked like when it was first formed. When you read this passage, it's evident that serving each other was at the centre of everything they did. Whether it be through finances, property, food, or anything else, everyone sought to meet the needs of each other. This concept of a selfless community is rare in the world we live in, especially in the western world today, where we are often encouraged to think of ourselves first. It is only in the church where this idea is turned on its head; where we first meet the needs of others and in turn allow them to meet our needs.

The church is a community that you can become a part of too. We would love to encourage you to find a local church and to get involved as much as you can. The Bible compares the church to a body and makes the point that each of us is a part of the body. Just as we need every part of our body to be strong, so we also need each other to build a strong church —the body of Christ is stronger if you play your part!

Just like the early believers in Acts, look to serve the people you come into contact with, look to share life with them and look for opportunities to use your God-given gifts and talents to build the church.

YOU WILL FIND YOURSELF GROWING AND STEPPING INTO SO MUCH MORE THAN YOU COULD EVER DREAM OR IMAGINE. THE CHURCH IS GOD'S VEHICLE FOR REACHING A BROKEN WORLD, AND IT'S AN AMAZING PRIVILEGE THAT WE ARE INCLUDED IN THIS PLAN!

Chapter Sixteen
The Pharisees and Sadducees Demand Signs

And the Pharisees and Sadducees came, and to test him they asked him to show them a sign from heaven. ² He answered them, "When it is evening, you say, 'It will be fair weather, for the sky is red.' ³ And in the morning, 'It will be stormy today, for the sky is red and threatening.' You know how to interpret the appearance of the sky, but you cannot interpret the signs of the times. ⁴ An evil and adulterous generation seeks for a sign, but no sign will be given to it except the sign of Jonah." So he left them and departed.

The Leaven of the Pharisees and Sadducees
⁵ When the disciples reached the other side, they had forgotten to bring any bread. ⁶ Jesus said to them, "Watch and beware of the leaven of the Pharisees and Sadducees." ⁷ And they began discussing it among themselves, saying, "We brought no bread." ⁸ But Jesus, aware of this, said, "O you of little faith, why are you discussing among yourselves the fact that you have no bread? ⁹ Do you not yet perceive? Do you not remember the five loaves for the five thousand, and how many baskets you gathered? ¹⁰ Or the seven loaves for the four thousand, and how many baskets you gathered? ¹¹ How is it that you fail to understand that I did not speak about bread? Beware of the leaven of the Pharisees and Sadducees." ¹² Then they understood that he did not tell them to beware of the leaven of bread, but of the teaching of the Pharisees and Sadducees.

Peter Confesses Jesus as the Christ
¹³ Now when Jesus came into the district of Caesarea Philippi, he asked his disciples, "Who do people say that the Son of Man is?" ¹⁴ And they said, "Some say John the Baptist, others say Elijah, and others Jeremiah or one of the prophets." ¹⁵ He said to them, "But who do you say that I am?" ¹⁶ Simon Peter replied, "You are the Christ, the Son of the living God." ¹⁷ And Jesus answered him, "Blessed are you, Simon Bar-Jonah! For flesh and blood has not revealed this to you, but my Father who is in heaven. ¹⁸ And I tell you, you are Peter, and on this rock I will build my church, and the gates of hell shall not prevail against

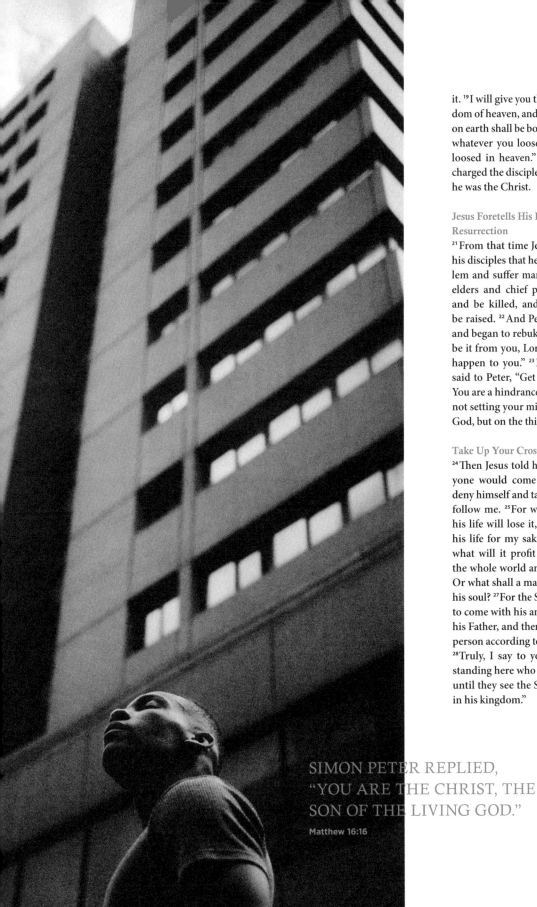

it. [19] I will give you the keys of the kingdom of heaven, and whatever you bind on earth shall be bound in heaven, and whatever you loose on earth shall be loosed in heaven." [20] Then he strictly charged the disciples to tell no one that he was the Christ.

Jesus Foretells His Death and Resurrection

[21] From that time Jesus began to show his disciples that he must go to Jerusalem and suffer many things from the elders and chief priests and scribes, and be killed, and on the third day be raised. [22] And Peter took him aside and began to rebuke him, saying, "Far be it from you, Lord! This shall never happen to you." [23] But he turned and said to Peter, "Get behind me, Satan! You are a hindrance to me. For you are not setting your mind on the things of God, but on the things of man."

Take Up Your Cross and Follow Jesus

[24] Then Jesus told his disciples, "If anyone would come after me, let him deny himself and take up his cross and follow me. [25] For whoever would save his life will lose it, but whoever loses his life for my sake will find it. [26] For what will it profit a man if he gains the whole world and forfeits his soul? Or what shall a man give in return for his soul? [27] For the Son of Man is going to come with his angels in the glory of his Father, and then he will repay each person according to what he has done. [28] Truly, I say to you, there are some standing here who will not taste death until they see the Son of Man coming in his kingdom."

SIMON PETER REPLIED,
"YOU ARE THE CHRIST, THE
SON OF THE LIVING GOD."

Matthew 16:16

Chapter Seventeen
The Transfiguration

"If you have faith like a grain of mustard seed, you will say to this mountain, 'Move from here to there', and it will move, and nothing will be impossible for you."

Matthew 17:20

And after six days Jesus took with him Peter and James, and John his brother, and led them up a high mountain by themselves. ² And he was transfigured before them, and his face shone like the sun, and his clothes became white as light. ³ And behold, there appeared to them Moses and Elijah, talking with him. ⁴ And Peter said to Jesus, "Lord, it is good that we are here. If you wish, I will make three tents here, one for you and one for Moses and one for Elijah." ⁵ He was still speaking when, behold, a bright cloud overshadowed them, and a voice from the cloud said, "This is my beloved Son, with whom I am well pleased; listen to him." ⁶ When the disciples heard this, they fell on their faces and were terrified. ⁷ But Jesus came and touched them, saying, "Rise, and have no fear." ⁸ And when they lifted up their eyes, they saw no one but Jesus only.

⁹ And as they were coming down the mountain, Jesus commanded them, "Tell no one the vision, until the Son of Man is raised from the dead." ¹⁰ And the disciples asked him, "Then why do the scribes say that first Elijah must come?" ¹¹ He answered, "Elijah does come, and he will restore all things. ¹²But I tell you that Elijah has already come, and they did not recognize him, but did to him whatever they pleased. So also the Son of Man will certainly suffer at their hands." ¹³ Then the disciples understood that he was speaking to them of John the Baptist.

Jesus Heals a Boy with a Demon
¹⁴ And when they came to the crowd, a man came up to him and, kneeling before him, ¹⁵ said, "Lord, have mercy on my son, for he has seizures and he suffers terribly. For often he falls into the fire, and often into the water. ¹⁶ And I brought him to your disciples, and they could not heal him." ¹⁷ And Jesus answered, "O faithless and twisted generation, how long am I to be with you? How long am I to bear with you? Bring him here to me." ¹⁸ And Jesus rebuked the demon, and it came out of him, and the boy was healed instantly. ¹⁹ Then the disciples came to Jesus privately and said, "Why could we not cast it out?" ²⁰ He said to them, "Because of your little faith. For truly, I say to you, if you have faith like a grain of mustard seed, you will say to this mountain, 'Move from here to there', and it will move, and nothing will be impossible for you."

Jesus Again Foretells Death, Resurrection
²² As they were gathering in Galilee, Jesus said to them, "The Son of Man is about to be delivered into the hands of men, ²³and they will kill him, and he will be raised on the third day." And they were greatly distressed.

The Temple Tax
²⁴ When they came to Capernaum, the collectors of the two-drachma tax went up to Peter and said, "Does your teacher not pay the tax?" ²⁵ He said, "Yes." And when he came into the house, Jesus spoke to him first, saying, "What do you think, Simon? From whom do kings of the earth take toll or tax? From their sons or from others?" ²⁶ And when he said, "From others", Jesus said to him, "Then the sons are free. ²⁷However, not to give offence to them, go to the lake and cast a hook and take the first fish that comes up, and when you open its mouth you will find a shekel. Take that and give it to them for me and for yourself."

Chapter Eighteen
Who is the Greatest?

A t that time the disciples came to Jesus, saying, "Who is the greatest in the kingdom of heaven?" ² And calling to him a child, he put him in the midst of them ³ and said, "Truly, I say to you, unless you turn and become like children, you will never enter the kingdom of heaven. ⁴Whoever humbles himself like this child is the greatest in the kingdom of heaven.

⁵"Whoever receives one such child in my name receives me, ⁶but whoever causes one of these little ones who believe in me to sin, it would be better for him to have a great millstone fastened round his neck and to be drowned in the depth of the sea.

Temptations to Sin
⁷"Woe to the world for temptations to sin! For it is necessary that temptations come, but woe to the one by whom the temptation comes! ⁸And if your hand or your foot causes you to sin, cut it off and throw it away. It is better for you to enter life crippled or lame than with two hands or two feet to be thrown into the eternal fire. ⁹And if your eye causes you to sin, tear it out and throw it away. It is better for you to enter life with one eye than with two eyes to be thrown into the hell of fire.

The Parable of the Lost Sheep
¹⁰"See that you do not despise one of these little ones. For I tell you that in heaven their angels always see the face of my Father who is in heaven. ¹²What do you think? If a man has a hundred sheep, and one of them has gone astray, does he not leave the ninety-nine on the mountains and go in search of the one that went astray? ¹³And if he finds it, truly, I say to you, he rejoices over it more than over the ninety-nine that never went astray. ¹⁴So it is not the will of my Father who is in heaven that one of these little ones should perish.

If Your Brother Sins Against You
¹⁵"If your brother sins against you, go and tell him his fault, between you and him alone. If he listens to you, you have gained your brother. ¹⁶But if he does not listen, take one or two others along with you, that every charge may be established by the evidence of two or three witnesses. ¹⁷If he refuses to listen to them, tell it to the church. And if he refuses to listen even to the church, let him be to you as a Gentile and a tax collector. ¹⁸Truly, I say to you, whatever you bind on earth shall be bound in heaven, and whatever you loose on earth shall be loosed in heaven. ¹⁹Again I say to you, if two of you agree on

earth about anything they ask, it will be done for them by my Father in heaven. [20]For where two or three are gathered in my name, there am I among them."

The Parable of the Unforgiving Servant

[21]Then Peter came up and said to him, "Lord, how often will my brother sin against me, and I forgive him? As many as seven times?" [22]Jesus said to him, "I do not say to you seven times, but seventy-seven times.

[23]"Therefore the kingdom of heaven may be compared to a king who wished to settle accounts with his servants. [24]When he began to settle, one was brought to him who owed him ten thousand talents. [25]And since he could not pay, his master ordered him to be sold, with his wife and children and all that he had, and payment to be made. [26]So the servant fell on his knees, imploring him, 'Have patience with me, and I will pay you everything.' [27]And out of pity for him, the master of that servant released him and forgave him the debt. [28]But when that same servant went out, he found one of his fellow servants who owed him a hundred denarii, and seizing him, he began to choke him, saying, 'Pay what you owe.' [29]So his fellow servant fell down and pleaded with him, 'Have patience with me, and I will pay you.' [30]He refused and went and put him in prison until he should pay the debt. [31]When his fellow servants saw what had taken place, they were greatly distressed, and they went and reported to their master all that had taken place. [32]Then his master summoned him and said to him, 'You wicked servant! I forgave you all that debt because you pleaded with me. [33]And should not you have had mercy on your fellow servant, as I had mercy on you?' [34]And in anger his master delivered him to the jailers, until he should pay all his debt. [35]So also my heavenly Father will do to every one of you, if you do not forgive your brother from your heart."

"...IF A MAN HAS

a hundred sheep, and one of them has gone astray, does he not leave the ninety-nine on the mountains and go in search of the one that went astray? And if he finds it, truly, I say to you, he rejoices over it more than over the ninety-nine that never went astray. So it is not the will of my Father who is in heaven that one of these little ones should perish."

Matthew 18:12-14

Chapter Nineteen
Teaching About Divorce

The disciples rebuked the people, but Jesus said, "Let the little children come to me and do not hinder them, for to such belongs the kingdom of heaven."

Matthew 19:13-14

Now when Jesus had finished these sayings, he went away from Galilee and entered the region of Judea beyond the Jordan. ² And large crowds followed him, and he healed them there.

³ And Pharisees came up to him and tested him by asking, "Is it lawful to divorce one's wife for any cause?" ⁴ He answered, "Have you not read that he who created them from the beginning made them male and female, ⁵ and said, 'Therefore a man shall leave his father and his mother and hold fast to his wife, and the two shall become one flesh'? ⁶ So they are no longer two but one flesh. What therefore God has joined together, let not man separate." ⁷ They said to him, "Why then did Moses command one to give a certificate of divorce and to send her away?" ⁸ He said to them, "Because of your hardness of heart Moses allowed you to divorce your wives, but from the beginning it was not so. ⁹ And I say to you: whoever divorces his wife, except for sexual immorality, and marries another, commits adultery."

¹⁰ The disciples said to him, "If such is the case of a man with his wife, it is better not to marry." ¹¹ But he said to them, "Not everyone can receive this saying, but only those to whom it is given. ¹² For there are eunuchs who have been so from birth, and there are eunuchs who have been made eunuchs by men, and there are eunuchs who have made themselves eunuchs for the sake of the kingdom of heaven. Let the one who is able to receive this receive it."

Let the Children Come to Me
¹³ Then children were brought to him that he might lay his hands on them and pray. The disciples rebuked the people, ¹⁴ but Jesus said, "Let the little children come to me and do not hinder them, for to such belongs the kingdom of heaven." ¹⁵ And he laid his hands on them and went away.

The Rich Young Man
¹⁶ And behold, a man came up to him, saying, "Teacher, what good deed must I do to have eternal life?" ¹⁷ And he said to him, "Why do you ask me about what is good? There is only one who is good. If you would enter life, keep the commandments." ¹⁸ He said to him, "Which ones?" And Jesus said, "You shall not murder, You shall not commit adultery, You shall not steal, You shall not bear false witness, ¹⁹ Honour your father and mother, and, You shall love your neighbour as yourself." ²⁰ The young man said to him, "All these I have kept. What do I still lack?" ²¹ Jesus said to him, "If you would be perfect, go, sell what you possess and give to the poor, and you will have treasure in heaven; and come, follow me." ²² When the young man heard this he went away sorrowful, for he had great possessions.

²³ And Jesus said to his disciples, "Truly, I say to you, only with difficulty will a rich person enter the kingdom of heaven. ²⁴ Again I tell you, it is easier for a camel to go through the eye of a needle than for a rich person to enter the kingdom of God." ²⁵ When the disciples heard this, they were greatly astonished, saying, "Who then can be saved?" ²⁶ But Jesus looked at them and said, "With man this is impossible, but with God all things are possible." ²⁷ Then Peter said in reply, "See, we have left everything and followed you. What then will we have?" ²⁸ Jesus said to them, "Truly, I say to you, in the new world, when the Son of Man will sit on his glorious throne, you who have followed me will also sit on twelve thrones, judging the twelve tribes of Israel. ²⁹ And everyone who has left houses or brothers or sisters or father or mother or children or lands, for my name's sake, will receive a hundredfold and will inherit eternal life. ³⁰ But many who are first will be last, and the last first.

✝

Chapter Twenty
Labourers in the Vineyard

For the kingdom of heaven is like a master of a house who went out early in the morning to hire labourers for his vineyard. ²After agreeing with the labourers for a denarius a day, he sent them into his vineyard. ³And going out about the third hour he saw others standing idle in the market-place, ⁴and to them he said, 'You go into the vineyard too, and whatever is right I will give you.' ⁵So they went. Going out again about the sixth hour and the ninth hour, he did the same.

⁶ And about the eleventh hour he went out and found others standing. And he said to them, 'Why do you stand here idle all day?'' They said to him, 'Because no one has hired us.' He said to them, 'You go into the vineyard too.'⁸And when evening came, the owner of the vineyard said to his foreman, 'Call the labourers

> AND STOPPING, JESUS CALLED THEM AND SAID,
> "WHAT DO YOU WANT ME TO DO FOR YOU?"
> THEY SAID TO HIM, "LORD, LET OUR EYES
> BE OPENED." AND JESUS IN PITY TOUCHED
> THEIR EYES, AND IMMEDIATELY THEY
> RECOVERED THEIR SIGHT AND
> FOLLOWED HIM.
>
> Matthew 20:32-34

and pay them their wages, beginning with the last, up to the first.' ⁹And when those hired about the eleventh hour came, each of them received a denarius. ¹⁰Now when those hired first came, they thought they would receive more, but each of them also received a denarius. ¹¹And on receiving it they grumbled at the master of the house, ¹²saying, 'These last worked only one hour, and you have made them equal to us who have borne the burden of the day and the scorching heat.' ¹³But he replied to one of them, 'Friend, I am doing you no wrong. Did you not agree with me for a denarius? ¹⁴Take what belongs to you and go. I choose to give to this last worker as I give to you. ¹⁵Am I not allowed to do what I choose with what belongs to me? Or do you begrudge my generosity?' ¹⁶So the last will be first, and the first last."

Jesus Foretells His Death a Third Time

¹⁷And as Jesus was going up to Jerusalem, he took the twelve disciples aside, and on the way he said to them, ¹⁸"See, we are going up to Jerusalem. And the Son of Man will be delivered over to the chief priests and scribes, and they will condemn him to death ¹⁹and deliver him over to the Gentiles to be mocked and flogged and crucified, and he will be raised on the third day."

A Mother's Request

²⁰Then the mother of the sons of Zebedee came up to him with her sons, and kneeling before him she asked him for something. ²¹And he said to her, "What do you want?" She said to him, "Say that these two sons of mine are to sit, one at your right hand and one at your left, in your kingdom." ²²Jesus answered, "You do not know what you are asking. Are you able to drink the cup that I am to drink?" They said to him, "We are able." ²³He said to them, "You will drink my cup, but to sit at my right hand and at my left is not mine to grant, but it is for those for whom it has been prepared by my Father." ²⁴And when the ten heard it, they were indignant at the two brothers. ²⁵But Jesus called them to him and said, "You know that the rulers of the Gentiles lord it over them, and their great ones exercise authority over them. ²⁶It shall not be so among you. But whoever would be great among you must be your servant, ²⁷and whoever would be first among you must be your slave, ²⁸even as the Son of Man came not to be served but to serve, and to give his life as a ransom for many."

Jesus Heals Two Blind Men

²⁹And as they went out of Jericho, a great crowd followed him. ³⁰And behold, there were two blind men sitting by the roadside, and when they heard that Jesus was passing by, they cried out, "Lord, have mercy on us, Son of David!" ³¹The crowd rebuked them, telling them to be silent, but they cried out all the more, "Lord, have mercy on us, Son of David!" ³²And stopping, Jesus called them and said, "What do you want me to do for you?" ³³They said to him, "Lord, let our eyes be opened." ³⁴And Jesus in pity touched their eyes, and immediately they recovered their sight and followed him.

Chapter Twenty-One

The Triumphal Entry

Now when they drew near to Jerusalem and came to Bethphage, to the Mount of Olives, then Jesus sent two disciples, [2] saying to them, "Go into the village in front of you, and immediately you will find a donkey tied, and a colt with her. Untie them and bring them to me. [3] If anyone says anything to you, you shall say, 'The Lord needs them', and he will send them at once." [4] This took place to fulfil what was spoken by the prophet, saying,

[5] "Say to the daughter of Zion,
   'Behold, your king is coming to
      you,
   humble, and mounted on a
      donkey,
      on a colt, the foal of a beast of
         burden.'"

[6] The disciples went and did as Jesus had directed them. [7] They brought the donkey and the colt and put on them their cloaks, and he sat on them. [8] Most of the crowd spread their cloaks on the road, and others cut branches from the trees and spread them on the road. [9] And the crowds that went before him and that followed him were shouting, "Hosanna to the Son of David! Blessed is he who comes in the name of the Lord! Hosanna in the highest!" [10] And when he entered Jerusalem, the whole city was stirred up, saying, "Who is this?" [11] And the crowds said, "This is the prophet Jesus, from Nazareth of Galilee."

Jesus Cleanses the Temple

[12] And Jesus entered the temple and drove out all who sold and bought in the temple, and he overturned the tables of the money-changers and the seats of those who sold pigeons. [13] He said to them, "It is written, 'My house shall be called a house of prayer', but you make it a den of robbers."

[14] And the blind and the lame came to him in the temple, and he healed them. [15] But when the chief priests and the scribes saw the wonderful things that he did, and the children crying out in the temple, "Hosanna to the Son of David!" they were indignant, [16] and they said to him, "Do you hear what these are saying?" And Jesus said to them, "Yes; have you never read,

"'Out of the mouth of infants and
      nursing babies
   you have prepared praise'?"

[17] And leaving them, he went out of the city to Bethany and lodged there.

Jesus Curses the Fig Tree

[18] In the morning, as he was returning to the city, he became hungry. [19] And seeing a fig tree by the wayside, he went to it and found nothing on it but only leaves. And he said to it, "May no fruit ever come from you again!" And the fig tree withered at once.

[20] When the disciples saw it, they marvelled, saying, "How did the fig tree wither at once?" [21] And Jesus answered them, "Truly, I say to you, if you have faith and do not doubt, you will not only do what has been done to the fig tree, but even if you say to this moun-

AND JESUS ENTERED THE TEMPLE AND DROVE OUT ALL WHO SOLD AND BOUGHT IN THE TEMPLE, AND HE OVERTURNED THE TABLES OF THE MONEY-CHANGERS AND THE SEATS OF THOSE WHO SOLD PIGEONS. HE SAID TO THEM, "IT IS WRITTEN, 'MY HOUSE SHALL BE CALLED A HOUSE OF PRAYER', BUT YOU MAKE IT A DEN OF ROBBERS."

Matthew 21:12-13

tain, 'Be taken up and thrown into the sea', it will happen. ²²And whatever you ask in prayer, you will receive, if you have faith."

The Authority of Jesus Challenged

²³ And when he entered the temple, the chief priests and the elders of the people came up to him as he was teaching, and said, "By what authority are you doing these things, and who gave you this authority?" ²⁴ Jesus answered them, "I also will ask you one question, and if you tell me the answer, then I also will tell you by what authority I do these things. ²⁵ The baptism of John, from where did it come? From heaven or from man?" And they discussed it among themselves, saying, "If we say, 'From heaven', he will say to us, 'Why then did you not believe him?' ²⁶ But if we say, 'From man', we are afraid of the crowd, for they all hold that John was a prophet." ²⁷ So they answered Jesus, "We do not know." And he said to them, "Neither will I tell you by what authority I do these things.

The Parable of the Two Sons

²⁸ "What do you think? A man had two sons. And he went to the first and said, 'Son, go and work in the vineyard today.' ²⁹ And he answered, 'I will not', but afterwards he changed his mind and went. ³⁰ And he went to the other son and said the same. And he answered, 'I go, sir', but did not go. ³¹ Which of the

two did the will of his father?" They said, "The first." Jesus said to them, "Truly, I say to you, the tax collectors and the prostitutes go into the kingdom of God before you. ³²For John came to you in the way of righteousness, and you did not believe him, but the tax collectors and the prostitutes believed him. And even when you saw it, you did not afterwards change your minds and believe him.

The Parable of the Tenants

³³"Hear another parable. There was a master of a house who planted a vineyard and put a fence round it and dug a wine press in it and built a tower and leased it to tenants, and went into another country. ³⁴When the season for fruit drew near, he sent his servants to the tenants to get his fruit. ³⁵And the tenants took his servants and beat one, killed another, and stoned another. ³⁶Again he sent other servants, more than at first. And they did the same to them. ³⁷Finally he sent his son to them, saying, 'They will respect my son.' ³⁸But when the tenants saw the son, they said to themselves, 'This is the heir. Come, let us kill him and have his inheritance.' ³⁹And they took him and threw him out of the vineyard and killed him. ⁴⁰When therefore the owner of the vineyard comes, what will he do to those tenants?" ⁴¹They said to him, "He will put those wretches to a miserable death

and let out the vineyard to other tenants who will give him the fruits in their seasons."

⁴²Jesus said to them, "Have you never read in the Scriptures:

"'The stone that the builders rejected
 has become the cornerstone;
this was the Lord's doing,
 and it is marvellous in our
 eyes'?

⁴³Therefore I tell you, the kingdom of God will be taken away from you and given to a people producing its fruits. ⁴⁴And the one who falls on this stone will be broken to pieces; and when it falls on anyone, it will crush him."

⁴⁵ When the chief priests and the Pharisees heard his parables, they perceived that he was speaking about them. ⁴⁶ And although they were seeking to arrest him, they feared the crowds, because they held him to be a prophet.

Chapter Twenty-Two
The Parable of the Wedding Feast

And again Jesus spoke to them in parables, saying, ²"The kingdom of heaven may be compared to a king who gave a wedding feast for his son, ³and sent his servants to call those who were invited to the wedding feast, but they would not come. ⁴Again he sent other servants, saying, 'Tell those who are invited, "See, I have prepared my dinner, my oxen and my fat calves have been slaughtered, and everything is ready. Come to the wedding feast."' ⁵But they paid no attention and went off, one to his farm, another to his business, ⁶while the rest seized his servants, treated them shamefully, and killed them. ⁷The king was angry, and he sent his troops and destroyed those murderers and burned their city. ⁸Then he said to his servants, 'The wedding feast is ready, but those invited were not worthy. ⁹Go therefore to the main roads and invite to the wedding feast as many as you find.' ¹⁰And those servants went out into the roads and gathered all whom they found, both bad and good. So the wedding hall was filled with guests.

¹¹"But when the king came in to look at the guests, he saw there a man who had no wedding garment. ¹²And he said to him, 'Friend, how did you get in here without a wedding garment?' And he was speechless. ¹³Then the king said to the attendants, 'Bind him hand and foot and cast him into the outer darkness. In that place there will be weeping and gnashing of teeth.' ¹⁴For many are called, but few are chosen."

Paying Taxes to Caesar
¹⁵ Then the Pharisees went and plotted how to entangle him in his words. ¹⁶ And they sent their disciples to him, along with the Herodians, saying,

"Teacher, we know that you are true and teach the way of God truthfully, and you do not care about anyone's opinion, for you are not swayed by appearances. [17] Tell us, then, what you think. Is it lawful to pay taxes to Caesar, or not?" [18] But Jesus, aware of their malice, said, "Why put me to the test, you hypocrites? [19] Show me the coin for the tax." And they brought him a denarius. [20] And Jesus said to them, "Whose likeness and inscription is this?" [21] They said, "Caesar's." Then he said to them, "Therefore render to Caesar the things that are Caesar's, and to God the things that are God's." [22] When they heard it, they marvelled. And they left him and went away.

Sadducees Ask About the Resurrection

[23] The same day Sadducees came to him, who say that there is no resurrection, and they asked him a question, [24] saying, "Teacher, Moses said, 'If a man dies having no children, his brother must marry the widow and raise up offspring for his brother.' [25] Now there were seven brothers among us. The first married and died, and having no offspring left his wife to his brother. [26] So too the second and third, down to the seventh. [27] After them all, the woman died. [28] In the resurrection, therefore, of the seven, whose wife will she be? For they all had her."

[29] But Jesus answered them, "You are wrong, because you know neither the Scriptures nor the power of God. [30] For in the resurrection they neither marry nor are given in marriage, but are like angels in heaven. [31] And as for the resurrection of the dead, have you not read what was said to you by God: [32] 'I am the God of Abraham, and the God of Isaac, and the God of Jacob'? He is not God of the dead, but of the living." [33] And when the crowd heard it, they were astonished at his teaching.

The Great Commandment

[34] But when the Pharisees heard that he had silenced the Sadducees, they gathered together. [35] And one of them, a lawyer, asked him a question to test him. [36] "Teacher, which is the great commandment in the Law?" [37] And he said to him, "You shall love the Lord your God with all your heart and with all your soul and with all your mind. [38] This is the great and first commandment. [39] And a second is like it: You shall love your neighbour as yourself. [40] On these two commandments depend all the Law and the Prophets."

Whose Son Is the Christ?

[41] Now while the Pharisees were gathered together, Jesus asked them a question, [42] saying, "What do you think about the Christ? Whose son is he?" They said to him, "The son of David." [43] He said to them, "How is it then that David, in the Spirit, calls him Lord, saying,

[44]   "'The Lord said to my Lord,
        "Sit at my right hand,
            until I put your enemies under
                your feet"'?

[45] If then David calls him Lord, how is he his son?" [46] And no one was able to answer him a word, nor from that day did anyone dare to ask him any more questions.

"TEACHER, WHICH IS THE GREAT COMMANDMENT IN THE LAW?" AND HE SAID TO HIM, "YOU SHALL LOVE THE LORD YOUR GOD WITH ALL YOUR HEART AND WITH ALL YOUR SOUL AND WITH ALL YOUR MIND. THIS IS THE GREAT AND FIRST COMMANDMENT."

Matthew 22:36-38

Chapter Twenty-Three
Seven Woes to the Scribes and Pharisees

Then Jesus said to the crowds and to his disciples, ²"The scribes and the Pharisees sit on Moses' seat, ³so do and observe whatever they tell you, but not the works they do. For they preach, but do not practise. ⁴They tie up heavy burdens, hard to bear, and lay them on people's shoulders, but they themselves are not willing to move them with their finger. ⁵They do all their deeds to be seen by others. For they make their phylacteries broad and their fringes long, ⁶and they love the place of honour at feasts and the best seats in the synagogues ⁷and greetings in the market-places and being called rabbi by others. ⁸But you are not to be called rabbi, for you have one teacher, and you are all brothers. ⁹And call no man your father on earth, for you have one Father, who is in heaven.

¹⁰Neither be called instructors, for you have one instructor, the Christ. ¹¹The greatest among you shall be your servant. ¹²Whoever exalts himself will be humbled, and whoever humbles himself will be exalted. ¹³"But woe to you, scribes and Pharisees, hypocrites! For you shut the kingdom of heaven in people's faces. For you neither enter yourselves nor allow those who would enter to go in. ¹⁵Woe to you, scribes and Pharisees, hypocrites! For you travel across sea and land to make a single proselyte, and when he becomes a proselyte, you make him twice as much a child of hell as yourselves.

¹⁶"Woe to you, blind guides, who say, 'If anyone swears by the temple, it is nothing, but if anyone swears by the gold of the temple, he is bound by his oath.' ¹⁷You blind fools! For which is greater, the gold or the temple that has made the gold sacred? ¹⁸And you say, 'If anyone swears by the altar, it is nothing, but if anyone swears by the gift that is on the altar, he is bound by his oath.' ¹⁹You blind men! For which is greater, the gift or the altar that makes the gift sacred? ²⁰So whoever swears by the altar swears by it and by everything on it. ²¹And whoever swears by the temple swears by it and by him who dwells in it. ²²And whoever swears by heaven swears by the throne of God and by him who sits upon it.

²³"Woe to you, scribes and Pharisees, hypocrites! For you tithe mint and dill and cumin, and have neglected the weightier matters of the law: justice and mercy and faithfulness. These you ought to have done, without neglecting the others. ²⁴You blind guides, straining out a gnat and swallowing a camel!

²⁵"Woe to you, scribes and Pharisees, hypocrites! For you clean the outside of the cup and the plate, but inside they are full of greed and self-indulgence. ²⁶You blind Pharisee! First clean the inside of the cup and the plate, that the outside also may be clean.

²⁷"Woe to you, scribes and Pharisees, hypocrites! For you are like whitewashed tombs, which outwardly appear beautiful, but within are full of dead people's bones and all uncleanness. ²⁸So you also outwardly appear righteous to others, but within you are full of hypocrisy and lawlessness.

²⁹"Woe to you, scribes and Pharisees, hypocrites! For you build the tombs of the prophets and decorate the monuments of the righteous, ³⁰saying, 'If we had lived in the days of our fathers, we would not have taken part with them in shedding the blood of the prophets.' ³¹Thus you witness against yourselves that you are sons of those who murdered the prophets. ³²Fill up, then, the measure of your fathers. ³³You serpents, you brood of vipers, how are you to escape being sentenced to hell? ³⁴Therefore I send you prophets and wise men and scribes, some of whom you will kill and crucify, and some you will flog in your synagogues and persecute from town to town, ³⁵so that on you may come all the righteous blood shed on earth, from the blood of righteous Abel to the blood of Zechariah the son of Barachiah, whom you murdered between the sanctuary and the altar. ³⁶Truly, I say to you, all these things will come upon this generation.

Lament over Jerusalem

³⁷ "O Jerusalem, Jerusalem, the city that kills the prophets and stones those who are sent to it! How often would I have gathered your children together as a hen gathers her brood under her wings, and you were not willing! ³⁸See, your house is left to you desolate. ³⁹For I tell you, you will not see me again, until you say, 'Blessed is he who comes in the name of the Lord.'"

Chapter Twenty-Four
Jesus Foretells Destruction of the Temple

"Truly, I say to you, this generation will not pass away until all these things take place. Heaven and earth will pass away, but my words will not pass away."

Matthew 24:34-35

Jesus left the temple and was going away, when his disciples came to point out to him the buildings of the temple. ² But he answered them, "You see all these, do you not? Truly, I say to you, there will not be left here one stone upon another that will not be thrown down."

Signs of the End of the Age

³ As he sat on the Mount of Olives, the disciples came to him privately, saying, "Tell us, when will these things be, and what will be the sign of your coming and of the end of the age?" ⁴ And Jesus answered them, "See that no one leads you astray. ⁵ For many will come in my name, saying, 'I am the Christ', and they will lead many astray. ⁶ And you will hear of wars and rumours of wars. See that you are not alarmed, for this must take place, but the end is not yet. ⁷ For nation will rise against nation, and kingdom against kingdom, and there will be famines and earthquakes in various places. ⁸ All these are but the beginning of the birth pains.

⁹ "Then they will deliver you up to tribulation and put you to death, and you will be hated by all nations for my name's sake. ¹⁰ And then many will fall away and betray one another and hate one another. ¹¹ And many false prophets will arise and lead many astray. ¹² And because lawlessness will be increased, the love of many will grow cold. ¹³ But the one who endures to the end will be saved. ¹⁴ And this gospel of the kingdom will be proclaimed throughout the whole world as a testimony to all nations, and then the end will come.

The Abomination of Desolation

¹⁵ "So when you see the abomination of desolation spoken of by the prophet Daniel, standing in the holy place (let the reader understand), ¹⁶ then let those who are in Judea flee to the mountains. ¹⁷ Let the one who is on the housetop not go down to take what is in his house, ¹⁸ and let the one who is in the field not turn back to take his cloak. ¹⁹ And alas for women who are pregnant and for those who are nursing infants in those days! ²⁰ Pray that your flight may not be in winter or on a Sabbath. ²¹ For then there will be great tribulation, such as has not been from the beginning of the world until now, no, and never will be. ²² And if those days had not been cut short, no human being would be saved. But for the sake of the elect those days will be cut short. ²³ Then if anyone says to you, 'Look, here is the Christ!' or 'There he is!' do not believe it. ²⁴ For false christs and false prophets will arise and perform great signs and wonders, so as to lead astray, if possible, even the elect. ²⁵ See, I have told you beforehand. ²⁶ So, if they say to you, 'Look, he is in the wilderness', do not go out. If they say, 'Look, he is in the inner rooms', do not believe it. ²⁷ For as the lightning comes from the east and shines as far as the west, so will be the coming of the Son of Man. ²⁸ Wherever the corpse is, there the vultures will gather.

The Coming of the Son of Man

²⁹ "Immediately after the tribulation of those days the sun will be darkened, and the moon will not give its light, and the stars will fall from heaven, and the powers of the heavens will be shaken. ³⁰ Then will appear in heaven the sign of the Son of Man, and then all the tribes of the earth will mourn, and they will see the Son of Man coming on the clouds of heaven with power and great glory. ³¹ And he will send out his angels with a loud trumpet call, and they will gather his elect from the four winds, from one end of heaven to the other.

<blockquote>
"WELL DONE, GOOD AND FAITHFUL SERVANT. YOU HAVE BEEN FAITHFUL OVER A LITTLE..."
</blockquote>

The Lesson of the Fig Tree

³²"From the fig tree learn its lesson: as soon as its branch becomes tender and puts out its leaves, you know that summer is near. ³³So also, when you see all these things, you know that he is near, at the very gates. ³⁴Truly, I say to you, this generation will not pass away until all these things take place. ³⁵Heaven and earth will pass away, but my words will not pass away.

No One Knows That Day and Hour

³⁶"But concerning that day and hour no one knows, not even the angels of heaven, nor the Son, but the Father only. ³⁷For as were the days of Noah, so will be the coming of the Son of Man. ³⁸For as in those days before the flood they were eating and drinking, marrying and giving in marriage, until the day when Noah entered the ark, ³⁹and they were unaware until the flood came and swept them all away, so will be the coming of the Son of Man. ⁴⁰Then two men will be in the field; one will be taken and one left. ⁴¹Two women will be grinding at the mill; one will be taken and one left. ⁴²Therefore, stay awake, for you do not know on what day your Lord is coming. ⁴³But know this, that if the master of the house had known in what part of the night the thief was coming, he would have stayed awake and would not have let his house be broken into. ⁴⁴Therefore you also must be ready, for the Son of Man is coming at an hour you do not expect.

⁴⁵"Who then is the faithful and wise servant, whom his master has set over his household, to give them their food at the proper time? ⁴⁶Blessed is that servant whom his master will find so doing when he comes. ⁴⁷Truly, I say to you, he will set him over all his possessions. ⁴⁸But if that wicked servant says to himself, 'My master is delayed', ⁴⁹and begins to beat his fellow servants and eats and drinks with drunkards, ⁵⁰the master of that servant will come on a day when he does not expect him and at an hour he does not know ⁵¹and will cut him in pieces and put him with the hypocrites. In that place there will be weeping and gnashing of teeth.

Chapter Twenty-Five
The Parable of the Ten Virgins

Then the kingdom of heaven will be like ten virgins who took their lamps and went to meet the bridegroom. ²Five of them were foolish, and five were wise. ³For when the foolish took their lamps, they took no oil with them, ⁴but the wise took flasks of oil with their lamps. ⁵As the bridegroom was delayed, they all became drowsy and slept. ⁶But at midnight there was a cry, 'Here is the bridegroom! Come out to meet him.' ⁷Then all those virgins rose and trimmed their lamps. ⁸And the foolish said to the wise, 'Give us some of your oil, for our lamps are going out.' ⁹But the wise answered, saying, 'Since there will not be enough for us and for you, go rather to the dealers and buy for yourselves.' ¹⁰And while they were going to buy, the bridegroom came, and those who were ready went in with him to the marriage feast, and the door was shut. ¹¹Afterwards the other virgins came also, saying, 'Lord, lord, open to us.' ¹²But he answered, 'Truly, I say to you, I do not know you.' ¹³Watch therefore, for you know neither the day nor the hour.

The Parable of the Talents

¹⁴"For it will be like a man going on a journey, who called his servants and entrusted to them his property. ¹⁵To one he gave five talents, to another two, to another one, to each according to his ability. Then he went away. ¹⁶He

who had received the five talents went at once and traded with them, and he made five talents more. ¹⁷So also he who had the two talents made two talents more. ¹⁸But he who had received the one talent went and dug in the ground and hid his master's money. ¹⁹Now after a long time the master of those servants came and settled accounts with them. ²⁰And he who had received the five talents came forward, bringing five talents more, saying, 'Master, you delivered to me five talents; here, I have made five talents more.' ²¹His master said to him, 'Well done, good and faithful servant. You have been faithful over a little; I will set you over much. Enter into the joy of your master.' ²²And he also who had the two talents came forward, saying, 'Master, you delivered to me two talents; here, I have made two talents more.' ²³His master said to him, 'Well done, good and faithful servant. You have been faithful over a little; I will set you over much. Enter into the joy of your master.' ²⁴He also who had received the one talent came forward, saying, 'Master, I knew you to be a hard man, reaping where you did not sow, and gathering where you scattered no seed, ²⁵so I was afraid, and I went and hid your talent in the ground. Here, you have what is yours.' ²⁶But his master answered him, 'You wicked and slothful servant! You knew that I reap where I have not sown and gather where I scattered no seed? ²⁷Then you ought to have invested my money with the bankers, and at my coming I should have received what was my own with interest. ²⁸So take the talent from him and give it to him who has the ten talents. ²⁹For to everyone who has will more be given, and he will have an abundance. But from the one who has not, even what he has will be taken away. ³⁰And cast the worthless servant into the outer darkness. In that place there will be weeping and gnashing of teeth.'

The Final Judgement

³¹"When the Son of Man comes in his glory, and all the angels with him, then he will sit on his glorious throne. ³²Before him will be gathered all the nations, and he will separate people one from another as a shepherd separates the sheep from the goats. ³³And he will place the sheep on his right, but the goats on the left. ³⁴Then the King will say to those on his right, 'Come, you who are blessed by my Father, inherit the kingdom prepared for you from the foundation of the world. ³⁵For I was hungry and you gave me food, I was thirsty and you gave me drink, I was a stranger and you welcomed me, ³⁶I was naked and you clothed me, I was sick and you visited me, I was in prison and you came to me.' ³⁷Then the righteous will answer him, saying, 'Lord, when did we see you hungry and feed you, or thirsty and give you drink? ³⁸And when did we see you a stranger and welcome you, or naked and clothe you? ³⁹And when did we see you sick or in prison and visit you?' ⁴⁰And the King will answer them, 'Truly, I say to you, as you did it to one of the least of these my brothers, you did it to me.'

⁴¹"Then he will say to those on his left, 'Depart from me, you cursed, into the eternal fire prepared for the devil and his angels. ⁴²For I was hungry and you gave me no food, I was thirsty and you gave me no drink, ⁴³I was a stranger and you did not welcome me, naked and you did not clothe me, sick and in prison and you did not visit me.' ⁴⁴Then they also will answer, saying, 'Lord, when did we see you hungry or thirsty or a stranger or naked or sick or in prison, and did not minister to you?' ⁴⁵Then he will answer them, saying, 'Truly, I say to you, as you did not do it to one of the least of these, you did not do it to me.' ⁴⁶And these will go away into eternal punishment, but the righteous into eternal life."

"...I WILL SET YOU OVER MUCH. ENTER INTO THE JOY OF YOUR MASTER."

Matthew 25:23

Chapter Twenty-Six
The Plot to Kill Jesus

When Jesus had finished all these sayings, he said to his disciples, ² "You know that after two days the Passover is coming, and the Son of Man will be delivered up to be crucified."

³ Then the chief priests and the elders of the people gathered in the palace of the high priest, whose name was Caiaphas, ⁴ and plotted together in order to arrest Jesus by stealth and kill him. ⁵ But they said, "Not during the feast, lest there be an uproar among the people."

Jesus Anointed at Bethany

⁶ Now when Jesus was at Bethany in the house of Simon the leper, ⁷ a woman came up to him with an alabaster flask of very expensive ointment, and she poured it on his head as he reclined at table. ⁸ And when the disciples saw it, they were indignant, saying, "Why this waste? ⁹ For this could have been sold for a large sum and given to the poor." ¹⁰ But Jesus, aware of this, said to them, "Why do you trouble the woman? For she has done a beautiful thing to me. ¹¹ For you always have the poor with you, but you will not always have me. ¹² In pouring this ointment on my body, she has done it to prepare me for burial. ¹³ Truly, I say to you, wherever this gospel is proclaimed in the whole world, what she has done will also be told in memory of her."

Judas to Betray Jesus

¹⁴ Then one of the twelve, whose name was Judas Iscariot, went to the chief priests ¹⁵ and said, "What will you give me if I deliver him over to you?" And they paid him thirty pieces of silver. ¹⁶ And from that moment he sought an opportunity to betray him.

The Passover with the Disciples

¹⁷ Now on the first day of Unleavened Bread the disciples came to Jesus, saying, "Where would you have us prepare for you to eat the Passover?" ¹⁸ He said, "Go into the city to a certain man and say to him, 'The Teacher says, My time is at hand. I will keep the Passover at your house with my disciples.' " ¹⁹ And the disciples did as Jesus had directed them, and they prepared the Passover.

²⁰ When it was evening, he reclined at table with the twelve. ²¹ And as they were eating, he said, "Truly, I say to you, one of you will betray me." ²² And they were very sorrowful and began

NOW THE BETRAYER
HAD GIVEN THEM A SIGN,
SAYING, "THE ONE I WILL KISS
IS THE MAN; SEIZE HIM." AND HE
CAME UP TO JESUS AT ONCE
AND SAID,"GREETINGS, RABBI!"
AND HE KISSED HIM.

Matthew 26:48-49

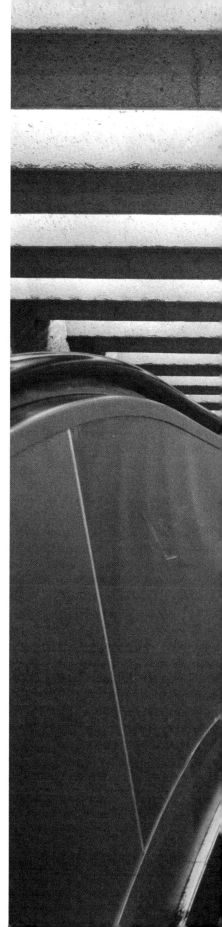

to say to him one after another, "Is it I, Lord?" ²³ He answered, "He who has dipped his hand in the dish with me will betray me. ²⁴ The Son of Man goes as it is written of him, but woe to that man by whom the Son of Man is betrayed! It would have been better for that man if he had not been born." ²⁵ Judas, who would betray him, answered, "Is it I, Rabbi?" He said to him, "You have said so."

Institution of the Lord's Supper

²⁶ Now as they were eating, Jesus took bread, and after blessing it broke it and gave it to the disciples, and said, "Take, eat; this is my body." ²⁷ And he took a cup, and when he had given thanks he gave it to them, saying, "Drink of it, all of you, ²⁸ for this is my blood of the covenant, which is poured out for many for the forgiveness of sins. ²⁹ I tell you I will not drink again of this fruit of the vine until that day when I drink it new with you in my Father's kingdom."

Jesus Foretells Peter's Denial

³⁰ And when they had sung a hymn, they went out to the Mount of Olives. ³¹ Then Jesus said to them, "You will all fall away because of me this night. For it is written, 'I will strike the shepherd, and the sheep of the flock will be scattered.' ³² But after I am raised up, I will go before you to Galilee." ³³ Peter answered him, "Though they all fall away because of you, I will never fall away." ³⁴ Jesus said to him, "Truly, I tell you, this very night, before the cock crows, you will deny me three times." ³⁵ Peter said to him, "Even if I must die with you, I will not deny you!" And all the disciples said the same.

Jesus Prays in Gethsemane

³⁶ Then Jesus went with them to a place called Gethsemane, and he said to his disciples, "Sit here, while I go over there and pray." ³⁷ And taking with him Peter and the two sons of Zebedee, he began to be sorrowful and troubled.

"MY SOUL IS VERY
SORROWFUL, EVEN TO
DEATH; REMAIN HERE,
AND WATCH WITH ME."
AND GOING A LITTLE
FARTHER HE FELL ON
HIS FACE AND PRAYED,
SAYING, "MY FATHER,
IF IT BE POSSIBLE, LET
THIS CUP PASS FROM
ME; NEVERTHELESS,
NOT AS I WILL, BUT
AS YOU WILL."

Matthew 26:38-39

[38] Then he said to them, "My soul is very sorrowful, even to death; remain here, and watch with me." [39] And going a little farther he fell on his face and prayed, saying, "My Father, if it be possible, let this cup pass from me; nevertheless, not as I will, but as you will." [40] And he came to the disciples and found them sleeping. And he said to Peter, "So, could you not watch with me one hour? [41] Watch and pray that you may not enter into temptation. The spirit indeed is willing, but the flesh is weak." [42] Again, for the second time, he went away and prayed, "My Father, if this cannot pass unless I drink it, your will be done." [43] And again he came and found them sleeping, for their eyes were heavy. [44] So, leaving them again, he went away and prayed for the third time, saying the same words again. [45] Then he came to the disciples and said to them, "Sleep and take your rest later on. See, the hour is at hand, and the Son of Man is betrayed into the hands of sinners. [46] Rise, let us be going; see, my betrayer is at hand."

Betrayal and Arrest of Jesus

[47] While he was still speaking, Judas came, one of the twelve, and with him a great crowd with swords and clubs, from the chief priests and the elders of the people. [48] Now the betrayer had given them a sign, saying, "The one I will kiss is the man; seize him." [49] And he came up to Jesus at once and said, "Greetings, Rabbi!" And he kissed him. [50] Jesus said to him, "Friend, do what you came to do." Then they came up and laid hands on Jesus and seized him. [51] And behold, one of those who were with Jesus stretched out his hand and drew his sword and struck the servant of the high priest and cut off his ear. [52] Then Jesus said to him, "Put your sword back into its place. For all who take the sword will perish by the sword. [53] Do you think that I cannot appeal to my Father, and he will at once send me more than twelve legions of angels? [54] But how then should the Scriptures be fulfilled, that it must be so?" [55] At that hour Jesus said to the crowds, "Have you come out as against a robber, with swords and clubs to capture me? Day after day I sat in the temple teaching, and you did not seize me. [56] But all this has taken place that the Scriptures of the prophets might be fulfilled." Then all the disciples left him and fled.

THEN HE
BEGAN TO
INVOKE A
CURSE ON
HIMSELF AND
TO SWEAR,
"I DO NOT
KNOW THE
MAN." AND
IMMEDIATELY
THE COCK
CROWED.
AND PETER
REMEMBERED
THE SAYING
OF JESUS,
"BEFORE THE
COCK CROWS,
YOU WILL
DENY ME
THREE TIMES."
AND HE
WENT OUT
AND WEPT
BITTERLY.

Matthew 26:74-75

Jesus Before Caiaphas and the Council

⁵⁷ Then those who had seized Jesus led him to Caiaphas the high priest, where the scribes and the elders had gathered. ⁵⁸ And Peter was following him at a distance, as far as the courtyard of the high priest, and going inside he sat with the guards to see the end. ⁵⁹ Now the chief priests and the whole council were seeking false testimony against Jesus that they might put him to death, ⁶⁰ but they found none, though many false witnesses came forward. At last two came forward ⁶¹ and said, "This man said, 'I am able to destroy the temple of God, and to rebuild it in three days.'" ⁶² And the high priest stood up and said, "Have you no answer to make? What is it that these men testify against you?" ⁶³ But Jesus remained silent. And the high priest said to him, "I adjure you by the living God, tell us if you are the Christ, the Son of God." ⁶⁴ Jesus said to him, "You have said so. But I tell you, from now on you will see the Son of Man seated at the right hand of Power and coming on the clouds of heaven." ⁶⁵ Then the high priest tore his robes and said, "He has uttered blasphemy. What further witnesses do we need? You have now heard his blasphemy. ⁶⁶ What is your judgement?" They answered, "He deserves death." ⁶⁷ Then they spat in his face and struck him. And some slapped him, ⁶⁸ saying, "Prophesy to us, you Christ! Who is it that struck you?"

Peter Denies Jesus

⁶⁹ Now Peter was sitting outside in the courtyard. And a servant girl came up to him and said, "You also were with Jesus the Galilean." ⁷⁰ But he denied it before them all, saying, "I do not know what you mean." ⁷¹ And when he went out to the entrance, another servant girl saw him, and she said to the bystanders, "This man was with Jesus of Nazareth." ⁷² And again he denied it with an oath: "I do not know the man." ⁷³ After a little while the bystanders came up and said to Peter, "Certainly you too are one of them, for your accent betrays you." ⁷⁴ Then he began to invoke a curse on himself and to swear, "I do not know the man." And immediately the cock crowed. ⁷⁵ And Peter remembered the saying of Jesus, "Before the cock crows, you will deny me three times." And he went out and wept bitterly.

JESUS BEFORE PILATE

THEN PILATE SAID
TO HIM, "DO YOU NOT
HEAR HOW MANY
THINGS THEY TESTIFY
AGAINST YOU?" BUT
HE GAVE HIM NO
ANSWER, NOT EVEN TO
A SINGLE CHARGE, SO
THAT THE GOVERNOR
WAS GREATLY
AMAZED.

Matthew 27:13-14

Chapter Twenty-Seven
Jesus Delivered to Pilate

When morning came, all the chief priests and the elders of the people took counsel against Jesus to put him to death. ² And they bound him and led him away and delivered him over to Pilate the governor.

Judas Hangs Himself

³ Then when Judas, his betrayer, saw that Jesus was condemned, he changed his mind and brought back the thirty pieces of silver to the chief priests and the elders, ⁴ saying, "I have sinned by betraying innocent blood." They said, "What is that to us? See to it yourself." ⁵ And throwing down the pieces of silver into the temple, he departed, and he went and hanged himself. ⁶ But the chief priests, taking the pieces of silver, said, "It is not lawful to put them into the treasury, since it is blood money." ⁷ So they took counsel and bought with them the potter's field as a burial place for strangers. ⁸ Therefore that field has been called the Field of Blood to this day. ⁹ Then was fulfilled what had been spoken by the prophet Jeremiah, saying, "And they took the thirty pieces of silver, the price of him on whom a price had been set by some of the sons of Israel, ¹⁰ and they gave them for the potter's field, as the Lord directed me."

Jesus Before Pilate

¹¹ Now Jesus stood before the governor, and the governor asked him, "Are you the King of the Jews?" Jesus said, "You have said so." ¹² But when he was accused by the chief priests and elders, he gave no answer. ¹³ Then Pilate said to him, "Do you not hear how many things they testify against you?" ¹⁴ But he gave him no answer, not even to a single charge, so that the governor was greatly amazed.

The Crowd Chooses Barabbas

¹⁵ Now at the feast the governor was accustomed to release for the crowd any one prisoner whom they wanted. ¹⁶ And they had then a notorious prisoner called Barabbas. ¹⁷ So when they had gathered, Pilate said to them, "Whom do you want me to release for you: Barabbas, or Jesus who is called Christ?" ¹⁸ For he knew that it was out of envy that they had delivered him up. ¹⁹ Besides, while he was sitting on the judgement seat, his wife sent word to him, "Have nothing to do with that righteous man, for I have suffered much because of him today in a dream." ²⁰ Now the chief priests and the elders persuaded the crowd to ask for Barabbas and destroy Jesus. ²¹ The governor again said to them, "Which of the two do you want me to release for you?" And they said, "Barabbas." ²² Pilate said to them, "Then what shall I do with Jesus who is called Christ?" They all said, "Let him be crucified!" ²³ And he said, "Why? What evil has he done?" But they shouted all the more, "Let him be crucified!"

Pilate Delivers Jesus to Be Crucified

²⁴ So when Pilate saw that he was gaining nothing, but rather that a riot was beginning, he took water and washed his hands before the crowd, saying, "I am innocent of this man's blood; see to it yourselves." ²⁵ And all the people answered, "His blood be on us and on our children!" ²⁶ Then he released for them Barabbas, and having scourged Jesus, delivered him to be crucified.

Jesus Is Mocked

²⁷ Then the soldiers of the governor took Jesus into the governor's headquarters,

and they gathered the whole battalion before him. [28] And they stripped him and put a scarlet robe on him, [29] and twisting together a crown of thorns, they put it on his head and put a reed in his right hand. And kneeling before him, they mocked him, saying, "Hail, King of the Jews!" [30] And they spat on him and took the reed and struck him on the head. [31] And when they had mocked him, they stripped him of the robe and put his own clothes on him and led him away to crucify him.

The Crucifixion

[32] As they went out, they found a man of Cyrene, Simon by name. They compelled this man to carry his cross. [33] And when they came to a place called Golgotha (which means Place of a Skull), [34] they offered him wine to drink, mixed with gall, but when he tasted it, he would not drink it. [35] And when they had crucified him, they divided his garments among them by casting lots. [36] Then they sat down and kept watch over him there. [37] And over his head they put the charge against him, which read, "This is Jesus, the King of the Jews." [38] Then two robbers were crucified with him, one on the right and one on the left. [39] And those who passed by derided him, wagging their heads [40] and saying, "You who would destroy the temple and rebuild it in three days, save yourself! If you are the Son of God, come down from the cross." [41] So also the chief priests, with the scribes and elders, mocked him, saying, [42] "He saved others; he cannot save himself. He is the King of Israel; let him come down now from the cross,

and we will believe in him. ⁴³He trusts in God; let God deliver him now, if he desires him. For he said, 'I am the Son of God.' " ⁴⁴And the robbers who were crucified with him also reviled him in the same way.

The Death of Jesus

⁴⁵Now from the sixth hour there was darkness over all the land until the ninth hour. ⁴⁶And about the ninth hour Jesus cried out with a loud voice, saying, "Eli, Eli, lema sabachthani?" that is, "My God, my God, why have you forsaken me?" ⁴⁷And some of the bystanders, hearing it, said, "This man is calling Elijah." ⁴⁸And one of them at once ran and took a sponge, filled it with sour wine, and put it on a reed and gave it to him to drink. ⁴⁹But the others said, "Wait, let us see whether Elijah will come to save him." ⁵⁰And Jesus cried out again with a loud voice and yielded up his spirit.

⁵¹And behold, the curtain of the temple was torn in two, from top to bottom. And the earth shook, and the rocks were split. ⁵²The tombs also were opened. And many bodies of the saints who had fallen asleep were raised, ⁵³and coming out of the tombs after his resurrection they went into the holy city and appeared to many. ⁵⁴When the centurion and those who were with him, keeping watch over Jesus, saw the earthquake and what took place, they were filled with awe and said, "Truly this was the Son of God!"

⁵⁵There were also many women there, looking on from a distance, who had followed Jesus from Galilee, ministering to him, ⁵⁶among whom were Mary Magdalene and Mary the mother of James and Joseph and the mother of the sons of Zebedee.

Jesus Is Buried

⁵⁷When it was evening, there came a rich man from Arimathea, named Joseph, who also was a disciple of Jesus. ⁵⁸He went to Pilate and asked for the body of Jesus. Then Pilate ordered it to be given to him. ⁵⁹And Joseph took the body and wrapped it in a clean linen shroud ⁶⁰and laid it in his own new tomb, which he had cut in the rock. And he rolled a great stone to the entrance of the tomb and went away. ⁶¹Mary Magdalene and the other Mary were there, sitting opposite the tomb.

The Guard at the Tomb

⁶²The next day, that is, after the day of Preparation, the chief priests and the Pharisees gathered before Pilate ⁶³and said, "Sir, we remember how that impostor said, while he was still alive, 'After three days I will rise.' ⁶⁴Therefore order the tomb to be made secure until the third day, lest his disciples go and steal him away and tell the people, 'He has risen from the dead', and the last fraud will be worse than the first." ⁶⁵Pilate said to them, "You have a guard of soldiers. Go, make it as secure as you can." ⁶⁶So they went and made the tomb secure by sealing the stone and setting a guard.

WHEN THE CENTURION AND THOSE WHO WERE WITH HIM, KEEPING WATCH OVER JESUS, SAW THE EARTHQUAKE AND WHAT TOOK PLACE, THEY WERE FILLED WITH AWE AND SAID, "TRULY THIS WAS THE SON OF GOD!"

Matthew 27:54

✝

Chapter Twenty-Eight
The Resurrection

Now after the Sabbath, towards the dawn of the first day of the week, Mary Magdalene and the other Mary went to see the tomb. ² And behold, there was a great earthquake, for an angel of the Lord descended from heaven and came and rolled back the stone and sat on it.³ His appearance was like lightning, and his clothing white as snow. ⁴ And for fear of him the guards trembled and became like dead men. ⁵ But the angel said to the women, "Do not be afraid, for I know that you seek Jesus who was crucified. ⁶ He is not here, for he has risen, as he said. Come, see the place where he lay. ⁷ Then go quickly and tell his disciples that he has risen from the dead, and behold, he is going before you to Galilee; there you will see him. See, I have told you." ⁸ So they departed quickly from the tomb with fear and great joy, and ran to tell his disciples. ⁹ And behold, Jesus met

"GO THEREFORE AND MAKE DISCIPLES OF ALL NATIONS, BAPTIZING THEM IN THE NAME OF THE FATHER AND OF THE SON AND OF THE HOLY SPIRIT, TEACHING THEM TO OBSERVE ALL THAT I HAVE COMMANDED YOU..."

"...AND BEHOLD, I AM
WITH YOU ALWAYS, TO
THE END OF THE AGE."

Matthew 28:19-20

them and said, "Greetings!" And they came up and took hold of his feet and worshipped him. [10] Then Jesus said to them, "Do not be afraid; go and tell my brothers to go to Galilee, and there they will see me."

The Report of the Guard

[11] While they were going, behold, some of the guard went into the city and told the chief priests all that had taken place. [12] And when they had assembled with the elders and taken counsel, they gave a sufficient sum of money to the soldiers [13] and said, "Tell people, 'His disciples came by night and stole him away while we were asleep.' [14] And if this comes to the governor's ears, we will satisfy him and keep you out of trouble." [15] So they took the money and did as they were directed. And this story has been spread among the Jews to this day.

The Great Commission

[16] Now the eleven disciples went to Galilee, to the mountain to which Jesus had directed them. [17] And when they saw him they worshipped him, but some doubted. [18] And Jesus came and said to them, "All authority in heaven and on earth has been given to me. [19] Go therefore and make disciples of all nations, baptizing them in the name of the Father and of the Son and of the Holy Spirit, [20] teaching them to observe all that I have commanded you. And behold, I am with you always, to the end of the age."

𝕴𝖓𝖘𝖕𝖎𝖗𝖊𝖉 𝖇𝖞 𝖙𝖍𝖊 𝕳𝖔𝖑𝖞 𝕾𝖕𝖎𝖗𝖎𝖙

EXPERIENCE MATTHEW

JESUS IS WISDOM AND THE FULFILMENT OF SCRIPTURE

AND HE SENT THEM TO BETHLEHEM, SAYING, "GO AND SEARCH DILIGENTLY FOR THE CHILD,
AND WHEN YOU HAVE FOUND HIM, BRING ME WORD, THAT I TOO MAY COME AND WORSHIP HIM."
Matthew 2:8

HOW MATTHEW FITS INTO GOD'S STORY AND MY STORY

God's rule has been inaugurated by Jesus. He reigns as king over the world Matthew 27:11
The life of Jesus changes the way that I live now in light of the future expectation of God's kingdom.

KEY CHARACTERS

Jesus, John the Baptist, Mary, Joseph, Peter, Scribes, Pharisees, Judas Iscariot

"THE WORDS OF JESUS BREATHE LIFE INTO COMMUNITIES AND PROVIDE UNITY, SUSTENANCE, PURPOSE AND MISSION."

KEY WORD IN MATTHEW: SPEAK

Greek: λέγω, legō, I speak

For Matthew, the first Evangelist, the Gospel is all about listening to what Jesus is saying. The verb to speak, *legō*, is the most frequently used verb in the Gospel of Matthew. This is not just because there is a lot of reported speech in the Gospel. Often, it is found on the very lips of Jesus himself (61 times). A frequent formula in the Gospel is when Jesus says, "You have heard it said... but I say to you" (e.g. Matthew 5:22). Jesus is the interpreter of the wisdom of the world, whether it be the Old Testament or something else. In order for us to be able to live according to his kingdom and in a way that enriches our humanity, we need to be attentive to what it is he is saying to us in the same way that Matthew wants his audience to be attentive to what Jesus is saying to them. The words of Jesus breathe life into communities and provide unity, sustenance, purpose and mission.

Matthew is unique among the Gospel writers when he characterizes Jesus as the embodiment of Wisdom. In Matthew 11, the author draws a correspondence between Jesus' actions (Matthew 11:2) with actions done by Wisdom (Matthew 11:19). He also uses language found in Jewish wisdom traditions in Matthew 11:28-30 to put the words of Wisdom in Jesus' mouth. In ancient Jewish traditions Wisdom was often personified as a partner who worked with God and the means through which the whole of creation was brought into being. Living according to wisdom (see the Old Testament book of Proverbs) was to live according to the way God intended. It is for Matthew a vital part of living under God's kingship and for Jesus an essential part of following after God's example.

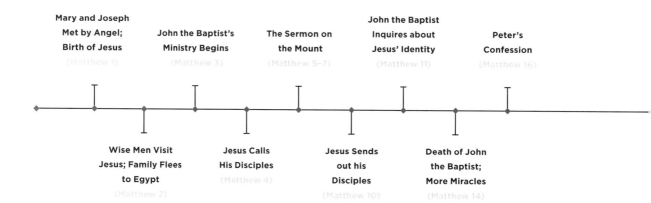

Mary and Joseph Met by Angel; Birth of Jesus
(Matthew 1)

John the Baptist's Ministry Begins
(Matthew 3)

The Sermon on the Mount
(Matthew 5-7)

John the Baptist Inquires about Jesus' Identity
(Matthew 11)

Peter's Confession
(Matthew 16)

Wise Men Visit Jesus; Family Flees to Egypt
(Matthew 2)

Jesus Calls His Disciples
(Matthew 4)

Jesus Sends out his Disciples
(Matthew 10)

Death of John the Baptist; More Miracles
(Matthew 14)

"YOU ARE THE LIGHT OF THE WORLD. A CITY SET ON A HILL CANNOT BE HIDDEN. NOR DO PEOPLE LIGHT A LAMP AND PUT IT UNDER A BASKET, BUT ON A STAND, AND IT GIVES LIGHT TO ALL IN THE HOUSE. IN THE SAME WAY, LET YOUR LIGHT SHINE BEFORE OTHERS, SO THAT THEY MAY SEE YOUR GOOD WORKS AND GIVE GLORY TO YOUR FATHER WHO IS IN HEAVEN."

Matthew 5:14-15

> "IN ANCIENT JEWISH TRADITIONS
> WISDOM WAS OFTEN PERSONIFIED AS
> A PARTNER WHO WORKED WITH GOD
> AND THE MEANS THROUGH WHICH
> THE WHOLE OF CREATION WAS
> BROUGHT INTO BEING."

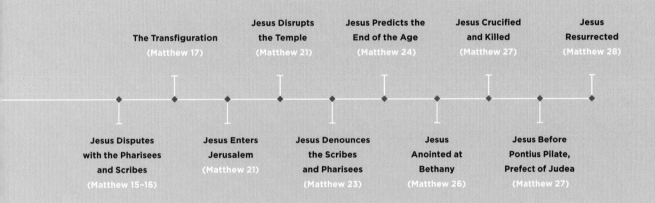

The Transfiguration (Matthew 17)

Jesus Disrupts the Temple (Matthew 21)

Jesus Predicts the End of the Age (Matthew 24)

Jesus Crucified and Killed (Matthew 27)

Jesus Resurrected (Matthew 28)

Jesus Disputes with the Pharisees and Scribes (Matthew 15–16)

Jesus Enters Jerusalem (Matthew 21)

Jesus Denounces the Scribes and Pharisees (Matthew 23)

Jesus Anointed at Bethany (Matthew 26)

Jesus Before Pontius Pilate, Prefect of Judea (Matthew 27)

KEY SECTION: THE SERMON ON THE MOUNT

The Sermon on the Mount (Matthew 5–7) is Jesus' longest speech in the New Testament. Though it is not found in the text, its title was made popular by a commentary by the early Church commentator Augustine. There is a shorter version called "The Sermon on the Plain" in Luke 6:17–49. In many ways, the Sermon on the Mount recalls the giving of the Torah (the Law) on Mount Sinai (Exodus 19–20). The "righteousness" of the "kingdom of heaven" found in this section outlines the way citizens behave and live in God's kingdom. But what is so striking about these chapters of Matthew is that its standards appear to be unattainable or unrealistic. How can people attain such a lifestyle on their own? Matthew assures us that it is possible with the help of Jesus. It is not so much that people earn their way into the kingdom of God. The very act of seeking out righteousness (Matthew 5:6) and God's kingship (Matthew 6:33) opens up the opportunity for God to give these things generously.

MARK

THE NEW TESTAMENT EXPERIENCE

SERVANT KING

WRITTEN BY MARK THE EVANGELIST

AND HE SAID TO THEM, "GO INTO ALL THE WORLD AND
PROCLAIM THE GOSPEL TO THE WHOLE CREATION."
Mark 16:15

IMPORTANT STORIES IN MARK

The Baptism of Jesus: Mark 1:9-11 **Jesus Heals a Paralytic:** Mark 2:1-12 **A Man with a Withered Hand:** Mark 3:1-6
Jesus Calms a Storm: Mark 4:35-41 **Jesus Heals a Woman and Jairus's Daughter:** Mark 5:21-43 **Jesus Walks on Water:** Mark 6:45-52
The Syrophoenician Woman's Faith: Mark 7:24-30 **Peter Confesses Jesus as the Christ:** Mark 8:27-30 **The Transfiguration:** Mark 9:2-7
Judas Betrays Jesus: Mark 14:10-11 **The Crucifixion:** Mark 15:21-32 **Jesus Appears to Mary Magdalene:** Mark 16:9-11

INTRODUCTION
TO MARK

NEW YORK CITY, USA

AUTHOR, DATE AND AUDIENCE

The apostle Peter passed on reports of the words and deeds of Jesus to his attendant, John Mark, who wrote this Gospel for the wider church as the record of Peter's apostolic testimony. The book was likely written from Rome during the mid- to late-50s AD (though the mid- or late-60s is also possible). Mark's audience, largely unfamiliar with Jewish customs, needed to become familiar with such customs in order to understand the coming of Jesus as the culmination of God's work with Israel and the entire world, so Mark explains them.

THEME AND PURPOSE

The ultimate purpose and theme of Mark's Gospel is to present and defend Jesus' universal call to discipleship. Mark returns often to this theme, categorizing his main audience as either followers or opponents of Jesus. Mark presents and supports this call to discipleship by narrating the identity and teaching of Jesus. For Mark, discipleship is essentially a relationship with Jesus, not merely following a certain code of conduct. Fellowship with Jesus marks the heart of the disciple's life, and this fellowship includes trusting Jesus, confessing him, observing his conduct, following his teaching, and being shaped by a relationship with him. Discipleship also means being prepared to face the kind of rejection that Jesus faced.

SHE WENT AND
TOLD THOSE
WHO HAD BEEN
WITH HIM, AS
THEY MOURNED
AND WEPT. BUT
WHEN THEY
HEARD THAT HE
WAS ALIVE AND
HAD BEEN SEEN
BY HER, THEY
WOULD NOT
BELIEVE IT.

Mark 16:10-11

Chapter One

John the Baptist Prepares the Way

The beginning of the gospel of Jesus Christ, the Son of God. [2] As it is written in Isaiah the prophet,

"Behold, I send my messenger
        before your face,
    who will prepare your way,
[3]   the voice of one crying in the
        wilderness:
    'Prepare the way of the Lord,
        make his paths straight,'"

[4] John appeared, baptizing in the wilderness and proclaiming a baptism of repentance for the forgiveness of sins. [5] And all the country of Judea and all Jerusalem were going out to him and were being baptized by him in the river Jordan, confessing their sins. [6] Now John was clothed with camel's hair and wore a leather belt round his waist and ate locusts and wild honey. [7] And he preached, saying, "After me comes he who is mightier than I, the strap of whose sandals I am not worthy to stoop down and untie. [8] I have baptized you with water, but he will baptize you with the Holy Spirit."

The Baptism of Jesus

[9] In those days Jesus came from Nazareth of Galilee and was baptized by John in the Jordan. [10] And when he came up out of the water, immediately he saw the heavens being torn open and the Spirit descending on him like a dove. [11] And a voice came from heaven, "You are my beloved Son; with you I am well pleased."

The Temptation of Jesus

[12] The Spirit immediately drove him out into the wilderness. [13] And he was in the wilderness forty days, being tempted by Satan. And he was with the wild animals, and the angels were ministering to him.

Jesus Begins His Ministry

[14] Now after John was arrested, Jesus came into Galilee, proclaiming the gospel of God, [15] and saying, "The time is fulfilled, and the kingdom of God is at hand; repent and believe in the gospel."

Jesus Calls the First Disciples

[16] Passing alongside the Sea of Galilee, he saw Simon and Andrew the brother of Simon casting a net into the sea, for they were fishermen. [17] And Jesus said to them, "Follow me, and I will make you become fishers of men." [18] And immediately they left their nets and followed him. [19] And going on a little farther, he saw James the son of Zebedee and John his brother, who were in their boat mending the nets. [20] And immediately he called them, and they left their father Zebedee in the boat with the hired servants and followed him.

"BEHOLD, I SEND MY MESSENGER BEFORE YOUR FACE, WHO WILL PREPARE YOUR WAY, THE VOICE OF ONE CRYING IN THE WILDERNESS: 'PREPARE THE WAY OF THE LORD, MAKE HIS PATHS STRAIGHT.'" Mark 1:2-3

Jesus Heals a Man with an Unclean Spirit

²¹ And they went into Capernaum, and immediately on the Sabbath he entered the synagogue and was teaching. ²² And they were astonished at his teaching, for he taught them as one who had authority, and not as the scribes. ²³ And immediately there was in their synagogue a man with an unclean spirit. And he cried out, ²⁴ "What have you to do with us, Jesus of Nazareth? Have you come to destroy us? I know who you are—the Holy One of God." ²⁵ But Jesus rebuked him, saying, "Be silent, and come out of him!" ²⁶ And the unclean spirit, convulsing him and crying out with a loud voice, came out of him. ²⁷ And they were all amazed, so that they questioned among themselves, saying, "What is this? A new teaching with authority! He commands even the unclean spirits, and they obey him." ²⁸ And at once his fame spread everywhere throughout all the surrounding region of Galilee.

Jesus Heals Many

²⁹ And immediately he left the synagogue and entered the house of Simon and Andrew, with James and John. ³⁰ Now Simon's mother-in-law lay ill with a fever, and immediately they told him about her. ³¹ And he came and took her by the hand and lifted her up, and the fever left her, and she began to serve them.

³² That evening at sunset they brought to him all who were sick or oppressed by demons. ³³ And the whole city was gathered together at the door. ³⁴ And he healed many who were sick with various diseases, and cast out many demons. And he would not permit the demons to speak, because they knew him.

Jesus Preaches in Galilee

³⁵ And rising very early in the morning, while it was still dark, he departed and went out to a desolate place, and there he prayed. ³⁶ And Simon and those who were with him searched for him, ³⁷ and they found him and said to him, "Everyone is looking for you." ³⁸ And he said to them, "Let us go on to the next towns, that I may preach there also, for that is what I came for." ³⁹ And he went throughout all Galilee, preaching in their synagogues and casting out demons.

Jesus Cleanses a Leper

⁴⁰ And a leper came to him, imploring him, and kneeling said to him, "If you will, you can make me clean." ⁴¹ Moved with pity, he stretched out his hand and touched him and said to him, "I will; be clean." ⁴² And immediately the leprosy left him, and he was made clean. ⁴³ And Jesus sternly charged him and sent him away at once, ⁴⁴ and said to him, "See that you say nothing to anyone, but go, show yourself to the priest and offer for your cleansing what Moses commanded, for a proof to them." ⁴⁵ But he went out and began to talk freely about it, and to spread the news, so that Jesus could no longer openly enter a town, but was out in desolate places, and people were coming to him from every quarter.

"WHAT HAVE YOU TO DO WITH US, JESUS OF NAZARETH? HAVE YOU COME TO DESTROY US? I KNOW WHO YOU ARE—THE HOLY ONE OF GOD." Mark 1:24

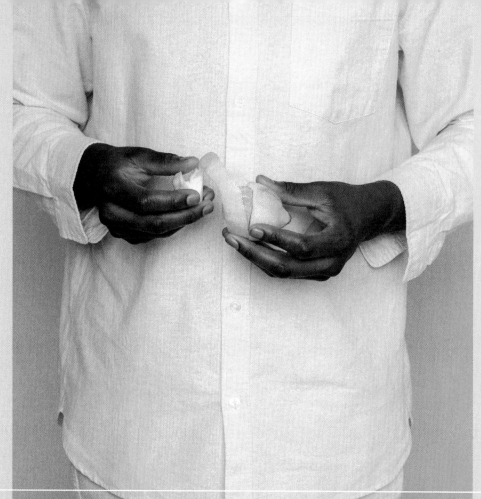

THE HOLY SPIRIT

WALKING IN RELATIONSHIP

The Gospel of Mark is the second account of Jesus' life that we have in the Bible, and in its opening chapter we are introduced to the Holy Spirit. The Gospel of Mark begins not with a story about Jesus' birth, childhood or any event from his adolescence; Mark instead chooses to tell his readers first and foremost about an experience that Jesus has with the Holy Spirit.

Today, people might shy away from talking about a "spirit". Discussion about spiritual things is quite alien to the culture we live in, and it is often frowned upon in our western, post-Enlightenment world, where we prefer to talk of things in language that we can define and observe with our own eyes. Although we can't rationalize and quantify the Holy Spirit, we can't let that stop us from learning about who he is, because knowing and understanding who the Holy Spirit is is one of the most important keys for us as Christians.

One misconception that people often have is that the Holy Spirit is a non-personal entity. But in fact, the Holy Spirit is a person, and he performs a crucial role of reconciling us as humanity back to God. We read in the book of Acts that after Jesus ascended to heaven, the

Christian believers received the Holy Spirit who was promised to them, and he moved among them, enabling them to share in the love of God. So, the Holy Spirit is the agent who facilitates our relationship with God. This clearly shows that the Holy Spirit is himself God, as only God could reconcile people to himself. No human being could bring another human being into fellowship with God; only God can do that!

This introduces us to the Trinity, which is the Christian belief that God is one being in three persons. He is one God but he has a plurality, in the sense of consisting of three persons; God the Father, God the Son and God the Holy Spirit. When we talk about the Father, Jesus, and the Holy Spirit, we are talking about three distinct persons who each share in being God. This is an amazing truth that gives us a deep understanding of who God is.

When you decide to accept Jesus and his complete forgiveness, the Bible teaches that the Holy Spirit has come to live within you. As he takes up residence in your life he produces fruit, and the fruit of that indwelling of the Holy Spirit gives you a confirmation that you are growing in your relationship with God. In Galatians 5, this fruit is described as being "love, joy, peace, patience, kindness, goodness, faithfulness, gentleness and self-control". If we see that we are growing in these areas, we can be assured that the Holy Spirit is living in us and working in our lives.

When you think about a fruit tree, it doesn't need to strain or work particularly hard to bear fruit; it's something that comes naturally. If the fruit tree is planted in good soil and if it receives the right nutrients, it will grow and be a healthy fruit tree. In the same way, the fruit of the Spirit is not something we need to work for in order to see the Holy Spirit work in our lives, but it's instead something that comes about naturally when we walk in relationship with God. Transformation comes from fixing our eyes on God and allowing his Spirit to work within us.

The amazing thing about the Holy Spirit is not just that through the Holy Spirit God works in our lives, but it's that he also empowers us to live a supernatural life. In 1 Corinthians 12, Paul talks about some of the different gifts that the Holy Spirit gives us. Each person will be gifted differently, but the point is that each of us has been gifted differently in order to build God's kingdom. Our purpose on earth is to build God's Church and one of the best ways we can do that is by using the gifts God has given us.

But what does that mean for each of us at an individual level? Well, just as the Spirit descended on Jesus in the first chapter of Mark, so he has also descended on each of us, to live in us and to be with us. The message of the Holy Spirit is ultimately that we can be assured of peace and comfort regardless of the circumstances of life. The Bible never promises the Christian believer that life will be perfect, but that in every situation God is with us, and that he is enough.

Whether life is going really well or if it couldn't be worse right now, God's Spirit is always with us, and he always wants to equip us to live our best lives. He is the one who personalizes who God is into our daily life and empowers us to witness to the world around us. He takes the sacrifice that Jesus made and weaves it into our personal life so that we can know that God loves us individually and that his plans and purposes are for us. He is the great comforter and provider of peace.

Chapter Two
Jesus Heals a Paralytic

And he rose and immediately picked up his bed and went out before them all, so that they were all amazed and glorified God, saying, "We never saw anything like this!"

Mark 2:12

And when he returned to Capernaum after some days, it was reported that he was at home. ² And many were gathered together, so that there was no more room, not even at the door. And he was preaching the word to them. ³ And they came, bringing to him a paralytic carried by four men. ⁴ And when they could not get near him because of the crowd, they removed the roof above him, and when they had made an opening, they let down the bed on which the paralytic lay. ⁵ And when Jesus saw their faith, he said to the paralytic, "Son, your sins are forgiven." ⁶ Now some of the scribes were sitting there, questioning in their hearts, ⁷ "Why does this man speak like that? He is blaspheming! Who can forgive sins but God alone?" ⁸ And immediately Jesus, perceiving in his spirit that they thus questioned within themselves, said to them, "Why do you question these things in your hearts? ⁹ Which is easier, to say to the paralytic, 'Your sins are forgiven', or to say, 'Rise, take up your bed and walk'? ¹⁰ But that you may know that the Son of Man has authority on earth to forgive sins"—he said to the paralytic— ¹¹ "I say to you, rise, pick up your bed, and go home." ¹² And he rose and immediately picked up his bed and went out before them all, so that they were all amazed and glorified God, saying, "We never saw anything like this!"

Jesus Calls Levi
¹³ He went out again beside the sea, and all the crowd was coming to him, and he was teaching them. ¹⁴ And as he passed by, he saw Levi the son of Alphaeus sitting at the tax booth, and he said to him, "Follow me." And he rose and followed him.

¹⁵ And as he reclined at table in his house, many tax collectors and sinners were reclining with Jesus and his disciples, for there were many who followed him. ¹⁶ And the scribes of the Pharisees, when they saw that he was eating with sinners and tax collectors, said to his disciples, "Why does he eat with tax collectors and sinners?" ¹⁷ And when Jesus heard it, he said to them, "Those who are well have no need of a physician, but those who are sick. I came not to call the righteous, but sinners."

A Question About Fasting
¹⁸ Now John's disciples and the Pharisees were fasting. And people came and said to him, "Why do John's disciples and the disciples of the Pharisees fast, but your disciples do not fast?" ¹⁹ And Jesus said to them, "Can the wedding guests fast while the bridegroom is with them? As long as they have the bridegroom with them, they cannot fast. ²⁰ The days will come when the bridegroom is taken away from them, and then they will fast in that day. ²¹ No one sews a piece of unshrunk cloth on an old garment. If he does, the patch tears away from it, the new from the old, and a worse tear is made. ²² And no one puts new wine into old wineskins. If he does, the wine will burst the skins—and the wine is destroyed, and so are the skins. But new wine is for fresh wineskins."

Jesus Is Lord of the Sabbath
²³ One Sabbath he was going through the cornfields, and as they made their way, his disciples began to pluck ears of corn. ²⁴ And the Pharisees were saying to him, "Look, why are they doing what is not lawful on the Sabbath?" ²⁵ And he said to them, "Have you never read what David did, when he was in need and was hungry, he and those who were with him: ²⁶ how he entered the house of God, in the time of Abiathar the high priest, and ate the bread of the Presence, which it is not lawful for any but the priests to eat, and also gave it to those who were with him?" ²⁷ And he said to them, "The Sabbath was made for man, not man for the Sabbath. ²⁸ So the Son of Man is lord even of the Sabbath."

Chapter Three

A Man with a Withered Hand

Again he entered the synagogue, and a man was there with a withered hand. ²And they watched Jesus, to see whether he would heal him on the Sabbath, so that they might accuse him. ³And he said to the man with the withered hand, "Come here." ⁴And he said to them, "Is it lawful on the Sabbath to do good or to do harm, to save life or to kill?" But they were silent. ⁵And he looked round at them with anger, grieved at their hardness of heart, and said to the man, "Stretch out your hand." He stretched it out, and his hand was restored. ⁶The Pharisees went out and immediately held counsel with the Herodians against him, how to destroy him.

A Great Crowd Follows Jesus

⁷Jesus withdrew with his disciples to the sea, and a great crowd followed, from Galilee and Judea ⁸and Jerusalem and Idumea and from beyond the Jordan and from around Tyre and Sidon. When the great crowd heard all that he was doing, they came to him. ⁹And he told his disciples to have a boat ready for him because of the crowd, lest they crush him, ¹⁰for he had healed many, so that all who had diseases pressed around him to touch him. ¹¹And whenever the unclean spirits saw him, they fell down before him and cried out, "You are the Son of God." ¹²And he strictly ordered them not to make him known.

The Twelve Apostles

¹³And he went up on the mountain and called to him those whom he desired, and they came to him. ¹⁴And he appointed twelve (whom he also named apostles) so that they might be with him and he might send them out to preach ¹⁵and have authority to cast out demons. ¹⁶He appointed the twelve: Simon (to whom he gave the name

AND HE SAID TO
THE MAN WITH
THE WITHERED
HAND, "COME
HERE." AND HE
SAID TO THEM,
"IS IT LAWFUL ON
THE SABBATH TO
DO GOOD OR TO
DO HARM, TO SAVE
LIFE OR TO KILL?"
BUT THEY WERE
SILENT. AND HE
LOOKED ROUND
AT THEM WITH
ANGER, GRIEVED
AT THEIR HARD-
NESS OF HEART,
AND SAID TO THE
MAN, "STRETCH
OUT YOUR HAND."
HE STRETCHED
IT OUT, AND HIS
HAND WAS
RESTORED.

Mark 3:3-5

Peter); [17] James the son of Zebedee and John the brother of James (to whom he gave the name Boanerges, that is, Sons of Thunder); [18] Andrew, and Philip, and Bartholomew, and Matthew, and Thomas, and James the son of Alphaeus, and Thaddaeus, and Simon the Zealot, [19] and Judas Iscariot, who betrayed him.

[20] Then he went home, and the crowd gathered again, so that they could not even eat. [21] And when his family heard it, they went out to seize him, for they were saying, "He is out of his mind."

Blasphemy Against the Holy Spirit

[22] And the scribes who came down from Jerusalem were saying, "He is possessed by Beelzebul," and "by the prince of demons he casts out the demons." [23] And he called them to him and said to them in parables, "How can Satan cast out Satan? [24] If a kingdom is divided against itself, that kingdom cannot stand. [25] And if a house is divided against itself, that house will not be able to stand. [26] And if Satan has risen up against himself and is divided, he cannot stand, but is coming to an end. [27] But no one can enter a strong man's house and plunder his goods, unless he first binds the strong man. Then indeed he may plunder his house.

[28] "Truly, I say to you, all sins will be forgiven the children of man, and whatever blasphemies they utter, [29] but whoever blasphemes against the Holy Spirit never has forgiveness, but is guilty of an eternal sin"— [30] for they were saying, "He has an unclean spirit."

Jesus' Mother and Brothers

[31] And his mother and his brothers came, and standing outside they sent to him and called him. [32] And a crowd was sitting around him, and they said to him, "Your mother and your brothers are outside, seeking you." [33] And he answered them, "Who are my mother and my brothers?" [34] And looking about at those who sat around him, he said, "Here are my mother and my brothers! [35] For whoever does the will of God, he is my brother and sister and mother."

AND HE ANSWERED THEM, "WHO ARE MY MOTHER AND MY BROTHERS?" AND LOOKING ABOUT AT THOSE WHO SAT AROUND HIM, HE SAID, "HERE ARE MY MOTHER AND MY BROTHERS! FOR WHOEVER DOES THE WILL OF GOD, HE IS MY BROTHER AND SISTER AND MOTHER."

Mark 3:33-35

Chapter Four
The Parable of the Sower

And he said to them, "Do you not understand this parable? How then will you understand all the parables?"

Mark 4:13

Again he began to teach beside the sea. And a very large crowd gathered about him, so that he got into a boat and sat in it on the sea, and the whole crowd was beside the sea on the land. ²And he was teaching them many things in parables, and in his teaching he said to them: ³"Listen! Behold, a sower went out to sow. ⁴And as he sowed, some seed fell along the path, and the birds came and devoured it. ⁵Other seed fell on rocky ground, where it did not have much soil, and immediately it sprang up, since it had no depth of soil. ⁶And when the sun rose, it was scorched, and since it had no root, it withered away. ⁷Other seed fell among thorns, and the thorns grew up and choked it, and it yielded no grain. ⁸And other seeds fell into good soil and produced grain, growing up and increasing and yielding thirtyfold and sixtyfold and a hundredfold." ⁹And he said, "He who has ears to hear, let him hear."

The Purpose of the Parables

¹⁰And when he was alone, those around him with the twelve asked him about the parables. ¹¹And he said to them, "To you has been given the secret of the kingdom of God, but for those outside everything is in parables, ¹²so that

"'they may indeed see but not
perceive,
and may indeed hear but not
understand,
lest they should turn and be
forgiven.'"

¹³And he said to them, "Do you not understand this parable? How then will you understand all the parables? ¹⁴The sower sows the word. ¹⁵And these are the ones along the path, where the word is sown: when they hear, Satan immediately comes and takes away the word that is sown in them. ¹⁶And these are the ones sown on rocky ground: the ones who, when they hear the word, immediately receive it with joy. ¹⁷And they have no root in themselves, but endure for a while; then, when tribulation or persecution arises on account of the word, immediately they fall away. ¹⁸And others are the ones sown among thorns. They are those who hear the word, ¹⁹but the cares of the world and the deceitfulness of riches and the desires for other things enter in and choke the word, and it proves unfruitful. ²⁰But those that were sown on the good soil are the ones who hear the word and accept it and bear fruit, thirtyfold and sixtyfold and a hundredfold."

A Lamp Under a Basket

²¹And he said to them, "Is a lamp brought in to be put under a basket, or under a bed, and not on a stand? ²²For nothing is hidden except to be made manifest; nor is anything secret

AND OTHERS ARE

the ones sown among thorns. They are those who hear the word, but the cares
of the world and the deceitfulness of riches and the desires for other things enter
in and choke the word, and it proves unfruitful. But those that were sown on
the good soil are the ones who hear the word and accept it and bear fruit,
thirtyfold and sixtyfold and a hundredfold."

Mark 4:18-20

HE SAID TO THEM, "WHY ARE YOU SO AFRAID? HAVE YOU STILL NO FAITH?" AND THEY WERE FILLED WITH GREAT FEAR AND SAID TO ONE ANOTHER, "WHO THEN IS THIS, THAT EVEN THE WIND AND THE SEA OBEY HIM?" Mark 4:40-41

except to come to light. ²³If anyone has ears to hear, let him hear." ²⁴And he said to them, "Pay attention to what you hear: with the measure you use, it will be measured to you, and still more will be added to you. ²⁵For to the one who has, more will be given, and from the one who has not, even what he has will be taken away."

The Parable of the Seed Growing

²⁶And he said, "The kingdom of God is as if a man should scatter seed on the ground. ²⁷He sleeps and rises night and day, and the seed sprouts and grows; he knows not how. ²⁸The earth produces by itself, first the blade, then the ear, then the full grain in the ear. ²⁹But when the grain is ripe, at once he puts in the sickle, because the harvest has come."

The Parable of the Mustard Seed

³⁰ And he said, "With what can we compare the kingdom of God, or what parable shall we use for it? ³¹It is like a grain of mustard seed, which, when sown on the ground, is the smallest of all the seeds on earth, ³²yet when it is sown it grows up and becomes larger than all the garden plants and puts out large branches, so that the birds of the air can make nests in its shade."

³³With many such parables he spoke the word to them, as they were able to hear it. ³⁴He did not speak to them without a parable, but privately to his own disciples he explained everything.

Jesus Calms a Storm

³⁵On that day, when evening had come, he said to them, "Let us go across to the other side." ³⁶And leaving the crowd, they took him with them in the boat, just as he was. And other boats were with him. ³⁷And a great windstorm arose, and the waves were breaking into the boat, so that the boat was already filling. ³⁸But he was in the stern, asleep on the cushion. And they woke him and said to him, "Teacher, do you not care that we are perishing?" ³⁹And he awoke and rebuked the wind and said to the sea, "Peace! Be still!" And the wind ceased, and there was a great calm. ⁴⁰He said to them, "Why are you so afraid? Have you still no faith?" ⁴¹And they were filled with great fear and said to one another, "Who then is this, that even the wind and the sea obey him?"

SHE HAD HEARD THE REPORTS ABOUT JESUS AND CAME UP BEHIND HIM IN THE CROWD AND TOUCHED HIS GARMENT. FOR SHE SAID, "IF I TOUCH EVEN HIS GARMENTS, I WILL BE MADE WELL." Mark 5:27-28

Chapter Five

Jesus Heals a Man with a Demon

They came to the other side of the lake, to the country of the Gerasenes. ²And when Jesus had stepped out of the boat, immediately there met him out of the tombs a man with an unclean spirit. ³He lived among the tombs. And no one could bind him any more, not even with a chain, ⁴for he had often been bound with shackles and chains, but he wrenched the chains apart, and he broke the shackles in pieces. No one had the strength to subdue him. ⁵Night and day among the tombs and on the mountains he was always crying out and cutting himself with stones. ⁶And when he saw Jesus from afar, he ran and fell down before him. ⁷And crying out with a loud voice, he said, "What have you to do with me, Jesus, Son of the Most High God? I adjure you by God, do not torment me." ⁸For he was saying to him, "Come out of the man, you unclean spirit!" ⁹And Jesus asked him, "What is your name?" He replied, "My name is Legion, for we are many." ¹⁰And he begged him earnestly not to send them out of the country. ¹¹Now a great herd of pigs was feeding there on the hillside, ¹²and they begged him, saying, "Send us to the pigs; let us enter

TAKING HER BY
THE HAND HE
SAID TO HER,
"TALITHA CUMI",
WHICH MEANS,
"LITTLE GIRL,
I SAY TO YOU,
ARISE." AND
IMMEDIATELY
THE GIRL GOT
UP AND BEGAN
WALKING
(FOR SHE WAS
TWELVE YEARS
OF AGE), AND
THEY WERE
IMMEDIATELY
OVERCOME WITH
AMAZEMENT.

Mark 5:41-42

them." [13] So he gave them permission. And the unclean spirits came out and entered the pigs; and the herd, numbering about two thousand, rushed down the steep bank into the sea and drowned in the sea.

[14] The herdsmen fled and told it in the city and in the country. And people came to see what it was that had happened. [15] And they came to Jesus and saw the demon-possessed man, the one who had had the legion, sitting there, clothed and in his right mind, and they were afraid. [16] And those who had seen it described to them what had happened to the demon-possessed man and to the pigs. [17] And they began to beg Jesus to depart from their region. [18] As he was getting into the boat, the man who had been possessed with demons begged him that he might be with him. [19] And he did not permit him but said to him, "Go home to your friends and tell them how much the Lord has done for you, and how he has had mercy on you." [20] And he went away and began to proclaim in the Decapolis how much Jesus had done for him, and everyone marvelled.

Jesus Heals a Woman and
Jairus's Daughter

[21] And when Jesus had crossed again in the boat to the other side, a great crowd gathered about him, and he was beside the sea. [22] Then came one of the rulers of the synagogue, Jairus by name, and seeing him, he fell at his feet [23] and implored him earnestly, saying, "My little daughter is at the point of death. Come and lay your hands on her, so that she may be made well and live." [24] And he went with him.

And a great crowd followed him and thronged about him. [25] And there was a woman who had had a discharge of blood for twelve years, [26] and who had suffered much under many physicians, and had spent all that she had, and was no better but rather grew worse. [27] She had heard the reports about Jesus and

came up behind him in the crowd and touched his garment. [28] For she said, "If I touch even his garments, I will be made well." [29] And immediately the flow of blood dried up, and she felt in her body that she was healed of her disease. [30] And Jesus, perceiving in himself that power had gone out from him, immediately turned about in the crowd and said, "Who touched my garments?" [31] And his disciples said to him, "You see the crowd pressing around you, and yet you say, 'Who touched me?'" [32] And he looked round to see who had done it. [33] But the woman, knowing what had happened to her, came in fear and trembling and fell down before him and told him the whole truth. [34] And he said to her, "Daughter, your faith has made you well; go in peace, and be healed of your disease."

[35] While he was still speaking, there came from the ruler's house some who said, "Your daughter is dead. Why trouble the Teacher any further?" [36] But overhearing what they said, Jesus said to the ruler of the synagogue, "Do not fear, only believe." [37] And he allowed no one to follow him except Peter and James and John the brother of James. [38] They came to the house of the ruler of the synagogue, and Jesus saw a commotion, people weeping and wailing loudly. [39] And when he had entered, he said to them, "Why are you making a commotion and weeping? The child is not dead but sleeping." [40] And they laughed at him. But he put them all outside and took the child's father and mother and those who were with him and went in where the child was. [41] Taking her by the hand he said to her, "Talitha cumi", which means, "Little girl, I say to you, arise." [42] And immediately the girl got up and began walking (for she was twelve years of age), and they were immediately overcome with amazement. [43] And he strictly charged them that no one should know this, and told them to give her something to eat.

Chapter Six
Jesus Rejected at Nazareth

And wherever he came, in villages, cities, or countryside, they laid the sick in the market-places and implored him that they might touch even the fringe of his garment. And as many as touched it were made well.

Mark 6:56

He went away from there and came to his home town, and his disciples followed him. ² And on the Sabbath he began to teach in the synagogue, and many who heard him were astonished, saying, "Where did this man get these things? What is the wisdom given to him? How are such mighty works done by his hands? ³ Is not this the carpenter, the son of Mary and brother of James and Joses and Judas and Simon? And are not his sisters here with us?" And they took offence at him. ⁴ And Jesus said to them, "A prophet is not without honour, except in his home town and among his relatives and in his own household." ⁵ And he could do no mighty work there, except that he laid his hands on a few sick people and healed them. ⁶ And he marvelled because of their unbelief.

And he went about among the villages teaching.

Jesus Sends Out the Twelve Apostles
⁷ And he called the twelve and began to send them out two by two, and gave them authority over the unclean spirits. ⁸ He charged them to take nothing for their journey except a staff—no bread, no bag, no money in their belts— ⁹ but to wear sandals and not put on two tunics. ¹⁰ And he said to them, "Whenever you enter a house, stay there until you depart from there. ¹¹ And if any place will not receive you and they will not listen to you, when you leave, shake off the dust that is on your feet as a testimony against them." ¹² So they went out and proclaimed that people should re-

pent. ¹³ And they cast out many demons and anointed with oil many who were sick and healed them.

The Death of John the Baptist
¹⁴ King Herod heard of it, for Jesus' name had become known. Some said, "John the Baptist has been raised from the dead. That is why these miraculous powers are at work in him." ¹⁵ But others said, "He is Elijah." And others said, "He is a prophet, like one of the prophets of old." ¹⁶ But when Herod heard of it, he said, "John, whom I beheaded, has been raised." ¹⁷ For it was Herod who had sent and seized John and bound him in prison for the sake of Herodias, his brother Philip's wife, because he had married her. ¹⁸ For John had been saying to Herod, "It is not lawful for

you to have your brother's wife." [19] And Herodias had a grudge against him and wanted to put him to death. But she could not, [20] for Herod feared John, knowing that he was a righteous and holy man, and he kept him safe. When he heard him, he was greatly perplexed, and yet he heard him gladly.

[21] But an opportunity came when Herod on his birthday gave a banquet for his nobles and military commanders and the leading men of Galilee. [22] For when Herodias's daughter came in and danced, she pleased Herod and his guests. And the king said to the girl, "Ask me for whatever you wish, and I will give it to you." [23] And he vowed to her, "Whatever you ask me, I will give you, up to half of my kingdom." [24] And she went out and said to her mother, "For what should I ask?" And she said, "The head of John the Baptist." [25] And she came in immediately with haste to the king and asked, saying, "I want you to give me at once the head of John the Baptist on a platter." [26] And the king was exceedingly sorry, but because of his oaths and his guests he did not want to break his word to her. [27] And immediately the king sent an executioner with orders to bring John's head. He went and beheaded him in the prison [28] and brought his head on a platter and gave it to the girl, and the girl gave it to her mother. [29] When his disciples heard of it, they came and took his body and laid it in a tomb.

Jesus Feeds the Five Thousand

[30] The apostles returned to Jesus and told him all that they had done and taught. [31] And he said to them, "Come away by yourselves to a desolate place and rest a while." For many were coming and going, and they had no leisure even to eat. [32] And they went away in the boat to a desolate place by themselves. [33] Now many saw them going and recognized them, and they ran there on foot from all the towns and got there ahead of them. [34] When he went ashore he saw a great crowd, and he had compassion on them, because they were like sheep without a shepherd. And he began to teach them many things. [35] And when it grew late, his disciples came to him and said, "This is a desolate place, and the hour is now late. [36] Send them away to go into the surrounding countryside and villages and buy themselves something to eat." [37] But he answered them, "You give them something to eat." And they said to him, "Shall we go and buy two hundred denarii worth of bread and give it to them to eat?" [38] And he said to them, "How many loaves do you have? Go and see." And when they had found out, they said, "Five, and two fish." [39] Then he commanded them all to sit down in groups on the green grass. [40] So they sat down in groups, by hundreds and by fifties. [41] And taking the five loaves and the two fish, he looked up to heaven and said a blessing and broke the loaves and gave them to the disciples to set before the people. And he divided the two fish among them all. [42] And they all ate and were satisfied. [43] And they took up twelve baskets full of broken pieces and of the fish. [44] And those who ate the loaves were five thousand men.

Jesus Walks on the Water

[45] Immediately he made his disciples get into the boat and go before him to the other side, to Bethsaida, while he dismissed the crowd. [46] And after he had taken leave of them, he went up on the mountain to pray. [47] And when evening came, the boat was out on the sea, and he was alone on the land. [48] And he saw that they were making headway painfully, for the wind was against them. And about the fourth watch of the night he came to them, walking on the sea. He meant to pass by them, [49] but when they saw him walking on the sea they thought it was a ghost, and cried out, [50] for they all saw him and were terrified. But immediately he spoke to them and said, "Take heart; it is I. Do not be afraid." [51] And he got into the boat with them, and the wind ceased. And they were utterly astounded, [52] for they did not understand about the loaves, but their hearts were hardened.

Jesus Heals the Sick in Gennesaret

[53] When they had crossed over, they came to land at Gennesaret and moored to the shore. [54] And when they got out of the boat, the people immediately recognized him [55] and ran about the whole region and began to bring the sick people on their beds to wherever they heard he was. [56] And wherever he came, in villages, cities, or countryside, they laid the sick in the market-places and implored him that they might touch even the fringe of his garment. And as many as touched it were made well.

Chapter Seven
Traditions and Commandments

Now when the Pharisees gathered to him, with some of the scribes who had come from Jerusalem, ²they saw that some of his disciples ate with hands that were defiled, that is, unwashed. ³(For the Pharisees and all the Jews do not eat unless they wash their hands properly, holding to the tradition of the elders, ⁴and when they come from the market-place, they do not eat unless they wash. And there are many other traditions that they observe, such as the washing of cups and pots and copper vessels and dining couches.) ⁵And the Pharisees and the scribes asked him, "Why do your disciples not walk according to the tradition of the elders, but eat with defiled hands?" ⁶And he said to them, "Well did Isaiah prophesy of you hypocrites, as it is written,

"'This people honours me with
their lips,
but their heart is far from me;
⁷ in vain do they worship me,
teaching as doctrines the
commandments of men.'

⁸You leave the commandment of God and hold to the tradition of men."

⁹And he said to them, "You have a fine way of rejecting the commandment of God in order to establish your tradition! ¹⁰For Moses said, 'Honour your father and your mother'; and, 'Whoever reviles father or mother must surely die.' ¹¹But you say, 'If a man tells his father or his mother, "Whatever you would have gained from me is Corban"' (that is, given to God)—¹²then you no longer permit him to do anything for his father or mother, ¹³thus making void the word of God by your tradition that you have handed down. And many such things you do."

What Defiles a Person

¹⁴And he called the people to him again and said to them, "Hear me, all of you, and understand: ¹⁵There is nothing outside a person that by going into him can defile him, but the things that come out of a person are what defile him." ¹⁷And when he had entered the house and left the people, his disciples asked him about the parable. ¹⁸And he said to them, "Then are you also without understanding? Do you not see that whatever goes into a person from outside cannot defile him, ¹⁹since it enters not his heart but his stomach, and is expelled?" (Thus he declared all foods clean.) ²⁰And he said, "What comes out of a person is what defiles him. ²¹For from within, out of the heart of man, come evil thoughts, sexual immorality, theft, murder, adultery, ²²coveting, wickedness, deceit, sensuality, envy, slander, pride, foolishness. ²³All these evil things come from within, and they defile a person."

The Syrophoenician Woman's Faith

²⁴And from there he arose and went away to the region of Tyre and Sidon. And he entered a house and did not want anyone to know, yet he could not be hidden. ²⁵But immediately a woman whose little daughter had an unclean spirit heard of him and came and fell down at his feet. ²⁶Now the woman was a Gentile, a Syrophoenician by birth. And she begged him to cast the demon out of her daughter. ²⁷And he said to her, "Let the children be fed first, for it is not right to take the children's bread and throw it to the dogs." ²⁸But she answered him, "Yes, Lord; yet even the dogs under the table eat the children's crumbs." ²⁹And he said to her, "For this statement you may go your way; the demon has left your daughter." ³⁰And she went home and found the child lying in bed and the demon gone.

Jesus Heals a Deaf Man

³¹Then he returned from the region of Tyre and went through Sidon to the Sea of Galilee, in the region of the Decapolis. ³²And they brought to him a man who was deaf and had a speech impediment, and they begged him to lay his hand on him. ³³And taking him aside from the crowd privately, he put his fingers into his ears, and after spitting touched his tongue. ³⁴And looking up to heaven, he sighed and said to him, "Ephphatha", that is, "Be opened." ³⁵And his ears were opened, his tongue was released, and he spoke plainly. ³⁶And Jesus charged them to tell no one. But the more he charged them, the more zealously they proclaimed it. ³⁷And they were astonished beyond measure, saying, "He has done all things well. He even makes the deaf hear and the mute speak."

BUT SHE ANSWERED HIM, "YES, LORD; YET EVEN THE DOGS UNDER THE TABLE EAT THE CHILDREN'S CRUMBS." AND HE SAID TO HER, "FOR THIS STATEMENT YOU MAY GO YOUR WAY; THE DEMON HAS LEFT YOUR DAUGHTER." AND SHE WENT HOME AND FOUND THE CHILD LYING IN BED AND THE DEMON GONE.

Mark 7:28-30

✝

Chapter Eight
Jesus Feeds the Four Thousand

In those days, when again a great crowd had gathered, and they had nothing to eat, he called his disciples to him and said to them, ²"I have compassion on the crowd, because they have been with me now three days and have nothing to eat. ³And if I send them away hungry to their homes, they will faint on the way. And some of them have come from far away." ⁴And his disciples answered him, "How can one feed these people with bread here in this desolate place?" ⁵And he asked them, "How many loaves do you have?" They said, "Seven." ⁶And he directed the crowd to sit down on the ground. And he took the seven loaves, and having given thanks, he broke them and gave them to his disciples to set before the people; and they set them before the crowd. ⁷And they had a few small fish. And having blessed them, he said that these also should be set before them. ⁸And they ate and were satisfied. And they took up the broken pieces left over, seven baskets full. ⁹And there were about four thousand people. And he sent them away. ¹⁰And immediately he got into the boat with his disciples and went to the district of Dalmanutha.

The Pharisees Demand a Sign
¹¹ The Pharisees came and began to argue with him, seeking from him a sign from heaven to test him. ¹²And he sighed deeply in his spirit and said, "Why does this generation seek a sign? Truly, I say to you, no sign will be given to this generation." ¹³And he left them, got into the boat again, and went to the other side.

The Leaven of the Pharisees and Herod

[14] Now they had forgotten to bring bread, and they had only one loaf with them in the boat. [15] And he cautioned them, saying, "Watch out; beware of the leaven of the Pharisees and the leaven of Herod." [16] And they began discussing with one another the fact that they had no bread. [17] And Jesus, aware of this, said to them, "Why are you discussing the fact that you have no bread? Do you not yet perceive or understand? Are your hearts hardened? [18] Having eyes do you not see, and having ears do you not hear? And do you not remember? [19] When I broke the five loaves for the five thousand, how many baskets full of broken pieces did you take up?" They said to him, "Twelve." [20] "And the seven for the four thousand, how many baskets full of broken pieces did you take up?" And they said to him, "Seven." [21] And he said to them, "Do you not yet understand?"

Jesus Heals a Blind Man at Bethsaida

[22] And they came to Bethsaida. And some people brought to him a blind man and begged him to touch him. [23] And he took the blind man by the hand and led him out of the village, and when he had spat on his eyes and laid his hands on him, he asked him, "Do you see anything?" [24] And he looked up and said, "I see people, but they look like trees, walking." [25] Then Jesus laid his hands on his eyes again; and he opened his eyes, his sight was restored, and he saw everything clearly. [26] And he sent him to his home, saying, "Do not even enter the village."

Peter Confesses Jesus as the Christ

[27] And Jesus went on with his disciples to the villages of Caesarea Philippi. And on the way he asked his disciples, "Who do people say that I am?" [28] And they told him, "John the Baptist; and others say, Elijah; and others, one of the prophets." [29] And he asked them, "But who do you say that I am?" Peter answered him, "You are the Christ." [30] And he strictly charged them to tell no one about him.

Jesus Foretells His Death and Resurrection

[31] And he began to teach them that the Son of Man must suffer many things and be rejected by the elders and the chief priests and the scribes and be killed, and after three days rise again. [32] And he said this plainly. And Peter took him aside and began to rebuke him. [33] But turning and seeing his disciples, he rebuked Peter and said, "Get behind me, Satan! For you are not setting your mind on the things of God, but on the things of man." [34] And calling the crowd to him with his disciples, he said to them, "If anyone would come after me, let him deny himself and take up his cross and follow me. [35] For whoever would save his life will lose it, but whoever loses his life for my sake and the gospel's will save it. [36] For what does it profit a man to gain the whole world and forfeit his soul? [37] For what can a man give in return for his soul? [38] For whoever is ashamed of me and of my words in this adulterous and sinful generation, of him will the Son of Man also be ashamed when he comes in the glory of his Father with the holy angels."

AND PETER TOOK HIM ASIDE AND BEGAN TO REBUKE HIM. BUT TURNING AND SEEING HIS DISCIPLES, HE REBUKED PETER AND SAID, "GET BEHIND ME, SATAN! FOR YOU ARE NOT SETTING YOUR MIND ON THE THINGS OF GOD, BUT ON THE THINGS OF MAN." Mark 8:32-33

AND A CLOUD
OVERSHADOWED
THEM, AND A
VOICE CAME OUT
OF THE CLOUD,
"THIS IS MY
BELOVED SON;
LISTEN TO HIM."

Mark 9:7

Chapter Nine

And he said to them, "Truly, I say to you, there are some standing here who will not taste death until they see the kingdom of God after it has come with power."

The Transfiguration

[2] And after six days Jesus took with him Peter and James and John, and led them up a high mountain by themselves. And he was transfigured before them, [3] and his clothes became radiant, intensely white, as no one on earth could bleach them. [4] And there appeared to them Elijah with Moses, and they were talking with Jesus. [5] And Peter said to Jesus, "Rabbi, it is good that we are here. Let us make three tents, one for you and one for Moses and one for Elijah." [6] For he did not know what to say, for they were terrified. [7] And a cloud overshadowed them, and a voice came out of the cloud, "This is my beloved Son; listen to him." [8] And suddenly, looking around, they no longer saw anyone with them but Jesus only.

[9] And as they were coming down the mountain, he charged them to tell no one what they had seen, until the Son of Man had risen from the dead. [10] So they kept the matter to themselves, questioning what this rising from the dead might mean. [11] And they asked him, "Why do the scribes say that first Elijah must come?" [12] And he said to them, "Elijah does come first to restore all things. And how is it written of the Son of Man that he should suffer many things and be treated with contempt? [13] But I tell you that Elijah has come, and they did to him whatever they pleased, as it is written of him."

Jesus Heals a Boy with an Unclean Spirit

[14] And when they came to the disciples, they saw a great crowd around them, and scribes arguing with them. [15] And immediately all the crowd, when they saw him, were greatly amazed and ran up to him and greeted him. [16] And he asked them, "What are you arguing about with them?" [17] And someone from the crowd answered him, "Teacher, I brought my son to you, for he has a spirit that makes him mute. [18] And whenever it seizes him, it throws him down, and he foams and grinds his teeth and becomes rigid. So I asked your disciples to cast it out, and they were not able." [19] And he answered them, "O faithless generation, how long am I to be with you? How long am I to bear with you? Bring him to me." [20] And they brought the boy to him. And when the spirit saw him, immediately it convulsed the boy, and he fell on the ground and rolled about, foaming at the mouth. [21] And Jesus asked his father, "How long has this been happening to him?" And he said, "From childhood. [22] And it has often cast him into fire

and into water, to destroy him. But if you can do anything, have compassion on us and help us." [23] And Jesus said to him, " 'If you can'! All things are possible for one who believes." [24] Immediately the father of the child cried out and said, "I believe; help my unbelief!" [25] And when Jesus saw that a crowd came running together, he rebuked the unclean spirit, saying to it, "You mute and deaf spirit, I command you, come out of him and never enter him again." [26] And after crying out and convulsing him terribly, it came out, and the boy was like a corpse, so that most of them said, "He is dead." [27] But Jesus took him by the hand and lifted him up, and he arose. [28] And when he had entered the house, his disciples asked him privately, "Why could we not cast it out?" [29] And he said to them, "This kind cannot be driven out by anything but prayer."

Jesus Again Foretells Death, Resurrection

[30] They went on from there and passed through Galilee. And he did not want anyone to know, [31] for he was teaching his disciples, saying to them, "The Son of Man is going to be delivered into the hands of men, and they will kill him. And when he is killed, after three days he will rise." [32] But they did not understand the saying, and were afraid to ask him.

Who Is the Greatest?

[33] And they came to Capernaum. And when he was in the house he asked them, "What were you discussing on the way?" [34] But they kept silent, for on the way they had argued with one another about who was the greatest. [35] And he sat down and called the twelve. And he said to them, "If anyone would be first, he must be last of all and servant of all." [36] And he

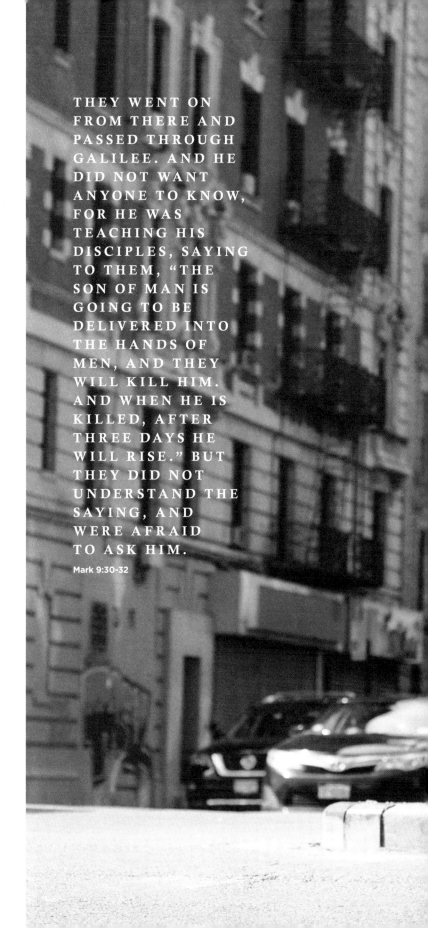

THEY WENT ON FROM THERE AND PASSED THROUGH GALILEE. AND HE DID NOT WANT ANYONE TO KNOW, FOR HE WAS TEACHING HIS DISCIPLES, SAYING TO THEM, "THE SON OF MAN IS GOING TO BE DELIVERED INTO THE HANDS OF MEN, AND THEY WILL KILL HIM. AND WHEN HE IS KILLED, AFTER THREE DAYS HE WILL RISE." BUT THEY DID NOT UNDERSTAND THE SAYING, AND WERE AFRAID TO ASK HIM.

Mark 9:30-32

took a child and put him in the midst of them, and taking him in his arms, he said to them, [37] "Whoever receives one such child in my name receives me, and whoever receives me, receives not me but him who sent me."

Anyone Not Against Us Is for Us

[38] John said to him, "Teacher, we saw someone casting out demons in your name, and we tried to stop him, because he was not following us." [39] But Jesus said, "Do not stop him, for no one who does a mighty work in my name will be able soon afterwards to speak evil of me. [40] For the one who is not against us is for us. [41] For truly, I say to you, whoever gives you a cup of water to drink because you belong to Christ will by no means lose his reward.

Temptations to Sin

[42] "Whoever causes one of these little ones who believe in me to sin, it would be better for him if a great millstone were hung round his neck and he were thrown into the sea. [43] And if your hand causes you to sin, cut it off. It is better for you to enter life crippled than with two hands to go to hell, to the unquenchable fire. [45] And if your foot causes you to sin, cut it off. It is better for you to enter life lame than with two feet to be thrown into hell. [47] And if your eye causes you to sin, tear it out. It is better for you to enter the kingdom of God with one eye than with two eyes to be thrown into hell, [48] 'where their worm does not die and the fire is not quenched.' [49] For everyone will be salted with fire. [50] Salt is good, but if the salt has lost its saltiness, how will you make it salty again? Have salt in yourselves, and be at peace with one another."

Chapter Ten

Teaching About Divorce

And he left there and went to the region of Judea and beyond the Jordan, and crowds gathered to him again. And again, as was his custom, he taught them.

² And Pharisees came up and in order to test him asked, "Is it lawful for a man to divorce his wife?" ³ He answered them, "What did Moses command you?" ⁴ They said, "Moses allowed a man to write a certificate of divorce and to send her away." ⁵ And Jesus said to them, "Because of your hardness of heart he wrote you this commandment. ⁶ But from the beginning of creation, 'God made them male and female.' ⁷ 'Therefore a man shall leave his father and mother and hold fast to his wife, ⁸ and the two shall become one flesh.' So they are no longer two but one flesh. ⁹ What therefore God has joined together, let not man separate."

¹⁰ And in the house the disciples asked him again about this matter. ¹¹ And he said to them, "Whoever divorces his wife and marries another commits adultery against her, ¹² and if she divorces her husband and marries another, she commits adultery."

Let the Children Come to Me

¹³ And they were bringing children to him that he might touch them, and the disciples rebuked them. ¹⁴ But when Jesus saw it, he was indignant and said to them, "Let the children come to me; do not hinder them, for to such belongs the kingdom of God. ¹⁵ Truly, I say to you, whoever does not receive the kingdom of God like a child shall not enter it." ¹⁶ And he took them in his arms and blessed them, laying his hands on them.

The Rich Young Man

¹⁷ And as he was setting out on his journey, a man ran up and knelt before him and asked him, "Good Teacher, what must I do to inherit eternal life?"

18 And Jesus said to him, "Why do you call me good? No one is good except God alone. 19 You know the commandments: 'Do not murder, Do not commit adultery, Do not steal, Do not bear false witness, Do not defraud, Honour your father and mother.'" 20 And he said to him, "Teacher, all these I have kept from my youth." 21 And Jesus, looking at him, loved him, and said to him, "You lack one thing: go, sell all that you have and give to the poor, and you will have treasure in heaven; and come, follow me." 22 Disheartened by the saying, he went away sorrowful, for he had great possessions.

23 And Jesus looked around and said to his disciples, "How difficult it will be for those who have wealth to enter the kingdom of God!" 24 And the disciples were amazed at his words. But Jesus said to them again, "Children, how difficult it is to enter the kingdom of God! 25 It is easier for a camel to go through the eye of a needle than for a rich person to enter the kingdom of God." 26 And they were exceedingly astonished, and said to him, "Then who can be saved?" 27 Jesus looked at them and said, "With man it is impossible, but not with God. For all things are possible with God." 28 Peter began to say to him, "See, we have left everything and followed you." 29 Jesus said, "Truly, I say to you, there is no one who has left house or brothers or sisters or mother or father or children or lands, for my sake and for the gospel, 30 who will not receive a hundredfold now in this time, houses and brothers and sisters and mothers and children and lands, with persecutions, and in the age to come eternal life. 31 But many who are first will be last, and the last first."

Jesus Foretells His Death a Third Time

32 And they were on the road, going up to Jerusalem, and Jesus was walking ahead of them. And they were

"IT IS EASIER FOR A CAMEL TO GO THROUGH THE EYE OF A NEEDLE THAN FOR A RICH PERSON TO ENTER THE KINGDOM OF GOD." AND THEY WERE EXCEEDINGLY ASTONISHED, AND SAID TO HIM, "THEN WHO CAN BE SAVED?" JESUS LOOKED AT THEM AND SAID, "WITH MAN IT IS IMPOSSIBLE, BUT NOT WITH GOD. FOR ALL THINGS ARE POSSIBLE WITH GOD."

Mark 10:25-27

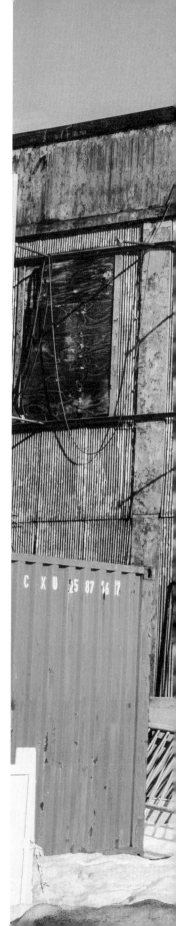

amazed, and those who followed were afraid. And taking the twelve again, he began to tell them what was to happen to him, [33] saying, "See, we are going up to Jerusalem, and the Son of Man will be delivered over to the chief priests and the scribes, and they will condemn him to death and deliver him over to the Gentiles. [34] And they will mock him and spit on him, and flog him and kill him. And after three days he will rise."

The Request of James and John

[35] And James and John, the sons of Zebedee, came up to him and said to him, "Teacher, we want you to do for us whatever we ask of you." [36] And he said to them, "What do you want me to do for you?" [37] And they said to him, "Grant us to sit, one at your right hand and one at your left, in your glory." [38] Jesus said to them, "You do not know what you are asking. Are you able to drink the cup that I drink, or to be baptized with the baptism with which I am baptized?" [39] And they said to him, "We are able." And Jesus said to them, "The cup that I drink you will drink, and with the baptism with which I am baptized, you will be baptized, [40] but to sit at my right hand or at my left is not mine to grant, but it is for those for whom it has been prepared." [41] And

when the ten heard it, they began to be indignant at James and John. [42] And Jesus called them to him and said to them, "You know that those who are considered rulers of the Gentiles lord it over them, and their great ones exercise authority over them. [43] But it shall not be so among you. But whoever would be great among you must be your servant, [44] and whoever would be first among you must be slave of all. [45] For even the Son of Man came not to be served but to serve, and to give his life as a ransom for many."

Jesus Heals Blind Bartimaeus

[46] And they came to Jericho. And as he was leaving Jericho with his disciples and a great crowd, Bartimaeus, a blind beggar, the son of Timaeus, was sitting by the roadside. [47] And when he heard that it was Jesus of Nazareth, he began to cry out and say, "Jesus, Son of David, have mercy on me!" [48] And many rebuked him, telling him to be silent. But he cried out all the more, "Son of David, have mercy on me!" [49] And Jesus stopped and said, "Call him." And they called the blind man, saying to him, "Take heart. Get up; he is calling you." [50] And throwing off his cloak, he sprang up and came to Jesus. [51] And Jesus said to him, "What do you want me to do

for you?" And the blind man said to him, "Rabbi, let me recover my sight." ⁵²And Jesus said to him, "Go your way; your faith has made you well." And immediately he recovered his sight and followed him on the way.

Chapter Eleven
The Triumphal Entry

Now when they drew near to Jerusalem, to Bethphage and Bethany, at the Mount of Olives, Jesus sent two of his disciples ²and said to them, "Go into the village in front of you, and immediately as you enter it you will find a colt tied, on which no one has ever sat. Untie it and bring it. ³If anyone says to you, 'Why are you doing this?' say, 'The Lord has need of it and will send it back here immediately.'" ⁴And they went away and found a colt tied at a door outside in the street, and they untied it. ⁵And some of those standing there said to them, "What are you doing, untying the colt?" ⁶And they told them what Jesus had said, and they let them go. ⁷And they brought the colt to Jesus and threw their cloaks on it, and he sat on it. ⁸And many spread their cloaks on the road, and others spread leafy branches that they had cut from the fields. ⁹And those who went before and those who followed were shouting, "Hosanna! Blessed is he who comes in the name of the Lord! ¹⁰Blessed is the coming kingdom of our father David! Hosanna in the highest!"

¹¹And he entered Jerusalem and went into the temple. And when he had looked around at everything, as it was already late, he went out to Bethany with the twelve.

Jesus Curses the Fig Tree
¹²On the following day, when they came from Bethany, he was hungry. ¹³And seeing in the distance a fig tree in leaf, he went to see if he could find anything on it. When he came to it, he found nothing but leaves, for it was not the season for figs. ¹⁴And he said to it, "May no one ever eat fruit from you again." And his disciples heard it.

Jesus Cleanses the Temple
¹⁵And they came to Jerusalem. And

"TRULY, I SAY TO YOU, WHOEVER SAYS TO THIS MOUNTAIN, 'BE TAKEN UP AND THROWN INTO THE SEA', AND DOES NOT DOUBT IN HIS HEART, BUT BELIEVES THAT WHAT HE SAYS WILL COME TO PASS, IT WILL BE DONE FOR HIM. THEREFORE I TELL YOU, WHATEVER YOU ASK IN PRAYER, BELIEVE THAT YOU HAVE RECEIVED IT, AND IT WILL BE YOURS."

Mark 11:23-24

he entered the temple and began to drive out those who sold and those who bought in the temple, and he overturned the tables of the money-changers and the seats of those who sold pigeons. ¹⁶And he would not allow anyone to carry anything through the temple. ¹⁷And he was teaching them and saying to them, "Is it not written, 'My house shall be called a house of prayer for all the nations'? But you have made it a den of robbers." ¹⁸And the chief priests and the scribes heard it and were seeking a way to destroy him, for they feared him, because all the crowd was astonished at his teaching. ¹⁹And when evening came they went out of the city.

The Lesson from the Withered Fig Tree

²⁰ As they passed by in the morning, they saw the fig tree withered away to its roots. ²¹And Peter remembered and said to him, "Rabbi, look! The fig tree that you cursed has withered." ²²And Jesus answered them, "Have faith in God. ²³Truly, I say to you, whoever says to this mountain, 'Be taken up and thrown into the sea', and does not doubt in his heart, but believes that what he says will come to pass, it will be done for him. ²⁴Therefore I tell you, whatever you ask in prayer, believe that you have received it, and it will be yours. ²⁵And whenever you stand praying, forgive, if you have anything against anyone, so that your Father also who is in heaven may forgive you your trespasses."

The Authority of Jesus Challenged

²⁷ And they came again to Jerusalem. And as he was walking in the temple, the chief priests and the scribes and the elders came to him, ²⁸and they said to him, "By what authority are you doing these things, or who gave you this authority to do them?" ²⁹Jesus said to them, "I will ask you one question; answer me, and I will tell you by what authority I do these things. ³⁰Was the baptism of John from heaven or from man? Answer me." ³¹And they discussed it with one another, saying, "If we say, 'From heaven', he will say, 'Why then did you not believe him?' ³²But shall we say, 'From man'?"—they were afraid of the people, for they all held that John really was a prophet. ³³So they answered Jesus, "We do not know." And Jesus said to them, "Neither will I tell you by what authority I do these things."

Chapter Twelve
The Parable of the Tenants

"Have you not read this Scripture: 'The stone that the builders rejected has become the cornerstone; this was the Lord's doing, and it is marvellous in our eyes'?"

Mark 12:10-11

And he began to speak to them in parables. "A man planted a vineyard and put a fence around it and dug a pit for the wine press and built a tower, and leased it to tenants and went into another country. ²When the season came, he sent a servant to the tenants to get from them some of the fruit of the vineyard. ³And they took him and beat him and sent him away emptyhanded. ⁴Again he sent to them another servant, and they struck him on the head and treated him shamefully. ⁵And he sent another, and him they killed. And so with many others: some they beat, and some they killed. ⁶He had still one other, a beloved son. Finally he sent him to them, saying, 'They will respect my son.' ⁷But those tenants said to one another, 'This is the heir. Come, let us kill him, and the inheritance will be ours.' ⁸And they took him and killed him and threw him out of the vineyard. ⁹What will the owner of the vineyard do? He will come and destroy the tenants and give the vineyard to others. ¹⁰Have you not read this Scripture:

"'The stone that the builders rejected
    has become the cornerstone;
¹¹   this was the Lord's doing,
        and it is marvellous in our
            eyes'?"

¹²And they were seeking to arrest him but feared the people, for they perceived that he had told the parable against them. So they left him and went away.

Paying Taxes to Caesar
¹³And they sent to him some of the Pharisees and some of the Herodians, to trap him in his talk. ¹⁴And they came and said to him, "Teacher, we know that you are true and do not care about anyone's opinion. For you are not swayed by appearances, but truly teach the way of God. Is it lawful to pay taxes to Caesar, or not? Should we pay them, or should we not?" ¹⁵But, knowing their hypocrisy, he said to them, "Why put me to the test? Bring me a denarius and let me look at it." ¹⁶And they brought one. And he said to them, "Whose likeness and inscription is this?" They said to him, "Caesar's." ¹⁷Jesus said to them, "Render to Caesar the things that are Caesar's, and to God the things that are God's." And they marvelled at him.

The Sadducees Ask About the Resurrection
¹⁸And Sadducees came to him, who say that there is no resurrection. And they asked him a question, saying, ¹⁹"Teacher, Moses wrote for us that if a man's brother dies and leaves a wife, but leaves no child, the man must take the widow and raise up offspring for his brother. ²⁰There were seven brothers; the first took a wife, and when he died left no offspring. ²¹And the second took her, and died, leaving no offspring. And the third likewise. ²²And the seven left no offspring. Last of all the woman also died. ²³In the resurrection, when they rise again, whose wife will she be? For the seven had her as wife."

²⁴Jesus said to them, "Is this not the reason you are wrong, because you know neither the Scriptures nor the power of God? ²⁵For when they rise from the dead, they neither marry nor are given in marriage, but are like angels in heaven. ²⁶And as for the dead being raised, have you not read in the book of Moses, in the passage about the bush, how God spoke to him, saying, 'I am the God of Abraham, and the God of Isaac, and the God of Jacob'? ²⁷He is not God of the dead, but of the living. You are quite wrong."

The Great Commandment
²⁸And one of the scribes came up and heard them disputing with one another, and seeing that he answered them well, asked him, "Which commandment is the most important of all?" ²⁹Jesus answered, "The most important is, 'Hear, O Israel: The Lord our God, the

Lord is one. ³⁰And you shall love the Lord your God with all your heart and with all your soul and with all your mind and with all your strength.' ³¹The second is this: 'You shall love your neighbour as yourself.' There is no other commandment greater than these." ³²And the scribe said to him, "You are right, Teacher. You have truly said that he is one, and there is no other besides him. ³³ And to love him with all the heart and with all the understanding and with all the strength, and to love one's neighbour as oneself, is much more than all whole burnt offerings and sacrifices." ³⁴And when Jesus saw that he answered wisely, he said to him, "You are not far from the kingdom of God." And after that no one dared to ask him any more questions.

Whose Son Is the Christ?

³⁵ And as Jesus taught in the temple, he said, "How can the scribes say that the Christ is the son of David? ³⁶David himself, in the Holy Spirit, declared,

"'The Lord said to my Lord,
  "Sit at my right hand,
      until I put your enemies under
          your feet."'

³⁷David himself calls him Lord. So how is he his son?" And the great throng heard him gladly.

Beware of the Scribes

³⁸ And in his teaching he said, "Beware of the scribes, who like to walk around in long robes and like greetings in the market-places ³⁹and have the best seats in the synagogues and the places of honour at feasts, ⁴⁰who devour widows' houses and for a pretence make long prayers. They will receive the greater condemnation."

The Widow's Offering

⁴¹ And he sat down opposite the treasury and watched the people putting money into the offering box. Many rich people put in large sums. ⁴²And a poor widow came and put in two small copper coins, which make a penny. ⁴³And he called his disciples to him and said to them, "Truly, I say to you, this poor widow has put in more than all those who are contributing to the offering box. ⁴⁴For they all contributed out of their abundance, but she out of her poverty has put in everything she had, all she had to live on."

AND HE CALLED HIS DISCIPLES TO HIM AND SAID TO THEM, "TRULY, I SAY TO YOU, THIS POOR WIDOW HAS PUT IN MORE THAN ALL THOSE WHO ARE CONTRIBUTING TO THE OFFERING BOX. FOR THEY ALL CONTRIBUTED OUT OF THEIR ABUNDANCE, BUT SHE OUT OF HER POVERTY HAS PUT IN EVERYTHING SHE HAD, ALL SHE HAD TO LIVE ON."

Mark 12:43-44

Chapter Thirteen

Jesus Foretells Destruction of the Temple

And as he came out of the temple, one of his disciples said to him, "Look, Teacher, what wonderful stones and what wonderful buildings!" ²And Jesus said to him, "Do you see these great buildings? There will not be left here one stone upon another that will not be thrown down."

Signs of the End of the Age

³And as he sat on the Mount of Olives opposite the temple, Peter and James and John and Andrew asked him privately, ⁴"Tell us, when will these things be, and what will be the sign when all these things are about to be accomplished?" ⁵And Jesus began to say to them, "See that no one leads you astray. ⁶Many will come in my name, saying, 'I am he!' and they will lead many astray. ⁷And when you hear of wars and rumours of wars, do not be alarmed. This must take place, but the end is not yet. ⁸For nation will rise against nation, and kingdom against kingdom. There will be earthquakes in various places; there will be famines. These are but the beginning of the birth pains.

⁹"But be on your guard. For they will deliver you over to councils, and you will be beaten in synagogues, and you will stand before governors and kings for my sake, to bear witness before them. ¹⁰And the gospel must first be proclaimed to all nations. ¹¹And when they bring you to trial and deliver you over, do not be anxious beforehand what you are to say, but say whatever is given you in that hour, for it is not you who speak, but the Holy Spirit. ¹²And brother will deliver brother over to death, and the father his child, and children will rise against parents and

have them put to death. ¹³And you will be hated by all for my name's sake. But the one who endures to the end will be saved.

The Abomination of Desolation
¹⁴"But when you see the abomination of desolation standing where he ought not to be (let the reader understand), then let those who are in Judea flee to the mountains. ¹⁵Let the one who is on the housetop not go down, nor enter his house, to take anything out, ¹⁶and let the one who is in the field not turn back to take his cloak. ¹⁷And alas for women who are pregnant and for those who are nursing infants in those days! ¹⁸Pray that it may not happen in winter. ¹⁹For in those days there will be such tribulation as has not been from the beginning of the creation that God created until now, and never will be. ²⁰And if the Lord had not cut short the days, no human being would be saved. But for the sake of the elect, whom he chose, he shortened the days. ²¹And then if anyone says to you, 'Look, here is the Christ!' or 'Look, there he is!' do not believe it. ²²For false christs and false prophets will arise and perform signs and wonders, to lead astray, if possible, the elect. ²³But be on guard; I have told you all things beforehand.

The Coming of the Son of Man
²⁴"But in those days, after that tribulation, the sun will be darkened, and the moon will not give its light, ²⁵and the stars will be falling from heaven, and the powers in the heavens will be shaken. ²⁶And then they will see the Son of Man coming in clouds with

great power and glory. ²⁷And then he will send out the angels and gather his elect from the four winds, from the ends of the earth to the ends of heaven.

The Lesson of the Fig Tree

²⁸"From the fig tree learn its lesson: as soon as its branch becomes tender and puts out its leaves, you know that summer is near. ²⁹So also, when you see these things taking place, you know that he is near, at the very gates. ³⁰Truly, I say to you, this generation will not pass away until all these things take place. ³¹Heaven and earth will pass away, but my words will not pass away.

No One Knows That Day or Hour

³²"But concerning that day or that hour, no one knows, not even the angels in heaven, nor the Son, but only the Father. ³³Be on guard, keep awake. For you do not know when the time will come. ³⁴It is like a man going on a journey, when he leaves home and puts his servants in charge, each with his work, and commands the doorkeeper to stay awake. ³⁵Therefore stay awake—for you do not know when the master of the house will come, in the evening, or at midnight, or when the cock crows, or in the morning— ³⁶lest he come suddenly and find you asleep. ³⁷And what I say to you I say to all: Stay awake."

Chapter Fourteen

The Plot to Kill Jesus

It was now two days before the Passover and the Feast of Unleavened Bread. And the chief priests and the scribes were seeking how to arrest him by stealth and kill him, ²for they said, "Not during the feast, lest there be an uproar from the people."

Jesus Anointed at Bethany

³And while he was at Bethany in the house of Simon the leper, as he was reclining at table, a woman came with an alabaster flask of ointment of pure nard, very costly, and she broke the flask and poured it over his head. ⁴There were some who said to themselves indignantly, "Why was the ointment wasted like that? ⁵For this ointment could have been sold for more than three hundred denarii and given to the poor." And they scolded her. ⁶But Jesus said, "Leave her alone. Why do you trouble her? She has done a beautiful thing to me. ⁷For you always have the poor with you, and whenever you want, you can do good for them. But you will not always have me. ⁸She has done what she could; she has anointed my body beforehand for burial. ⁹And truly, I say to you, wherever the gospel is proclaimed in the whole world, what she has done will be told in memory of her."

Judas to Betray Jesus

¹⁰Then Judas Iscariot, who was one of the twelve, went to the chief priests in order to betray him to them. ¹¹And when they heard it, they were glad and promised to give him money. And he sought an opportunity to betray him.

The Passover with the Disciples

¹²And on the first day of Unleavened Bread, when they sacrificed the Passover lamb, his disciples said to him, "Where will you have us go and prepare for you to eat the Passover?" ¹³And he sent two of his disciples and said to them, "Go into the city, and a man carrying a jar of water will meet you. Follow him, ¹⁴and wherever he enters, say to the master of the house, 'The

Teacher says, Where is my guest room, where I may eat the Passover with my disciples?' ¹⁵ And he will show you a large upper room furnished and ready; there prepare for us." ¹⁶ And the disciples set out and went to the city and found it just as he had told them, and they prepared the Passover.

¹⁷ And when it was evening, he came with the twelve. ¹⁸ And as they were reclining at table and eating, Jesus said, "Truly, I say to you, one of you will betray me, one who is eating with me." ¹⁹ They began to be sorrowful and to say to him one after another, "Is it I?" ²⁰ He said to them, "It is one of the twelve, one who is dipping bread into the dish with me. ²¹ For the Son of Man goes as it is written of him, but woe to that man by whom the Son of Man is betrayed! It would have been better for that man if he had not been born."

Institution of the Lord's Supper

²² And as they were eating, he took bread, and after blessing it broke it and gave it to them, and said, "Take; this is my body." ²³ And he took a cup, and when he had given thanks he gave it to them, and they all drank of it. ²⁴ And he said to them, "This is my blood of the covenant, which is poured out for many. ²⁵ Truly, I say to you, I will not drink again of the fruit of the vine until that day when I drink it new in the kingdom of God."

Jesus Foretells Peter's Denial

²⁶ And when they had sung a hymn, they went out to the Mount of Olives. ²⁷ And Jesus said to them, "You will all fall away, for it is written, 'I will strike the shepherd, and the sheep will be scattered.' ²⁸ But after I am raised up, I will go before you to Galilee." ²⁹ Peter said to him, "Even though they all fall away, I will not." ³⁰ And Jesus said to him, "Truly, I tell

you, this very night, before the cock crows twice, you will deny me three times." [31] But he said emphatically, "If I must die with you, I will not deny you." And they all said the same.

Jesus Prays in Gethsemane

[32] And they went to a place called Gethsemane. And he said to his disciples, "Sit here while I pray." [33] And he took with him Peter and James and John, and began to be greatly distressed and troubled. [34] And he said to them, "My soul is very sorrowful, even to death. Remain here and watch." [35] And going a little farther, he fell on the ground and prayed that, if it were possible, the hour might pass from him. [36] And he said, "Abba, Father, all things are possible for you. Remove this cup from me. Yet not what I will, but what you will." [37] And he came and found them sleeping, and he said to Peter, "Simon, are you asleep? Could you not watch one hour? [38] Watch and pray that you may not enter into temptation. The spirit indeed is willing, but the flesh is weak." [39] And again he went away and prayed, saying the same words. [40] And again he came and found them sleeping, for their eyes were very heavy, and they did not know what to answer him. [41] And he came the third time and said to them, "Are you still sleeping and taking your rest? It is enough; the hour has come. The Son of Man is betrayed into the hands of sinners. [42] Rise, let us be going; see, my betrayer is at hand."

Betrayal and Arrest of Jesus

[43] And immediately, while he was still speaking, Judas came, one of the twelve, and with him a crowd with swords and clubs, from the chief priests and the scribes and the elders. [44] Now the betrayer had given them a sign, saying, "The one I will kiss is the man. Seize him and lead him away under guard." [45] And when he came, he went up to him at once and said, "Rabbi!" And he kissed him. [46] And they laid hands on him and seized him. [47] But one of those who stood by drew his sword and struck the servant of the high priest and cut off his ear. [48] And Jesus said to them, "Have you come out as against a robber, with swords and clubs to capture me? [49] Day after day I was with you in the temple teaching, and you did not seize me. But let the Scriptures be fulfilled." [50] And they all left him and fled.

A Young Man Flees

[51] And a young man followed him, with nothing but a linen cloth about his body. And they seized him, [52] but he left the linen cloth and ran away naked.

Jesus Before the Council

[53] And they led Jesus to the high priest. And all the chief priests and the elders and the scribes came together. [54] And Peter had followed him at a distance, right into the courtyard of the high priest. And he was sitting with the guards and warming himself at the fire. [55] Now the chief priests and the whole council were seeking testimony against Jesus to put him to death, but they found none. [56] For many bore false witness against him, but their testimony did not agree. [57] And some stood up and bore false witness against him, saying, [58] "We heard him say, 'I will destroy this temple that is made with hands, and in three days I will build another, not made with hands.'" [59] Yet even about this their testimony did not agree. [60] And the high priest stood up in the midst and asked Jesus, "Have you no answer to make? What is it that these men testify against you?" [61] But he remained silent and made no answer. Again the high priest asked him, "Are you the Christ, the Son of the Blessed?" [62] And Jesus said, "I am,

BUT HE DENIED IT, SAYING, "I NEITHER KNOW NOR UNDERSTAND WHAT YOU MEAN." AND HE WENT OUT INTO THE GATEWAY AND THE COCK CROWED.

Mark 14:68

and you will see the Son of Man seated at the right hand of Power, and coming with the clouds of heaven." ⁶³And the high priest tore his garments and said, "What further witnesses do we need? ⁶⁴You have heard his blasphemy. What is your decision?" And they all condemned him as deserving death. ⁶⁵And some began to spit on him and to cover his face and to strike him, saying to him, "Prophesy!" And the guards received him with blows.

Peter Denies Jesus

⁶⁶ And as Peter was below in the courtyard, one of the servant girls of the high priest came, ⁶⁷ and seeing Peter warming himself, she looked at him and said, "You also were with the Nazarene, Jesus." ⁶⁸But he denied it, saying, "I neither know nor understand what you mean." And he went out into the gateway and the cock crowed. ⁶⁹And the servant girl saw him and began again to say to the bystanders, "This man is one of them." ⁷⁰But again he denied it. And after a little while the bystanders again said to Peter, "Certainly you are one of them, for you are a Galilean." ⁷¹But he began to invoke a curse on himself and to swear, "I do not know this man of whom you speak." ⁷²And immediately

the cock crowed a second time. And Peter remembered how Jesus had said to him, "Before the cock crows twice, you will deny me three times." And he broke down and wept.

Chapter Fifteen
Jesus Delivered to Pilate

And as soon as it was morning, the chief priests held a consultation with the elders and scribes and the whole council. And they bound Jesus and led him away and delivered him over to Pilate. ² And Pilate asked him, "Are you the King of the Jews?" And he answered him, "You have said so." ³And the chief priests accused him of many things. ⁴And Pilate again asked him, "Have you no answer to make? See how many charges they bring against you." ⁵But Jesus made no further answer, so that Pilate was amazed.

Pilate Delivers Jesus to Be Crucified

⁶ Now at the feast he used to release for them one prisoner for whom they asked. ⁷And among the rebels in prison, who had committed murder in the

insurrection, there was a man called Barabbas. ⁸And the crowd came up and began to ask Pilate to do as he usually did for them. ⁹And he answered them, saying, "Do you want me to release for you the King of the Jews?" ¹⁰For he perceived that it was out of envy that the chief priests had delivered him up. ¹¹But the chief priests stirred up the crowd to have him release for them Barabbas instead. ¹²And Pilate again said to them, "Then what shall I do with the man you call the King of the Jews?" ¹³And they cried out again, "Crucify him." ¹⁴And Pilate said to them, "Why? What evil has he done?" But they shouted all the more, "Crucify him." ¹⁵So Pilate, wishing to satisfy the crowd, released for them Barabbas, and having scourged Jesus, he delivered him to be crucified.

Jesus Is Mocked

¹⁶ And the soldiers led him away inside the palace (that is, the governor's headquarters), and they called together the whole battalion. ¹⁷And they clothed him in a purple cloak, and twisting together a crown of thorns, they put it on him. ¹⁸And they began to salute him, "Hail, King of the Jews!" ¹⁹And they were striking his head with a reed and

spitting on him and kneeling down in homage to him. ²⁰ And when they had mocked him, they stripped him of the purple cloak and put his own clothes on him. And they led him out to crucify him.

The Crucifixion

²¹ And they compelled a passer-by, Simon of Cyrene, who was coming in from the country, the father of Alexander and Rufus, to carry his cross. ²² And they brought him to the place called Golgotha (which means Place of a Skull). ²³ And they offered him wine mixed with myrrh, but he did not take it. ²⁴ And they crucified him and divided his garments among them, casting lots for them, to decide what each should take. ²⁵ And it was the third hour when they crucified him. ²⁶ And the inscription of the charge against him read, "The King of the Jews." ²⁷ And with him they crucified two robbers, one on his right and one on his left. ²⁹ And those who passed by derided him, wagging their heads and saying, "Aha! You who would destroy the temple and rebuild it in three days, ³⁰ save yourself, and come down from the cross!" ³¹ So also the chief priests with the scribes mocked him to one another, saying, "He saved others; he cannot save himself. ³² Let the Christ, the King of Israel, come down now from the cross that we may see and believe." Those who were crucified with him also reviled him.

The Death of Jesus

³³ And when the sixth hour had come, there was darkness over the whole land until the ninth hour. ³⁴ And at the ninth hour Jesus cried with a loud voice, "Eloi, Eloi, lema sabachthani?" which means, "My God, my God, why have you forsaken me?" ³⁵ And some of the bystanders hearing it said, "Behold, he is calling Elijah." ³⁶ And someone ran and filled a sponge with sour wine, put it on a reed and gave it to him to drink, saying, "Wait, let us see whether Elijah will come to take him down." ³⁷ And Jesus uttered a loud cry and breathed his last. ³⁸ And the curtain of the temple was torn in two, from top to bottom. ³⁹ And when the centurion, who stood facing him, saw that in this way he breathed his last, he said, "Truly this man was the Son of God!"

⁴⁰ There were also women looking on from a distance, among whom were Mary Magdalene, and Mary the mother of James the younger and of Joses, and Salome. ⁴¹ When he was in Galilee, they followed him and ministered to him, and there were also many other women who came up with him to Jerusalem.

Jesus Is Buried

⁴² And when evening had come, since it was the day of Preparation, that is, the day before the Sabbath, ⁴³ Joseph of Arimathea, a respected member of the council, who was also himself looking for the kingdom of God, took courage and went to Pilate and asked for the body of Jesus. ⁴⁴ Pilate was surprised to hear that he should have already died. And summoning the centurion, he asked him whether he was already dead. ⁴⁵ And when he learned from the centurion that he was dead, he granted the corpse to Joseph. ⁴⁶ And Joseph bought a linen shroud, and taking him down, wrapped him in the linen shroud and laid him in a tomb that had been cut out of the rock. And he rolled a stone against the entrance of the tomb. ⁴⁷ Mary Magdalene and Mary the mother of Joses saw where he was laid.

AND AT THE NINTH HOUR JESUS CRIED WITH A LOUD VOICE, "ELOI, ELOI, LEMA SABACHTHANI?" WHICH MEANS, "MY GOD, MY GOD, WHY HAVE YOU FORSAKEN ME?"

Mark 15:34

Chapter Sixteen

The Resurrection

When the Sabbath was past, Mary Magdalene, Mary the mother of James, and Salome bought spices, so that they might go and anoint him. ²And very early on the first day of the week, when the sun had risen, they went to the tomb. ³And they were saying to one another, "Who will roll away the stone for us from the entrance of the tomb?" ⁴And looking up, they saw that the stone had been rolled back—it was very large. ⁵And entering the tomb, they saw a young man sitting on the right side, dressed in a white robe, and they were alarmed. ⁶And he said to them, "Do not be alarmed. You seek Jesus of Nazareth, who was crucified. He has risen; he is not here. See the place where they laid him. ⁷But go, tell his disciples and Peter that he is going before you to Galilee. There you will see him, just as he told you." ⁸And they went out and fled from the tomb, for trembling and astonishment had seized them, and they said nothing to anyone, for they were afraid.

[Some of the earliest manuscripts do not include 16:9–20.]

Jesus Appears to Mary Magdalene

⁹[[Now when he rose early on the first day of the week, he appeared first to Mary Magdalene, from whom he had cast out seven demons. ¹⁰She went and told those who had been with him, as they mourned and wept. ¹¹But when they heard that he was alive and had been seen by her, they would not believe it.

Jesus Appears to Two Disciples

¹²After these things he appeared in another form to two of them, as they were walking into the country. ¹³And they went back and told the rest, but they did not believe them.

The Great Commission

¹⁴Afterwards he appeared to the eleven themselves as they were reclining at table, and he rebuked them for their unbelief and hardness of heart, because they had not believed those who saw him after he had risen. ¹⁵And he said to them, "Go into all the world and proclaim the gospel to the whole creation. ¹⁶Whoever believes and is baptized will be saved, but whoever does not believe will be condemned. ¹⁷And these signs will accompany those who believe: in my name they will cast out demons; they will speak in new tongues; ¹⁸they will pick up serpents with their hands; and if they drink any deadly poison, it will not hurt them; they will lay their hands on the sick, and they will recover."

¹⁹So then the Lord Jesus, after he had spoken to them, was taken up into heaven and sat down at the right hand of God. ²⁰And they went out and preached everywhere, while the Lord worked with them and confirmed the message by accompanying signs.]]

AND HE SAID TO THEM, "DO NOT BE ALARMED. YOU SEEK JESUS OF NAZARETH, WHO WAS CRUCIFIED. HE HAS RISEN; HE IS NOT HERE. SEE THE PLACE WHERE THEY LAID HIM."

Mark 16:6

EXPERIENCE MARK

JESUS IS THE SON OF GOD UNVEILED

AND ON THE SABBATH HE BEGAN TO TEACH IN THE SYNAGOGUE, AND MANY WHO HEARD HIM WERE ASTONISHED, SAYING, "WHERE DID THIS MAN GET THESE THINGS? WHAT IS THE WISDOM GIVEN TO HIM? HOW ARE SUCH MIGHTY WORKS DONE BY HIS HANDS?" Mark 6:2

HOW MARK FITS INTO GOD'S STORY AND MY STORY
Like an oasis in the desert, Jesus is good news to the whole world.
God uses everyday people to change the world.

KEY CHARACTERS
Jesus, John the Baptist, Peter, Mary Magdalene, Jewish leaders (Pharisees, Sadducees, Scribes), Blind Bartimaeus

HE GAINED TWICE THE AMOUNT OF SIGHT THAT DAY, A PHYSICAL SIGHT AND A SPIRITUAL FAITH.

KEY WORD IN MARK: SIGHT

Greek: ἀναβλέπω, *anablepō*, to look up, regain sight, gain sight

The sense of sight is an important part of the Gospel of Mark, as it was in the ancient Graeco-Roman world. For Mark, sight was important on two levels. One the one hand, Jesus did indeed come to restore sight to those who did not have it. Healing is an important part of Jesus' power. On the other hand, in order to follow Jesus, a certain level of sight (or "faith") was required. The disciples in Mark's Gospel don't seem to be the most ideal followers for Jesus. They try to exclude children from seeing Jesus (Mark 10:13-16), they abandon him when he is arrested (Mark 14:50-52), and at the climax of understanding Jesus' identity, Peter, the chief disciple, is rebuked with the famous saying, "Get behind me, Satan!" (Mark 8:33). Some scholars believe that the disciples act as an example of how not to follow Jesus in faith. This has led some to read the blind man healed in Mark 8:22-26 as a metaphor for the disciples. In contrast, a man named Bartimaeus in Mark 10:46-52 merely asks Jesus in faith and immediately he is healed and follows Jesus. He gained twice the amount of sight that day, a physical sight and a spiritual faith.

KEY THEME: MARK'S "MESSIANIC SECRET"

If you closely read Mark's Gospel you'll notice an odd feature of the narrative: Jesus tries to hide his identity as the Messiah (a long-awaited liberator of the Jewish people). After cleansing a leper, Jesus tells him to tell no one (Mark 1:43-45). In the parable of the sower in Mark 4, Jesus talks about how his teaching is veiled in a mystery. When Peter successfully pinpoints Jesus' identity in Mark 8:29-30, Jesus immediately tells the disciples to reveal it to no one. Why does Mark portray Jesus in this way? From a historical perspective, it is likely that Jesus spoke in such a manner. Judea, the region where Jesus lived, was politically unstable. Many revolutionaries came as "messiahs" to try and liberate the people only to be crushed by the iron hand of the Roman empire. Were Jesus to announce that he was the Messiah and that he had come foretelling the destruction of the temple (a cornerstone of Judea and a political/religious moot point for the Jewish people), then it is likely he would have been swiftly excommunicated or executed. From a scriptural perspective, Mark did not want Jesus' identity to be separated from his suffering on the cross. Yes, Jesus healed people, walked on water and told the future. But he also died the death of a slave. This turned people's expectations about a liberator on their heads. It makes sense why Jesus tries to "hide" his identity in Mark's Gospel.

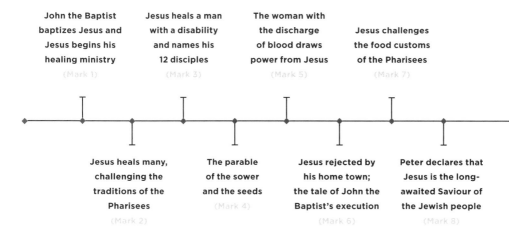

John the Baptist baptizes Jesus and Jesus begins his healing ministry
(Mark 1)

Jesus heals a man with a disability and names his 12 disciples
(Mark 3)

The woman with the discharge of blood draws power from Jesus
(Mark 5)

Jesus challenges the food customs of the Pharisees
(Mark 7)

Jesus heals many, challenging the traditions of the Pharisees
(Mark 2)

The parable of the sower and the seeds
(Mark 4)

Jesus rejected by his home town; the tale of John the Baptist's execution
(Mark 6)

Peter declares that Jesus is the long-awaited Saviour of the Jewish people
(Mark 8)

UNIQUE LITERARY MOTIF: SON OF MAN STATEMENTS

While the phrase "Son of Man" occurs in Matthew, Luke, and John, Mark is the earliest Gospel and it influenced all the other Gospel writers. The phrase "Son of Man" is confusing. For example, in Mark 2:28 Jesus says, "the Son of Man is lord even of the Sabbath". Who is Jesus referring to? Who is this Son of Man? For the most part, the "Son of Man" is obviously a reference to Jesus. For the first time this phrase is employed in Mark and in the other Gospels with reference to a specific person: Jesus. Outside of the New Testament, "Son of Man" is not known as a set title for any specific thing, whether it be an expected leader, liberator or person. It has a whole range of meanings. But, in Mark's Gospel for the first time we see it used by someone to refer to themselves. When Jesus does this in Mark's Gospel, it not only contributes to the mysterious nature of Jesus' identity but in some ways, appears to grant him authority. More significantly, it serves as a counterpart to Jesus's other title in Mark's Gospel: Son of God. Therein lies the mystery about Jesus Christ, Son of Man (human) and Son of God (divine).

MARK: QUICK FACTS

• Was written, in part, to preserve traditions about Jesus that were circulating at the time. • Early Church traditions hold that "Mark" was the disciple Peter's translator. Also known as "John Mark." • If it was written by John Mark, then he also accompanied the Apostle Paul on a missionary journey. • The earliest form of the Gospel that we have begins and ends abruptly. The first sentence of the Gospel in Greek is an incomplete sense and could actually have been a title or a note from a scribe about the contents of the work. The earliest form of the Gospel we have ends at Mark 16:8 ("they were afraid"). Such an ending was unsatisfying for a number of reasons, so Mark's ending was ex-

tended, drawing on material from Matthew, Luke, and Acts. • Mark is used by both Matthew and Luke (large parts are copied verbatim or developed). John also shows signs that it has been influenced by Mark. • The narrative structure of Mark (from John the Baptist to the resurrection) has been a defining feature of the Gospel story in early Christian literature. • We cannot know for sure if Mark contains accounts from the Apostle Peter, but it is certainly possible. • While we do not have sources that pre-date Mark's Gospel, it is likely he drew on earlier written versions of Jesus' teaching (anecdotes kept here or there) and oral tradition that circulated.

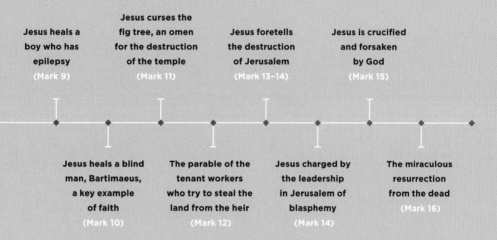

Jesus heals a boy who has epilepsy (Mark 9)

Jesus curses the fig tree, an omen for the destruction of the temple (Mark 11)

Jesus foretells the destruction of Jerusalem (Mark 13–14)

Jesus is crucified and forsaken by God (Mark 15)

Jesus heals a blind man, Bartimaeus, a key example of faith (Mark 10)

The parable of the tenant workers who try to steal the land from the heir (Mark 12)

Jesus charged by the leadership in Jerusalem of blasphemy (Mark 14)

The miraculous resurrection from the dead (Mark 16)

KEY PATTERN: WRESTLING WITH ANCIENT JEWISH TRADITIONS

At various points in Mark's Gospel (Mark 2-3, 7, etc.) we come across Jesus butting heads with Jewish leaders (Pharisees, Sadduccees, scribes). It is important to remember that Christianity came from and took form in ancient Judaism. Jesus was Jewish. His disciples were Jewish. The core of early Christianity in its first fifty years was Jewish. The Jewish scriptures (the Hebrew Bible known to us as the Old Testament) were and are vital for understanding who Jesus is. Jesus had certain qualms about how various passages of the Hebrew Bible were interpreted. For the Jewish people, the Hebrew scriptures (and specifically the first five books of the Old Testament,

Genesis-Deuteronomy, known as the Torah) were divine revelation about how best to live. You might hear some people talk about the Torah as the "Law" but this is a misnomer. The Torah was a way of life. As such it was subject to interpretations. While Jesus interprets the Hebrew Scriptures differently from his contemporaries, he did not seek to do away with Judaism altogether. The snapshot of Jesus's teaching in Mark's Gospel shows us an educated Jewish man wrestling with how the Hebrew Scriptures can bring abundant supernatural life to those who live within it. In this way Christianity is the daughter of ancient Judaism.

LUKE

THE NEW TESTAMENT EXPERIENCE

Inspired by the Holy Spirit

SAVIOUR FOR ALL

WRITTEN BY LUKE THE EVANGELIST

"FOR NOTHING WILL BE IMPOSSIBLE WITH GOD." AND MARY SAID, "BEHOLD, I AM THE SERVANT OF THE LORD; LET IT BE TO ME ACCCORDING TO YOUR WORD." AND THE ANGEL DEPARTED FROM HER. Luke 1:37-38

IMPORTANT STORIES IN LUKE

Birth of Jesus Foretold: Luke 1:26-45 **John the Baptist Prepares the Way:** Luke 3:3-9 **Temptation of Jesus:** Luke 4:1-13
Jesus Calls the First Disciples: Luke 5:1-45 **A Sinful Women Forgiven:** Luke 7:36-50 **Peter Confesses Jesus as the Christ:** Luke 9:18-20
Lament over Jerusalem: Luke 13:31-35 **The Parable of the Lost Sheep:** Luke 15:3-7 **Jesus and Zacchaeus:** Luke 19:1-10
Judas Betrays Jesus: Luke 22:3-6 **Pilate Delivers Jesus to Be Crucified:** Luke 23:18 **The Resurrection:** Luke 24:1-12

INTRODUCTION
TO LUKE

SYDNEY, AUSTRALIA

THEN HE SAID TO THEM, "THESE ARE MY WORDS THAT I SPOKE TO YOU WHILE I WAS STILL WITH YOU, THAT EVERYTHING WRITTEN ABOUT ME IN THE LAW OF MOSES AND THE PROPHETS AND THE PSALMS MUST BE FULFILLED." Luke 24:44

AUTHOR, DATE AND AUDIENCE

Luke lived 80-90 AD (the time of the Gospel's writing). Unknown date of birth or death.
Early Christian tradition says that he was Paul's "fellow worker" (Philemon 24, see Acts) and
a physician (Colossians 4:14). Had an advanced education in Greek grammar, rhetoric and
literature as well as the Jewish scriptures and historical techniques (historiography).
Very little is known about who Luke was.

THEME AND PURPOSE

He obviously wrote to supplement Mark's Gospel (as he draws on Markan material).
His narrative focus suggests that he wanted to generate a document about Jesus' life according
to the standards of Jewish and Graeco-Roman historians.

"THEREFORE I TELL YOU, HER SINS, WHICH ARE MANY, ARE FORGIVEN—FOR SHE LOVED MUCH. BUT HE WHO IS FORGIVEN LITTLE, LOVES LITTLE." AND HE SAID TO HER, "YOUR SINS ARE FORGIVEN." THEN THOSE WHO WERE AT TABLE WITH HIM BEGAN TO SAY AMONG THEMSELVES, "WHO IS THIS, WHO EVEN FORGIVES SINS?" AND HE SAID TO THE WOMAN, "YOUR FAITH HAS SAVED YOU; GO IN PEACE."

Luke 7:47-50

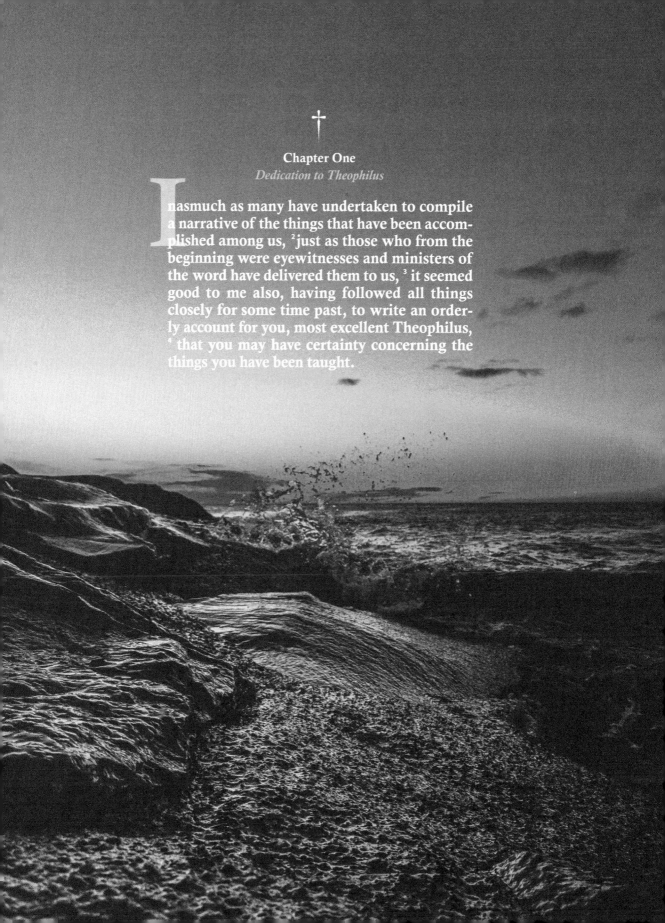

✝

Chapter One
Dedication to Theophilus

Inasmuch as many have undertaken to compile a narrative of the things that have been accomplished among us, ²just as those who from the beginning were eyewitnesses and ministers of the word have delivered them to us, ³ it seemed good to me also, having followed all things closely for some time past, to write an orderly account for you, most excellent Theophilus, ⁴ that you may have certainty concerning the things you have been taught.

Birth of John the Baptist Foretold

[5] In the days of Herod, king of Judea, there was a priest named Zechariah, of the division of Abijah. And he had a wife from the daughters of Aaron, and her name was Elizabeth. [6] And they were both righteous before God, walking blamelessly in all the commandments and statutes of the Lord. [7] But they had no child, because Elizabeth was barren, and both were advanced in years.

[8] Now while he was serving as priest before God when his division was on duty, [9] according to the custom of the priesthood, he was chosen by lot to enter the temple of the Lord and burn incense. [10] And the whole multitude of the people were praying outside at the hour of incense. [11] And there appeared to him an angel of the Lord standing on the right side of the altar of incense. [12] And Zechariah was troubled when he saw him, and fear fell upon him. [13] But the angel said to him, "Do not be afraid, Zechariah, for your prayer has been heard, and your wife Elizabeth will bear you a son, and you shall call his name John. [14] And you will have joy and gladness, and many will rejoice at his birth, [15] for he will be great before the Lord. And he must not drink wine or strong drink, and he will be filled with the Holy Spirit, even from his mother's womb. [16] And he will turn many of the children of Israel to the Lord their God, [17] and he will go before him in the spirit and power of Elijah, to turn the hearts of the fathers to the children, and the disobedient to the wisdom of the just, to make ready for the Lord a people prepared."

[18] And Zechariah said to the angel, "How shall I know this? For I am an old man, and my wife is advanced in years." [19] And the angel answered him, "I am Gabriel. I stand in the presence of God, and I was sent to speak to you and to bring you this good news. [20] And behold, you will be silent and unable to speak until the day that these things take place, because you did not believe my words, which will be fulfilled in their time." [21] And the people were waiting for Zechariah, and they were wondering at his delay in the temple. [22] And when he came out, he was unable to speak to them, and they realized that he had seen a vision in the temple. And he kept making signs to them and remained mute. [23] And when his time of service was ended, he went to his home.

[24] After these days his wife Elizabeth conceived, and for five months she kept herself hidden, saying, [25] "Thus the Lord has done for me in the days when he looked on me, to take away my reproach among people."

Birth of Jesus Foretold

[26] In the sixth month the angel Gabriel was sent from God to a city of Galilee named Nazareth, [27] to a virgin betrothed to a man whose name was Joseph, of the house of David. And the virgin's name was Mary. [28] And he came to her and said, "Greetings, O favoured one, the Lord is with you!" [29] But she was greatly troubled at the saying, and tried to discern what sort of greeting this might be. [30] And the angel said to

AND MARY SAID, "MY SOUL MAGNIFIES
THE LORD, AND MY SPIRIT REJOICES IN GOD MY
SAVIOUR, FOR HE HAS LOOKED ON THE HUMBLE
ESTATE OF HIS SERVANT. FOR BEHOLD, FROM NOW ON
ALL GENERATIONS WILL CALL ME BLESSED; FOR HE
WHO IS MIGHTY HAS DONE GREAT THINGS
FOR ME, AND HOLY IS HIS NAME.

Luke 1:46-49

her, "Do not be afraid, Mary, for you have found favour with God. [31] And behold, you will conceive in your womb and bear a son, and you shall call his name Jesus. [32] He will be great and will be called the Son of the Most High. And the Lord God will give to him the throne of his father David, [33] and he will reign over the house of Jacob for ever, and of his kingdom there will be no end."

[34] And Mary said to the angel, "How will this be, since I am a virgin?"

[35] And the angel answered her, "The Holy Spirit will come upon you, and the power of the Most High will overshadow you; therefore the child to be born will be called holy— the Son of God. [36] And behold, your relative Elizabeth in her old age has also conceived a son, and this is the sixth month with her who was called barren. [37] For nothing will be impossible with God." [38] And Mary said, "Behold, I am the servant of the Lord; let it be to me according to your word." And the angel departed from her.

Mary Visits Elizabeth

[39] In those days Mary arose and went with haste into the hill country, to a town in Judah, [40] and she entered the house of Zechariah and greeted Elizabeth. [41] And when Elizabeth heard the greeting of Mary, the baby leaped in her womb. And Elizabeth was filled with the Holy Spirit, [42] and she exclaimed with a loud cry, "Blessed are you among women, and blessed is the fruit of your womb! [43] And why is this granted to me that the mother of my Lord should come to me? [44] For behold, when the sound of your greeting came to my ears, the baby in my womb leaped for joy. [45] And blessed is she who believed that there would be a fulfilment of what was spoken to her from the Lord."

Mary's Song of Praise: The Magnificat

[46] And Mary said,

"My soul magnifies the Lord,
[47]   and my spirit rejoices in God
       my Saviour,
[48]   for he has looked on the humble

       estate of his servant.
    For behold, from now on all
       generations will call me
       blessed;
[49] for he who is mighty has done
       great things for me,
    and holy is his name.
[50] And his mercy is for those who
       fear him
       from generation to generation.
[51] He has shown strength with his
       arm;
       he has scattered the proud in
       the thoughts of their hearts;
[52] he has brought down the mighty
       from their thrones and exalted
       those of humble
       estate;
[53] he has filled the hungry with
       good things,
       and the rich he has sent away
       empty.
[54] He has helped his servant Israel,
       in remembrance of his mercy,
[55] as he spoke to our fathers,
       to Abraham and to his
       offspring for ever."

⁵⁶ And Mary remained with her about three months and returned to her home.

The Birth of John the Baptist
⁵⁷ Now the time came for Elizabeth to give birth, and she bore a son. ⁵⁸ And her neighbours and relatives heard that the Lord had shown great mercy to her, and they rejoiced with her. ⁵⁹ And on the eighth day they came to circumcise the child. And they would have called him Zechariah after his father, ⁶⁰ but his mother answered, "No; he shall be called John." ⁶¹ And they said to her, "None of your relatives is called by this name." ⁶² And they made signs to his father, enquiring what he wanted him to be called. ⁶³ And he asked for a writing tablet and wrote, "His name is John." And they all wondered. ⁶⁴ And immediately his mouth was opened and his tongue loosed, and he spoke, blessing God. ⁶⁵ And fear came on all their neighbours. And all these things were talked about through all the hill country of Judea, ⁶⁶ and all who heard them laid them up in their hearts, saying, "What then will this child be?" For the hand of the Lord was with him.

Zechariah's Prophecy
⁶⁷ And his father Zechariah was filled with the Holy Spirit and prophesied, saying,

⁶⁸ "Blessed be the Lord God of Israel,
for he has visited and
redeemed his people
⁶⁹ and has raised up a horn of
salvation for us
in the house of his servant
David,
⁷⁰ as he spoke by the mouth of his
holy prophets from of old,
⁷¹ that we should be saved from
our enemies
and from the hand of all who
hate us;
⁷² to show the mercy promised to
our fathers
and to remember his holy
covenant,
⁷³ the oath that he swore to our
father Abraham, to grant us
⁷⁴ that we, being delivered from
the hand of our enemies,
might serve him without fear,
⁷⁵ in holiness and righteousness
before him all our days.
⁷⁶ And you, child, will be called the
prophet of the Most High;
for you will go before the Lord
to prepare his ways,
⁷⁷ to give knowledge of salvation to
his people
in the forgiveness of their sins,
⁷⁸ because of the tender mercy of
our God,
whereby the sunrise shall visit
us from on high
⁷⁹ to give light to those who sit in
darkness and in the shadow
of death,
to guide our feet into the way
of peace."

⁸⁰ And the child grew and became strong in spirit, and he was in the wilderness until the day of his public appearance to Israel.

AND HIS FATHER ZECHARIAH
WAS FILLED WITH THE HOLY SPIRIT
AND PROPHESIED, SAYING, "BLESSED BE THE
LORD GOD OF ISRAEL, FOR HE HAS VISITED
AND REDEEMED HIS PEOPLE AND HAS
RAISED UP A HORN OF SALVATION FOR US
IN THE HOUSE OF HIS SERVANT DAVID."

Luke 1:67-69

AND THE ANGEL

said to them, "Fear not, for behold, I bring you good news of great joy that will be for all the people. For unto you is born this day in the city of David a Saviour, who is Christ the Lord. And this will be a sign for you: you will find a baby wrapped in swaddling cloths and lying in a manger."

Luke 2:10-12

Chapter Two
The Birth of Jesus Christ

In those days a decree went out from Caesar Augustus that all the world should be registered. ²This was the first registration when Quirinius was governor of Syria. ³And all went to be registered, each to his own town. ⁴And Joseph also went up from Galilee, from the town of Nazareth, to Judea, to the city of David, which is called Bethlehem, because he was of the house and lineage of David, ⁵to be registered with Mary, his betrothed, who was with child. ⁶And while they were there, the time came for her to give birth. ⁷And she gave birth to her firstborn son and wrapped him in swaddling cloths and laid him in a manger, because there was no place for them in the inn.

The Shepherds and the Angels
⁸And in the same region there were shepherds out in the field, keeping watch over their flock by night. ⁹And an angel of the Lord appeared to them, and the glory of the Lord shone around them, and they were filled with great fear. ¹⁰And the angel said to them, "Fear not, for behold, I bring you good news of great joy that will be for all the people. ¹¹For unto you is born this day in the city of David a Saviour, who is Christ the Lord. ¹²And this will be a sign for you: you will find a baby wrapped in swaddling cloths and lying in a manger." ¹³And suddenly there was with the angel a multitude of the heavenly host praising God and saying,

¹⁴   "Glory to God in the highest,
        and on earth peace among
            those with whom he is
            pleased!"

¹⁵When the angels went away from them into heaven, the shepherds said to one another, "Let us go over to Bethlehem and see this thing that has happened, which the Lord has made known to us." ¹⁶And they went with haste and found Mary and Joseph, and the baby lying in a manger. ¹⁷And when they saw it, they made known the saying that had been told them concerning this child. ¹⁸And all who heard it wondered at what the shepherds told them. ¹⁹But Mary treasured up all these things, pondering them in her heart. ²⁰And the shepherds returned, glorifying and praising God for all they had heard and seen, as it had been told them.

²¹And at the end of eight days, when he was circumcised, he was called Jesus, the name given by the angel before he was conceived in the womb.

Jesus Presented at the Temple
²²And when the time came for their purification according to the Law of Moses, they brought him up to Jerusalem to present him to the Lord ²³(as it is

written in the Law of the Lord, "Every male who first opens the womb shall be called holy to the Lord") [24] and to offer a sacrifice according to what is said in the Law of the Lord, "a pair of turtle-doves, or two young pigeons". [25] Now there was a man in Jerusalem, whose name was Simeon, and this man was righteous and devout, waiting for the consolation of Israel, and the Holy Spirit was upon him. [26] And it had been revealed to him by the Holy Spirit that he would not see death before he had seen the Lord's Christ. [27] And he came in the Spirit into the temple, and when the parents brought in the child Jesus, to do for him according to the custom of the Law, [28] he took him up in his arms and blessed God and said,

[29] "Lord, now you are letting your
      servant depart in peace,
      according to your word;
[30] for my eyes have seen your
      salvation
[31] that you have prepared in the
      presence of all peoples,
[32] a light for revelation to the
      Gentiles,
      and for glory to your people
      Israel."

[33] And his father and his mother marvelled at what was said about him. [34] And Simeon blessed them and said to Mary his mother, "Behold, this child is appointed for the fall and rising of many in Israel, and for a sign that is opposed [35] (and a sword will pierce through your own soul also), so that thoughts from many hearts may be revealed."

[36] And there was a prophetess, Anna, the daughter of Phanuel, of the tribe of Asher. She was advanced in years, having lived with her husband seven years from when she was a virgin, [37] and then as a widow until she was eighty-four. She did not depart from the temple, worshipping with fasting and prayer night and day. [38] And coming up at that very hour she began to give thanks to God and to speak of him to all who were waiting for the redemption of Jerusalem.

The Return to Nazareth

[39] And when they had performed everything according to the Law of the Lord, they returned into Galilee, to their own town of Nazareth. [40] And the child grew and became strong, filled with wisdom. And the favour of God was upon him.

AND WHEN HIS PARENTS SAW HIM, THEY WERE ASTONISHED. AND HIS MOTHER SAID TO HIM, "SON, WHY HAVE YOU TREATED US SO? BEHOLD, YOUR FATHER AND I HAVE BEEN SEARCHING FOR YOU IN GREAT DISTRESS."

AND HE SAID TO THEM,
"WHY WERE YOU LOOKING
FOR ME? DID YOU NOT KNOW
THAT I MUST BE IN MY
FATHER'S HOUSE?"

Luke 2:48-49

The Boy Jesus in the Temple

⁴¹ Now his parents went to Jerusalem every year at the Feast of the Passover. ⁴² And when he was twelve years old, they went up according to custom. ⁴³ And when the feast was ended, as they were returning, the boy Jesus stayed behind in Jerusalem. His parents did not know it, ⁴⁴ but supposing him to be in the group they went a day's journey, but then they began to search for him among their relatives and acquaintances, ⁴⁵ and when they did not find him, they returned to Jerusalem, searching for him. ⁴⁶ After three days they found him in the temple, sitting among the teachers, listening to them and asking them questions. ⁴⁷ And all who heard him were amazed at his understanding and his answers. ⁴⁸ And when his parents saw him, they were astonished. And his mother said to him, "Son, why have you treated us so? Behold, your father and I have been searching for you in great distress." ⁴⁹ And he said to them, "Why were you looking for me? Did you not know that I must be in my Father's house?" ⁵⁰ And they did not understand the saying that he spoke to them. ⁵¹ And he went down with them and came to Nazareth and was submissive to them. And his mother treasured up all these things in her heart.

⁵² And Jesus increased in wisdom and in stature and in favour with God and man.

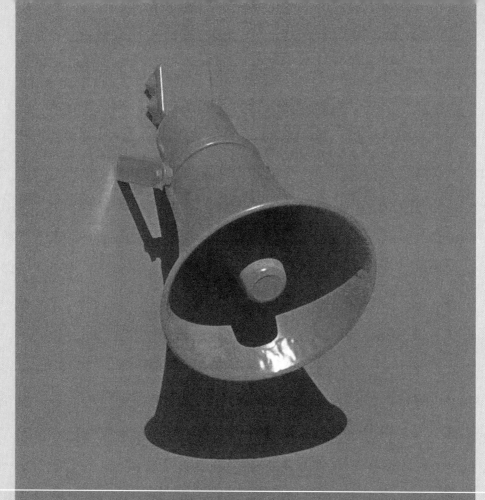

THE GOSPEL

"GOOD NEWS"

The four books in this New Testament Experience Bible are commonly called "Gospels", or "Gospel accounts". Following on from Matthew and Mark, Luke's is the third account of the life of Jesus that we find in the Bible. It has an introduction that sets out the intent of the author, Luke, to write a "narrative" and "orderly account" of the life, death and legacy of Jesus. In other words, Luke intended to write a kind of "Jesus biography" for his readers.

You may have heard people refer to these books as "Gospels", and although it is a useful description for these books of the Bible, the word "gospel" is a lot broader than just a genre of the New Testament. It is actually the heart of the whole Christian message, and it is the key to understanding what Jesus' life was all about, and what he wanted to accomplish through his time on earth.

The word "gospel" today is often considered to be a religious word, and it's not commonly used in general conversation. For this reason, there is a bit of mystery surrounding its meaning. So, you might be thinking "what does the word 'gospel' actually mean? I've heard Christians talk about it, but I've never really known what it means." Well, the English word "gospel" is a translation of the Greek word *euangelion*, which literally means "good news". It's no more complicated than that; "gospel" means that the Christian message is good news!

Although nowadays the word "gospel" is mainly used in religious circles, at the time of Jesus it was actually a secular word, used in different contexts, to describe any positive announcement of good news. Jesus and the early Christians who used this term to talk about Jesus' mission hadn't come up with a new term when they talked about the *euangelion*, but they had actually re-framed a non-religious term that people would have been aware of. They endeavoured to re-define what good news looked like, in an attempt to help people to think differently about what good news could be. They took a popular cultural piece of dialogue and shed a new light on its scope and potential; they located *euangelion* in Jesus himself, suggesting that the greatest announcement of good news is that God has made himself known to us in a personal way.

The root of the word "gospel" also had military connotations. In ancient times, when soldiers went out to fight, the people from their community had no news sources or social media accounts to follow to keep them updated on the progress of their army. They had no idea whether their army had been victorious or if they had been defeated until a messenger was sent to run back to the people to either announce defeat or the "good news" of victory. "Gospel" was a declaration of victory, and it was one that led to great joy and celebration!

In the world we live in, good news is often hard to come by. Most of the time, we hear more about the negative things that are taking place. Whether it be on social media or in the newspapers we read, bad news sells better. You don't often hear of the first item on a news programme being a piece of good news! Yet, by emphasising that the heart of his ministry was "gospel", Jesus chose to define his message and life's work as being good news! What a counter-cultural idea for the world we live in today.

For many people today, the last thing they would think about the Christian message is that it is good news! It's more likely that they'll think of God's word as being restrictive or irrelevant; bad news for the individual rights and freedoms that we should have in the world we live in. Yet, time and time again the Bible declares that the message of Jesus is "good news", *euangelion*; the greatest news we could ever dream of or imagine.

The Bible teaches us that by dying on a cross and rising from the grave, Jesus defeated death, sin and shame. Those things, although they can still be a part of our life here on earth, have lost their power in the work of Jesus. Perhaps you just made a decision to follow Jesus — that is great news! But if you haven't yet made that decision, why not continue reading the story for yourself in light of this good news being announced for you too?

Jesus has been victorious on your behalf, and because of him you get to share in his victory. You no longer need to worry about the power of death, sin or shame, because in Christ we are all victorious. If we accept the good news that is on offer to us, we can confidently be assured that our new life in Christ has begun and that ultimately, we are victorious because he is victorious.

As you read the Gospel of Luke, know that the intention of the author is to inform you about the good news of Jesus; his life, death and resurrection. If you have ever been told that the Christian message is anything but good news, I would encourage you to look at the life of Jesus and what he offers to those who put their trust in him, and work out for yourself if there is any better news in the world.

THE ENGLISH WORD "GOSPEL" IS A TRANSLATION OF THE GREEK WORD *EUANGELION*, WHICH LITERALLY MEANS "GOOD NEWS". IT'S NO MORE COMPLICATED THAN THAT; "GOSPEL" MEANS THAT THE CHRISTIAN MESSAGE IS GOOD NEWS!

Chapter Three
John the Baptist Prepares the Way

"The voice of one crying in the wilderness: 'Prepare the way of the Lord, make his paths straight… and all flesh shall see the salvation of God.'"

Luke 3:4, 6

n the fifteenth year of the reign of Tiberius Caesar, Pontius Pilate being governor of Judea, and Herod being tetrarch of Galilee, and his brother Philip tetrarch of the region of Ituraea and Trachonitis, and Lysanias tetrarch of Abilene, ² during the high priesthood of Annas and Caiaphas, the word of God came to John the son of Zechariah in the wilderness. ³ And he went into all the region around the Jordan, proclaiming a baptism of repentance for the forgiveness of sins. ⁴ As it is written in the book of the words of Isaiah the prophet,

"The voice of one crying in the
    wilderness:
'Prepare the way of the Lord,
    make his paths straight.
⁵ Every valley shall be filled,
    and every mountain and hill
        shall be made low,
and the crooked shall become
        straight,
    and the rough places shall
        become level ways,
⁶ and all flesh shall see the salvation
        of God.'"

⁷ He said therefore to the crowds that came out to be baptized by him, "You brood of vipers! Who warned you to flee from the wrath to come? ⁸ Bear fruits in keeping with repentance. And do not begin to say to yourselves, 'We have Abraham as our father.' For I tell you, God is able from these stones to raise up children for Abraham. ⁹ Even now the axe is laid to the root of the trees. Every tree therefore that does not bear good fruit is cut down and thrown into the fire."

¹⁰ And the crowds asked him, "What then shall we do?" ¹¹ And he answered them, "Whoever has two tunics is to share with him who has none, and whoever has food is to do likewise." ¹² Tax collectors also came to be baptized and said to him, "Teacher, what shall we do?" ¹³ And he said to them, "Collect no more than you are authorized to do." ¹⁴ Soldiers also asked him, "And we, what shall we do?" And he said to them, "Do not extort money from anyone by threats or by false accusation, and be content with your wages."

¹⁵ As the people were filled with expectation, and all were questioning in their hearts concerning John, whether he might be the Christ, ¹⁶ John answered them all, saying, "I baptize you with water, but he who is mightier than I is coming, the strap of whose sandals I am not worthy to untie. He will baptize you with the Holy Spirit and fire. ¹⁷ His winnowing fork is in his hand, to clear his threshing floor and to gather the wheat into his barn, but the chaff he will burn with unquenchable fire."

¹⁸ So with many other exhortations he preached good news to the people. ¹⁹ But Herod the tetrarch, who had been reproved by him for Herodias, his brother's wife, and for all the evil things that Herod had done, ²⁰ added this to them all, that he locked up John in prison.

²¹ Now when all the people were baptized, and when Jesus also had been baptized and was praying, the heavens were opened, ²² and the Holy Spirit descended on him in bodily form, like a dove; and a voice came from heaven, "You are my beloved Son; with you I am well pleased."

The Genealogy of Jesus Christ

²³ Jesus, when he began his ministry, was about thirty years of age, being the son (as was supposed) of Joseph, the son of Heli, ²⁴ the son of Matthat, the son of Levi, the son of Melchi, the son of Jannai, the son of Joseph, ²⁵ the son of Mattathias, the son of Amos, the son of Nahum, the son of Esli, the son of Naggai, ²⁶ the son of Maath, the son of Mattathias, the son of Semein, the son of Josech, the son of Joda, ²⁷ the son of Joanan, the son of Rhesa, the son of Zerubbabel, the son of Shealtiel, the son of Neri, ²⁸ the son of Melchi, the son of Addi, the son of Cosam, the son of Elmadam, the son of Er, ²⁹ the son of Joshua, the son of Eliezer, the son of Jorim, the son of Matthat, the son of Levi, ³⁰ the son of Simeon, the son of Judah,

AND JESUS ANSWERED HIM, "IT IS WRITTEN, 'YOU SHALL WORSHIP THE LORD YOUR GOD, AND HIM ONLY SHALL YOU SERVE.' "

Luke 4:8

the son of Joseph, the son of Jonam, the son of Eliakim, ³¹the son of Melea, the son of Menna, the son of Mattatha, the son of Nathan, the son of David, ³²the son of Jesse, the son of Obed, the son of Boaz, the son of Sala, the son of Nahshon, ³³the son of Amminadab, the son of Admin, the son of Arni, the son of Hezron, the son of Perez, the son of Judah, ³⁴the son of Jacob, the son of Isaac, the son of Abraham, the son of Terah, the son of Nahor, ³⁵the son of Serug, the son of Reu, the son of Peleg, the son of Eber, the son of Shelah, ³⁶the son of Cainan, the son of Arphaxad, the son of Shem, the son of Noah, the son of Lamech, ³⁷the son of Methuselah, the son of Enoch, the son of Jared, the son of Mahalaleel, the son of Cainan, ³⁸the son of Enos, the son of Seth, the son of Adam, the son of God.

✝

Chapter Four

The Temptation of Jesus

And Jesus, full of the Holy Spirit, returned from the Jordan and was led by the Spirit in the wilderness ²for forty days, being tempted by the devil. And he ate nothing during those days. And when they were over, he was hungry.

³The devil said to him, "If you are the Son of God, command this stone to become bread." ⁴And Jesus answered him, "It is written, 'Man shall not live by bread alone.' " ⁵And the devil took him up and showed him all the kingdoms of the world in a moment of time, ⁶and said to him, "To you I will give all this authority and their glory, for it has been delivered to me, and I give it to whom I will. ⁷If you, then, will worship me, it will all be yours." ⁸And Jesus answered him, "It is written,

"'You shall worship the Lord your God,
    and him only shall you serve.'"

⁹And he took him to Jerusalem and set him on the pinnacle of the temple and said to him, "If you are the Son of God, throw yourself down from here, ¹⁰for it is written,

"'He will command his angels concerning you,
    to guard you',

¹¹and

"'On their hands they will bear you up,
    lest you strike your foot against a stone.'"

¹²And Jesus answered him, "It is said, 'You shall not put the Lord your God to the test.' " ¹³And when the devil had ended every temptation, he departed from him until an opportune time.

Jesus Begins His Ministry

¹⁴And Jesus returned in the power of the Spirit to Galilee, and a report about him went out through all the surrounding country. ¹⁵And he taught in their synagogues, being glorified by all.

Jesus Rejected at Nazareth

¹⁶And he came to Nazareth, where he had been brought up. And as was his custom, he went to the synagogue on the Sabbath day, and he stood up to read. ¹⁷And the scroll of the prophet Isaiah was given to him. He unrolled the scroll and found the place where it was written,

¹⁸   "The Spirit of the Lord is upon me,
        because he has anointed me
        to proclaim good news to the poor.
    He has sent me to proclaim liberty to the captives
        and recovering of sight to the blind,
        to set at liberty those who are oppressed,
¹⁹   to proclaim the year of the Lord's favour."

²⁰ And he rolled up the scroll and gave it back to the attendant and sat down. And the eyes of all in the synagogue were fixed on him. ²¹ And he began to say to them, "Today this Scripture has been fulfilled in your hearing." ²² And all spoke well of him and marvelled at the gracious words that were coming from his mouth. And they said, "Is not this Joseph's son?" ²³ And he said to them, "Doubtless you will quote to me this proverb, "'Physician, heal yourself.' What we have heard you did at Capernaum, do here in your home town as well.'" ²⁴ And he said, "Truly, I say to you, no prophet is acceptable in his home town. ²⁵ But in truth, I tell you, there were many widows in Israel in the days of Elijah, when the heavens were shut up three years and six months, and a great famine came over all the land, ²⁶ and Elijah was sent to none of them but only to Zarephath, in the land of Sidon, to a woman who was a widow. ²⁷ And there were many lepers in Israel in the time of the prophet Elisha, and none of them was cleansed, but only Naaman the Syrian." ²⁸ When they heard these things, all in the synagogue were filled with wrath. ²⁹ And they rose up and drove him out of the town and brought him to the brow of the hill on which their town was built, so that they could throw him down the cliff. ³⁰ But passing through their midst, he went away.

Jesus Heals a Man with an Unclean Demon

³¹ And he went down to Capernaum, a city of Galilee. And he was teaching them on the Sabbath, ³² and they were astonished at his teaching, for his word possessed authority. ³³ And in the synagogue there was a man who had the spirit of an unclean demon, and he cried out with a loud voice, ³⁴ "Ha! What have you to do with us, Jesus of Nazareth? Have you come to destroy us? I know who you are—the Holy One of God." ³⁵ But Jesus rebuked him, saying, "Be silent and come out of him!" And when the demon had thrown him down in their midst, he came out of him, having done him no harm. ³⁶ And they were all amazed and said to one another, "What is this word? For with authority and power he commands the unclean spirits, and they come out!" ³⁷ And reports about him went out into every place in the surrounding region.

Jesus Heals Many

³⁸ And he arose and left the synagogue and entered Simon's house. Now Simon's mother-in-law was ill with a high fever, and they appealed to him on her behalf. ³⁹ And he stood over her and rebuked the fever, and it left her, and immediately she rose and began to serve them.

⁴⁰ Now when the sun was setting, all those who had any who were sick with various diseases brought them to him, and he laid his hands on every one of them and healed them. ⁴¹ And demons also came out of many, crying, "You are the Son of God!" But he rebuked them and would not allow them to speak, because they knew that he was the Christ.

Jesus Preaches in Synagogues

⁴² And when it was day, he departed and went into a desolate place. And the people sought him and came to him, and would have kept him from leaving them, ⁴³ but he said to them, "I must preach the good news of the kingdom of God to the other towns as well; for I was sent for this purpose." ⁴⁴ And he was preaching in the synagogues of Judea.

NOW WHEN THE SUN WAS
SETTING, ALL THOSE WHO HAD
ANY WHO WERE SICK WITH
VARIOUS DISEASES BROUGHT
THEM TO HIM, AND HE LAID HIS
HANDS ON EVERY ONE OF THEM
AND HEALED THEM.

Luke 4:40

Chapter Five

Jesus Calls the First Disciples

On one occasion, while the crowd was pressing in on him to hear the word of God, he was standing by the lake of Gennesaret, ²and he saw two boats by the lake, but the fishermen had gone out of them and were washing their nets. ³Getting into one of the boats, which was Simon's, he asked him to put out a little from the land. And he sat down and taught the people from the boat. ⁴And when he had finished speaking, he said to Simon, "Put out into the deep and let down your nets for a catch." ⁵And Simon answered, "Master, we toiled all night and took nothing! But at your word I will let down the nets." ⁶And when they had done this, they enclosed a large number of fish, and their nets were breaking. ⁷They signalled to their partners in the other boat to come and help them. And they came and filled both the boats, so that they began to sink. ⁸But when Simon Peter saw it, he fell down at Jesus' knees, saying, "Depart from me, for I am a sinful man, O Lord." ⁹For he and all who were with him were astonished at the catch of fish that they had taken, ¹⁰and so also were James and John, sons of Zebedee, who were partners with Simon. And Jesus said to Simon, "Do not be afraid; from now on you will be catching men." ¹¹And when they had brought their boats to land, they left everything and followed him.

Jesus Cleanses a Leper

¹²While he was in one of the cities, there came a man full of leprosy.

And when he saw Jesus, he fell on his face and begged him, "Lord, if you will, you can make me clean." ¹³ And Jesus stretched out his hand and touched him, saying, "I will; be clean." And immediately the leprosy left him. ¹⁴ And he charged him to tell no one, but "go and show yourself to the priest, and make an offering for your cleansing, as Moses commanded, for a proof to them." ¹⁵ But now even more the report about him went abroad, and great crowds gathered to hear him and to be healed of their infirmities. ¹⁶ But he would withdraw to desolate places and pray.

Jesus Heals a Paralytic

¹⁷ On one of those days, as he was teaching, Pharisees and teachers of the law were sitting there, who had come from every village of Galilee and Judea and from Jerusalem. And the power of the Lord was with him to heal. ¹⁸ And behold, some men were bringing on a bed a man who was paralysed, and they were seeking to bring him in and lay him before Jesus, ¹⁹ but finding no way to bring him in, because of the crowd, they went up on the roof and let him down with his bed through the tiles into the midst before Jesus. ²⁰ And when he saw their faith, he said, "Man, your sins are forgiven you." ²¹ And the scribes and the Pharisees began to question, saying, "Who is this who speaks blasphemies? Who can forgive sins but God alone?" ²² When Jesus perceived their thoughts, he answered them, "Why do you question in your hearts? ²³ Which is easier, to say, 'Your sins are forgiven you', or to say, 'Rise and walk'? ²⁴ But that you may know that the Son of Man has authority on earth to forgive sins"—he said to the man who was paralysed—"I say to you, rise, pick up your bed and go home." ²⁵ And immediately he rose up before them and picked up what he had been lying on and went home, glorifying God. ²⁶ And amazement seized them all, and they glorified God and were filled with awe, saying, "We have seen extraordinary things today."

Jesus Calls Levi

²⁷ After this he went out and saw a tax collector named Levi, sitting at the tax booth. And he said to him, "Follow me." ²⁸ And leaving everything, he rose and followed him.

²⁹ And Levi made him a great feast in his house, and there was a large company of tax collectors and others reclining at table with them. ³⁰ And the Pharisees and their scribes grumbled at his disciples, saying, "Why do you eat and drink with tax collectors and sinners?" ³¹ And Jesus answered them, "Those who are well have no need of a physician, but those who are sick. ³² I have not come to call the righteous but sinners to repentance."

A Question About Fasting

³³ And they said to him, "The disciples of John fast often and offer prayers, and so do the disciples of the Pharisees, but yours eat and drink." ³⁴ And Jesus said to them, "Can you make wedding guests fast while the bridegroom is with them? ³⁵ The days will come when the bridegroom is taken away from them, and then they will fast in those days." ³⁶ He also told them a parable: "No one tears a piece from a new garment and puts it on an old garment. If he does, he will tear the new, and the piece from the new will not match the old. ³⁷ And no one puts new wine into old wineskins. If he does, the new wine will burst the skins and it will be spilled, and the skins will be destroyed. ³⁸ But new wine must be put into fresh wineskins. ³⁹ And no one after drinking old wine desires new, for he says, 'The old is good.'"

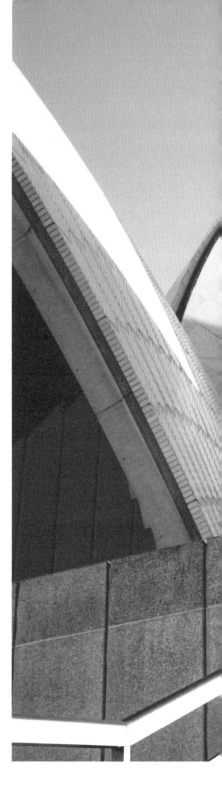

... AND JESUS SAID TO SIMON, "DO NOT BE AFRAID; FROM NOW ON YOU WILL BE CATCHING MEN." AND WHEN THEY HAD BROUGHT THEIR BOATS TO LAND, THEY LEFT EVERYTHING AND FOLLOWED HIM.

Luke 5:10-11

"GIVE, AND IT WILL BE GIVEN TO YOU.
GOOD MEASURE, PRESSED DOWN,
SHAKEN TOGETHER, RUNNING OVER,
WILL BE PUT INTO YOUR LAP. FOR
WITH THE MEASURE YOU USE IT
WILL BE MEASURED BACK TO YOU."

Luke 6:38

Chapter Six
Jesus Is Lord of the Sabbath

On a Sabbath, while he was going through the cornfields, his disciples plucked and ate some ears of corn, rubbing them in their hands. [2] But some of the Pharisees said, "Why are you doing what is not lawful to do on the Sabbath?" [3] And Jesus answered them, "Have you not read what David did when he was hungry, he and those who were with him: [4] how he entered the house of God and took and ate the bread of the Presence, which is not lawful for any but the priests to eat, and also gave it to those with him?" [5] And he said to them, "The Son of Man is lord of the Sabbath."

A Man with a Withered Hand

[6] On another Sabbath, he entered the synagogue and was teaching, and a man was there whose right hand was withered. [7] And the scribes and the Pharisees watched him, to see whether he would heal on the Sabbath, so that they might find a reason to accuse him. [8] But he knew their thoughts, and he said to the man with the withered hand, "Come and stand here." And he rose and stood there. [9] And Jesus said to them, "I ask you, is it lawful on the Sabbath to do good or to do harm, to save life or to destroy it?" [10] And after looking around at them all he said to him, "Stretch out your hand." And he did so, and his hand was restored. [11] But they were filled with fury and discussed with one another what they might do to Jesus.

The Twelve Apostles

[12] In these days he went out to the mountain to pray, and all night he continued in prayer to God. [13] And when day came, he called his disciples and chose from them twelve, whom he named apostles: [14] Simon, whom he named Peter, and Andrew his brother, and James and John, and Philip, and Bartholomew, [15] and Matthew, and Thomas, and James the son of Alphaeus, and Simon who was called the Zealot, [16] and Judas the son of James, and Judas Iscariot, who became a traitor.

Jesus Ministers to a Great Multitude

[17] And he came down with them and stood on a level place, with a great crowd of his disciples and a great multitude of people from all Judea and Jerusalem and the sea coast of Tyre and Sidon, [18] who came to hear him and to be healed of their diseases. And those who were troubled with unclean spirits were cured. [19] And all the crowd sought to touch him, for power came out from him and healed them all.

The Beatitudes

[20] And he lifted up his eyes on his disciples, and said:

"Blessed are you who are poor, for yours is the kingdom of God.

[21] "Blessed are you who are hungry now, for you shall be satisfied.

"Blessed are you who weep now, for you shall laugh.

[22] "Blessed are you when people hate you and when they exclude you and revile you and spurn your name as evil, on account of the Son of Man! [23] Rejoice in that day, and leap for joy, for behold, your reward is great in heaven; for so their fathers did to the prophets.

Jesus Pronounces Woes

²⁴ "But woe to you who are rich, for you have received your consolation.

²⁵ "Woe to you who are full now, for you shall be hungry.

"Woe to you who laugh now, for you shall mourn and weep.

²⁶ "Woe to you, when all people speak well of you, for so their fathers did to the false prophets.

Love Your Enemies

²⁷ "But I say to you who hear, Love your enemies, do good to those who hate you, ²⁸ bless those who curse you, pray for those who abuse you. ²⁹ To one who strikes you on the cheek, offer the other also, and from one who takes away your cloak do not withhold your tunic either. ³⁰ Give to everyone who begs from you, and from one who takes away your goods do not demand them back. ³¹ And as you wish that others would do to you, do so to them.

³² "If you love those who love you, what benefit is that to you? For even sinners love those who love them. ³³ And if you do good to those who do good to you, what benefit is that to you? For even sinners do the same. ³⁴ And if you lend to those from whom you expect to receive, what credit is that to you? Even sinners lend to sinners, to get back the same amount. ³⁵ But love your enemies, and do good, and lend, expecting nothing in return, and your reward will be great, and you will be sons of the Most High, for he is kind to the ungrateful and the evil. ³⁶ Be merciful, even as your Father is merciful.

Judging Others

³⁷ "Judge not, and you will not be judged; condemn not, and you will not be condemned; forgive, and you will be forgiven; ³⁸ give, and it will be given to you. Good measure, pressed down, shaken together, running over, will be put into your lap. For with the measure you use it will be measured back to you."

³⁹ He also told them a parable: "Can a blind man lead a blind man? Will they not both fall into a pit? ⁴⁰ A disciple is not above his teacher, but everyone

"HOW CAN YOU SAY TO YOUR BROTHER, 'BROTHER, LET ME TAKE OUT THE SPECK THAT IS IN YOUR EYE', WHEN YOU YOURSELF DO NOT SEE THE LOG THAT IS IN YOUR OWN EYE? YOU HYPOCRITE, FIRST TAKE THE LOG OUT OF YOUR OWN EYE, AND THEN YOU WILL SEE CLEARLY TO TAKE OUT THE SPECK THAT IS IN YOUR BROTHER'S EYE." **Luke 6:42**

when he is fully trained will be like his teacher. ⁴¹ Why do you see the speck that is in your brother's eye, but do not notice the log that is in your own eye? ⁴² How can you say to your brother, 'Brother, let me take out the speck that is in your eye', when you yourself do not see the log that is in your own eye? You hypocrite, first take the log out of your own eye, and then you will see clearly to take out the speck that is in your brother's eye.

A Tree and Its Fruit

⁴³"For no good tree bears bad fruit, nor again does a bad tree bear good fruit, ⁴⁴for each tree is known by its own fruit. For figs are not gathered from thorn bushes, nor are grapes picked from a bramble bush. ⁴⁵The good person out of the good treasure of his heart produces good, and the evil person out of his evil treasure produces evil, for out of the abundance of the heart his mouth speaks.

Build Your House on the Rock

⁴⁶"Why do you call me 'Lord, Lord', and not do what I tell you? ⁴⁷Everyone who comes to me and hears my words and does them, I will show you what he is like: ⁴⁸he is like a man building a house, who dug deep and laid the foundation on the rock. And when a flood arose, the stream broke against that house and could not shake it, because it had been well built. ⁴⁹But the one who hears and does not do them is like a man who built a house on the ground without a foundation. When the stream broke against it, immediately it fell, and the ruin of that house was great."

Chapter Seven
Jesus Heals a Centurion's Servant

"Therefore I tell you, her sins, which are many, are forgiven—for she loved much. But he who is forgiven little, loves little." And he said to her, "Your sins are forgiven." Luke 7:47-48

After he had finished all his sayings in the hearing of the people, he entered Capernaum. ²Now a centurion had a servant who was sick and at the point of death, who was highly valued by him. ³When the centurion heard about Jesus, he sent to him elders of the Jews, asking him to come and heal his servant. ⁴And when they came to Jesus, they pleaded with him earnestly, saying, "He is worthy to have you do this for him, ⁵for he loves our nation, and he is the one who built us our synagogue." ⁶And Jesus went with them. When he was not far from the house, the centurion sent friends, saying to him, "Lord, do not trouble yourself, for I am not worthy to have you come under my roof. ⁷Therefore I did not presume to come to you. But say the word, and let my servant be healed. ⁸For I too am a man set under authority, with soldiers under me: and I say to one, 'Go', and he goes; and to another, 'Come', and he comes; and to my servant, 'Do this', and he does it."

⁹When Jesus heard these things, he marvelled at him, and turning to the crowd that followed him, said, "I tell you, not even in Israel have I found such faith." ¹⁰And when those who had been sent returned to the house, they found the servant well.

Jesus Raises a Widow's Son
¹¹Soon afterwards he went to a town called Nain, and his disciples and a great crowd went with him. ¹²As he drew near to the gate of the town, behold, a man who had died was being carried out, the only son of his mother, and she was a widow, and a considerable crowd from the town was with her. ¹³And when the Lord saw her, he had compassion on her and said to her, "Do not weep." ¹⁴Then he came up and touched the bier, and the bearers stood still. And he said, "Young man, I say to you, arise." ¹⁵And the dead man sat up and began to speak, and Jesus gave him to his mother. ¹⁶Fear seized them

all, and they glorified God, saying, "A great prophet has arisen among us!" and "God has visited his people!" ¹⁷And this report about him spread through the whole of Judea and all the surrounding country.

Messengers from John the Baptist
¹⁸The disciples of John reported all these things to him. And John, ¹⁹calling two of his disciples to him, sent them to the Lord, saying, "Are you the one who is to come, or shall we look for another?" ²⁰And when the men had come to him, they said, "John the Baptist has sent us to you, saying, 'Are you the one who is to come, or shall we look for another?'" ²¹In that hour he healed many people of diseases and plagues and evil spirits, and on many who were blind he bestowed sight. ²²And he answered them, "Go and tell John what you have seen and heard: the blind receive their sight, the lame walk, lepers are cleansed, and the deaf hear, the dead

are raised up, the poor have good news preached to them. ²³And blessed is the one who is not offended by me."

²⁴When John's messengers had gone, Jesus began to speak to the crowds concerning John: "What did you go out into the wilderness to see? A reed shaken by the wind? ²⁵What then did you go out to see? A man dressed in soft clothing? Behold, those who are dressed in splendid clothing and live in luxury are in kings' courts. ²⁶What then did you go out to see? A prophet? Yes, I tell you, and more than a prophet. ²⁷This is he of whom it is written,

"'Behold, I send my messenger
before your face,
who will prepare your way
before you.'

²⁸I tell you, among those born of women none is greater than John. Yet the one who is least in the kingdom of God is greater than he." ²⁹(When all the people heard this, and the tax collectors too, they declared God just, having been baptized with the baptism of John, ³⁰but the Pharisees and the lawyers rejected the purpose of God for themselves, not having been baptized by him.)

³¹"To what then shall I compare the people of this generation, and what are they like? ³²They are like children sitting in the market-place and calling to one another,

"'We played the flute for you, and
you did not dance;
we sang a dirge, and you did
not weep.'

³³For John the Baptist has come eating no bread and drinking no wine, and you say, 'He has a demon.' ³⁴The Son of Man has come eating and drinking, and you say, 'Look at him! A glutton and a drunkard, a friend of tax collectors and sinners!' ³⁵Yet wisdom is justified by all her children."

A Sinful Woman Forgiven

³⁶One of the Pharisees asked him to eat with him, and he went into the Pharisee's house and reclined at table. ³⁷And behold, a woman of the city, who was a sinner, when she learned that he was reclining at table in the Pharisee's house, brought an alabaster flask of ointment, ³⁸and standing behind him at his feet, weeping, she began to wet his feet with her tears and wiped them with the hair of her head and kissed his feet and anointed them with the ointment. ³⁹Now when the Pharisee who had invited him saw this, he said to himself, "If this man were a prophet, he would have known who and what sort of woman this is who is touching him, for she is a sinner." ⁴⁰And Jesus answering said to him, "Simon, I have something to say to you." And he answered, "Say it, Teacher."

⁴¹"A certain money-lender had two debtors. One owed five hundred denarii, and the other fifty. ⁴²When they could not pay, he cancelled the debt of both. Now which of them will love him more?" ⁴³Simon answered, "The one, I suppose, for whom he cancelled the larger debt." And he said to him, "You have judged rightly." ⁴⁴Then turning towards the woman he said to Simon, "Do you see this woman? I entered your house; you gave me no water for my feet, but she has wet my feet with her tears and wiped them with her hair. ⁴⁵You gave me no kiss, but from the time I came in she has not ceased to kiss my feet. ⁴⁶You did not anoint my head with oil, but she has anointed my feet with ointment. ⁴⁷Therefore I tell you, her sins, which are many, are forgiven—for she loved much. But he who is forgiven little, loves little." ⁴⁸And he said to her, "Your sins are forgiven." ⁴⁹Then those who were at table with him began to say among themselves, "Who is this, who even forgives sins?" ⁵⁰And he said to the woman, "Your faith has saved you; go in peace."

"WHAT THEN DID YOU GO OUT TO SEE? A PROPHET? YES, I TELL YOU, AND MORE THAN A PROPHET. THIS IS HE OF WHOM IT IS WRITTEN, 'BEHOLD, I SEND MY MESSENGER BEFORE YOUR FACE, WHO WILL PREPARE YOUR WAY BEFORE YOU.'"

Luke 7.26-27

Chapter Eight
Women Accompanying Jesus

Soon afterwards he went on through cities and villages, proclaiming and bringing the good news of the kingdom of God. And the twelve were with him, ² and also some women who had been healed of evil spirits and infirmities: Mary, called Magdalene, from whom seven demons had gone out, ³ and Joanna, the wife of Chuza, Herod's household manager, and Susanna, and many others, who provided for them out of their means.

The Parable of the Sower
⁴ And when a great crowd was gathering and people from town after town came to him, he said in a parable, ⁵ "A sower went out to sow his seed. And as he sowed, some fell along the path and was trampled underfoot, and the birds of the air devoured it. ⁶ And some fell on the rock, and as it grew up, it withered away, because it had no moisture. ⁷ And some fell among thorns, and the thorns grew up with it and choked it. ⁸ And some fell into good soil and grew and yielded a hundredfold." As he said these things, he called out, "He who has ears to hear, let him hear."

The Purpose of the Parables
⁹ And when his disciples asked him what this parable meant, ¹⁰ he said, "To you it has been given to know the secrets of the kingdom of God, but for others they are in parables, so that 'seeing they may not see, and hearing they may not understand'. ¹¹ Now the parable is this: The seed is the word of God. ¹² The ones along the path are those who have heard; then the devil comes and takes away the word from their hearts, so that they may not believe and be saved. ¹³ And the ones on the rock are those who, when they hear

the word, receive it with joy. But these have no root; they believe for a while, and in time of testing fall away. ¹⁴And as for what fell among the thorns, they are those who hear, but as they go on their way they are choked by the cares and riches and pleasures of life, and their fruit does not mature. ¹⁵As for that in the good soil, they are those who, hearing the word, hold it fast in an honest and good heart, and bear fruit with patience.

A Lamp Under a Jar

¹⁶"No one after lighting a lamp covers it with a jar or puts it under a bed, but puts it on a stand, so that those who enter may see the light. ¹⁷For nothing is hidden that will not be made manifest, nor is anything secret that will not be known and come to light. ¹⁸Take care

then how you hear, for to the one who has, more will be given, and from the one who has not, even what he thinks that he has will be taken away."

Jesus' Mother and Brothers

¹⁹Then his mother and his brothers came to him, but they could not reach him because of the crowd. ²⁰And he was told, "Your mother and your brothers are standing outside, desiring to see you." ²¹But he answered them, "My mother and my brothers are those who hear the word of God and do it."

Jesus Calms a Storm

²²One day he got into a boat with his disciples, and he said to them, "Let us go across to the other side of the lake." So they set out, ²³and as they sailed he fell asleep. And a windstorm came

down on the lake, and they were filling with water and were in danger. ²⁴And they went and woke him, saying, "Master, Master, we are perishing!" And he awoke and rebuked the wind and the raging waves, and they ceased, and there was a calm. ²⁵He said to them, "Where is your faith?" And they were afraid, and they marvelled, saying to one another, "Who then is this, that he commands even winds and water, and they obey him?"

Jesus Heals a Man with a Demon

²⁶Then they sailed to the country of the Gerasenes, which is opposite Galilee. ²⁷When Jesus had stepped out on land, there met him a man from the city who had demons. For a long time he had worn no clothes, and he had not lived in a house but among the tombs. ²⁸When

HE SAID TO THEM, "WHERE IS YOUR FAITH?" AND THEY WERE AFRAID, AND THEY MARVELLED, SAYING TO ONE ANOTHER, "WHO THEN IS THIS, THAT HE COMMANDS EVEN WINDS AND WATER, AND THEY OBEY HIM?"

Luke 8:25

he saw Jesus, he cried out and fell down before him and said with a loud voice, "What have you to do with me, Jesus, Son of the Most High God? I beg you, do not torment me." ²⁹ For he had commanded the unclean spirit to come out of the man. (For many a time it had seized him. He was kept under guard and bound with chains and shackles, but he would break the bonds and be driven by the demon into the desert.) ³⁰ Jesus then asked him, "What is your name?" And he said, "Legion", for many demons had entered him. ³¹ And they begged him not to command them to depart into the abyss. ³² Now a large herd of pigs was feeding there on the hillside, and they begged him to let them enter these. So he gave them permission. ³³ Then the demons came out of the man and entered the pigs, and the herd rushed down the steep bank into the lake and drowned.

³⁴ When the herdsmen saw what had happened, they fled and told it in the city and in the country. ³⁵ Then people went out to see what had happened, and they came to Jesus and found the man from whom the demons had gone, sitting at the feet of Jesus, clothed and in his right mind, and they were afraid. ³⁶ And those who had seen it told them how the demon-possessed man had been healed. ³⁷ Then all the people of the surrounding country of the Gerasenes asked him to depart from them, for they were seized with great fear. So he got into the boat and returned. ³⁸ The man from whom the demons had gone begged that he might be with him, but Jesus sent him away, saying, ³⁹ "Return to your home, and declare how much God has done for you." And he went away, proclaiming throughout the whole city how much Jesus had done for him.

Jesus Heals a Woman and Jairus's Daughter

⁴⁰ Now when Jesus returned, the crowd welcomed him, for they were all waiting for him. ⁴¹ And there came a man named Jairus, who was a ruler of the synagogue. And falling at Jesus' feet, he implored him to come to his house, ⁴² for he had an only daughter, about twelve years of age, and she was dying. As Jesus went, the people pressed around him. ⁴³ And there was a woman who had had a discharge of blood for twelve years, and though she had spent all her living on physicians, she could not be healed by anyone. ⁴⁴ She came up behind him and touched the fringe of his garment, and immediately her discharge of blood ceased. ⁴⁵ And Jesus said, "Who was it that touched me?" When all denied it, Peter said, "Master, the crowds surround you and are pressing in on you!" ⁴⁶ But Jesus said, "Someone touched me, for I perceive that power has gone out from me." ⁴⁷ And when the woman saw that she was not hidden, she came trembling, and falling down before him declared in the presence of all the people why she had touched him, and how she had been immediately healed. ⁴⁸ And he said to her, "Daughter, your faith has made you well; go in peace."

⁴⁹ While he was still speaking, someone from the ruler's house came and said, "Your daughter is dead; do not trouble the Teacher any more." ⁵⁰ But Jesus on hearing this answered him, "Do not fear; only believe, and she will be well." ⁵¹ And when he came to the house, he allowed no one to enter with him, except Peter and John and James, and the father and mother of the child. ⁵² And all were weeping and mourning for her, but he said, "Do not weep, for she is not dead but sleeping." ⁵³ And they laughed at him, knowing that she was dead. ⁵⁴ But taking her by the hand he called, saying, "Child, arise." ⁵⁵ And her spirit returned, and she got up at once. And he directed that something should be given to her to eat. ⁵⁶ And her parents were amazed, but he charged them to tell no one what had happened.

Chapter Nine

Jesus Sends Out the Twelve Apostles

And he called the twelve together and gave them power and authority over all demons and to cure diseases, ²and he sent them out to proclaim the kingdom of God and to heal. ³And he said to them, "Take nothing for your journey, no staff, nor bag, nor bread, nor money; and do not have two tunics. ⁴And whatever house you enter, stay there, and from there depart. ⁵And wherever they do not receive you, when you leave that town shake off the dust from your feet as a testimony against them." ⁶And they departed and went through the villages, preaching the gospel and healing everywhere.

Herod Is Perplexed by Jesus

⁷Now Herod the tetrarch heard about all that was happening, and he was perplexed, because it was said by some that John had been raised from the dead, ⁸by some that Elijah had appeared, and by others that one of the prophets of old had risen. ⁹Herod said, "John I beheaded, but who is this about whom I hear such things?" And he sought to see him.

Jesus Feeds the Five Thousand

¹⁰On their return the apostles told him all that they had done. And he took them and withdrew apart to a town called Bethsaida. ¹¹When the crowds learned it, they followed him, and he welcomed them and spoke to them of the kingdom of God and cured those who needed healing. ¹²Now the day began to wear away, and the twelve came and said to him, "Send the crowd away to go into the surrounding villages and countryside to find lodging and get provisions, for we are here in a desolate place."

¹³But he said to them, "You give them something to eat." They said, "We have no more than five loaves and two fish—unless we are to go and buy food for all these people." ¹⁴For there were about five thousand men. And he said to his disciples, "Make them sit down in groups of about fifty each." ¹⁵And they did so, and made them all sit down. ¹⁶And taking the five loaves and the two fish, he looked up to heaven and said a blessing over them. Then he broke the loaves and gave them to the disciples to set before the crowd. ¹⁷And they all ate and were satisfied. And what was left over was picked up, twelve baskets of broken pieces.

Peter Confesses Jesus as the Christ

¹⁸Now it happened that as he was praying alone, the disciples were with him. And he asked them, "Who do the crowds say that I am?" ¹⁹And they answered, "John the Baptist. But others say, Elijah, and others, that one of

the prophets of old has risen." ²⁰ Then he said to them, "But who do you say that I am?" And Peter answered, "The Christ of God."

Jesus Foretells His Death

²¹ And he strictly charged and commanded them to tell this to no one, ²² saying, "The Son of Man must suffer many things and be rejected by the elders and chief priests and scribes, and be killed, and on the third day be raised."

Take Up Your Cross and Follow Jesus

²³ And he said to all, "If anyone would come after me, let him deny himself and take up his cross daily and follow me. ²⁴ For whoever would save his life will lose it, but whoever loses his life for my sake will save it. ²⁵ For what does it profit a man if he gains the whole world and loses or forfeits himself? ²⁶ For whoever is ashamed of me and of my words, of him will the Son of Man be ashamed when he comes in his glory and the glory of the Father and of the holy angels. ²⁷ But I tell you truly, there are some standing here who will not taste death until they see the kingdom of God."

The Transfiguration

²⁸ Now about eight days after these sayings he took with him Peter and John and James and went up on the mountain to pray. ²⁹ And as he was praying, the appearance of his face was altered, and his clothing became dazzling white. ³⁰ And behold, two men were talking with him, Moses and Elijah, ³¹ who appeared in glory and spoke of his departure, which he was about to accomplish at Jerusalem. ³² Now Peter and those who were with him were heavy with sleep, but when they became fully awake they saw his glory and the two men who stood with him. ³³ And as the men were parting from him, Peter said to Jesus, "Master, it is good that

AND HE CALLED THE TWELVE TOGETHER AND GAVE THEM POWER AND AUTHORITY OVER ALL DEMONS AND TO CURE DISEASES, AND HE SENT THEM OUT TO PROCLAIM THE KINGDOM OF GOD AND TO HEAL.

Luke 9:1-2

we are here. Let us make three tents, one for you and one for Moses and one for Elijah"—not knowing what he said. ³⁴ As he was saying these things, a cloud came and overshadowed them, and they were afraid as they entered the cloud. ³⁵ And a voice came out of the cloud, saying, "This is my Son, my Chosen One; listen to him!" ³⁶ And when the voice had spoken, Jesus was found alone. And they kept silent and told no one in those days anything of what they had seen.

Jesus Heals a Boy with an Unclean Spirit

³⁷ On the next day, when they had come down from the mountain, a great crowd met him. ³⁸ And behold, a man from the crowd cried out, "Teacher, I beg you to look at my son, for he is my only child. ³⁹ And behold, a spirit seizes him, and he suddenly cries out. It convulses him so that he foams at the mouth, and shatters him, and will hardly leave him. ⁴⁰ And I begged your disciples to cast it out, but they could not." ⁴¹ Jesus answered, "O faithless and twisted generation, how long am I to be with you and bear with you? Bring your son here." ⁴² While he was coming, the demon threw him to the ground and convulsed him. But Jesus rebuked the unclean spirit and healed the

boy, and gave him back to his father. ⁴³ And all were astonished at the majesty of God.

Jesus Again Foretells His Death

But while they were all marvelling at everything he was doing, Jesus said to his disciples, ⁴⁴ "Let these words sink into your ears: The Son of Man is about to be delivered into the hands of men." ⁴⁵ But they did not understand this saying, and it was concealed from them, so that they might not perceive it. And they were afraid to ask him about this saying.

Who Is the Greatest?

⁴⁶ An argument arose among them as to which of them was the greatest. ⁴⁷ But Jesus, knowing the reasoning of their hearts, took a child and put him by his side ⁴⁸ and said to them, "Whoever receives this child in my name receives me, and whoever receives me receives him who sent me. For he who is least among all of you is the one who is great."

Anyone Not Against Us Is For Us

⁴⁹ John answered, "Master, we saw someone casting out demons in your name, and we tried to stop him, because he does not follow with us." ⁵⁰ But Jesus said to him, "Do not stop him, for the one who is not against you is for you."

A Samaritan Village Rejects Jesus

⁵¹ When the days drew near for him to be taken up, he set his face to go to Jerusalem. ⁵² And he sent messengers ahead of him, who went and entered a village of the Samaritans, to make preparations for him. ⁵³ But the people did not receive him, because his face was set towards Jerusalem. ⁵⁴ And when his disciples James and John saw it, they said, "Lord, do you want us to tell fire to come down from heaven and consume them?" ⁵⁵ But he turned and rebuked them. ⁵⁶ And they went on to another village.

The Cost of Following Jesus

⁵⁷ As they were going along the road, someone said to him, "I will follow you wherever you go." ⁵⁸ And Jesus said to him, "Foxes have holes, and birds of the air have nests, but the Son of Man has nowhere to lay his head." ⁵⁹ To another he said, "Follow me." But he said, "Lord, let me first go and bury my father." ⁶⁰ And Jesus said to him, "Leave the dead to bury their own dead. But as for you, go and proclaim the kingdom of God." ⁶¹ Yet another said, "I will follow you, Lord, but let me first say farewell to those at my home." ⁶² Jesus said to him, "No one who puts his hand to the plough and looks back is fit for the kingdom of God."

"WHOEVER RECEIVES THIS CHILD
IN MY NAME RECEIVES ME, AND WHOEVER
RECEIVES ME RECEIVES HIM WHO SENT ME.
FOR HE WHO IS LEAST AMONG ALL OF YOU
IS THE ONE WHO IS GREAT."

Luke 9:48

Chapter Ten
Jesus Sends Out the Seventy-Two

And he said to them, "The harvest is plentiful, but the labourers are few. Therefore pray earnestly to the Lord of the harvest to send out labourers into his harvest."

Luke 10:2

After this the Lord appointed seventy-two others and sent them on ahead of him, two by two, into every town and place where he himself was about to go. ²And he said to them, "The harvest is plentiful, but the labourers are few. Therefore pray earnestly to the Lord of the harvest to send out labourers into his harvest. ³Go your way; behold, I am sending you out as lambs in the midst of wolves. ⁴Carry no money bag, no knapsack, no sandals, and greet no one on the road. ⁵Whatever house you enter, first say, 'Peace be to this house!' ⁶And if a son of peace is there, your peace will rest upon him. But if not, it will return to you. ⁷And remain in the same house, eating and drinking what they provide, for the labourer deserves his wages. Do not go from house to house. ⁸Whenever you enter a town and they receive you, eat what is set before you. ⁹Heal the sick in it and say to them, 'The kingdom of God has come near to you.' ¹⁰But when-ever you enter a town and they do not receive you, go into its streets and say, ¹¹'Even the dust of your town that clings to our feet we wipe off against you. Nevertheless know this, that the kingdom of God has come near.' ¹²I tell you, it will be more bearable on that day for Sodom than for that town.

Woe to Unrepentant Cities
¹³"Woe to you, Chorazin! Woe to you, Bethsaida! For if the mighty works done in you had been done in Tyre and Sidon, they would have repented long ago, sitting in sackcloth and ashes. ¹⁴But it will be more bearable in the judge-ment for Tyre and Sidon than for you. ¹⁵And you, Capernaum, will you be ex-alted to heaven? You shall be brought down to Hades.

¹⁶"The one who hears you hears me, and the one who rejects you rejects me, and the one who rejects me rejects him who sent me."

The Return of the Seventy-Two
¹⁷The seventy-two returned with joy, saying, "Lord, even the demons are subject to us in your name!" ¹⁸And he said to them, "I saw Satan fall like light-ning from heaven. ¹⁹Behold, I have giv-en you authority to tread on serpents and scorpions, and over all the power of the enemy, and nothing shall hurt you. ²⁰Nevertheless, do not rejoice in this, that the spirits are subject to you, but rejoice that your names are written in heaven."

Jesus Rejoices in the Father's Will
²¹In that same hour he rejoiced in the Holy Spirit and said, "I thank you, Fa-ther, Lord of heaven and earth, that you have hidden these things from the wise and understanding and revealed them to little children; yes, Father, for such was your gracious will. ²²All things have been handed over to me by my Father, and no one knows who the Son

is except the Father, or who the Father is except the Son and anyone to whom the Son chooses to reveal him."

²³ Then turning to the disciples he said privately, "Blessed are the eyes that see what you see! ²⁴ For I tell you that many prophets and kings desired to see what you see, and did not see it, and to hear what you hear, and did not hear it."

The Parable of the Good Samaritan

²⁵ And behold, a lawyer stood up to put him to the test, saying, "Teacher, what shall I do to inherit eternal life?" ²⁶ He said to him, "What is written in the Law? How do you read it?" ²⁷ And he answered, "You shall love the Lord your God with all your heart and with all your soul and with all your strength and with all your mind, and your neighbour as yourself." ²⁸ And he said to him, "You have answered correctly; do this, and you will live."

²⁹ But he, desiring to justify himself, said to Jesus, "And who is my neighbour?" ³⁰ Jesus replied, "A man was going down from Jerusalem to Jericho, and he fell among robbers, who stripped him and beat him and departed, leaving him half dead. ³¹ Now by chance a priest was going down that road, and when he saw him he passed by on the other side. ³² So likewise a Levite, when he came to the place and saw him, passed by on the other side. ³³ But a Samaritan, as he journeyed, came to where he was, and when he saw him, he had compassion. ³⁴ He went to him and bound up his wounds, pouring on oil and wine. Then he set him on his own animal and brought him to an inn and took care of him. ³⁵ And the next day he took out two denarii and gave them to the innkeeper, saying,

'Take care of him, and whatever more you spend, I will repay you when I come back.' ³⁶ Which of these three, do you think, proved to be a neighbour to the man who fell among the robbers?" ³⁷ He said, "The one who showed him mercy." And Jesus said to him, "You go, and do likewise."

Martha and Mary

³⁸ Now as they went on their way, Jesus entered a village. And a woman named Martha welcomed him into her house. ³⁹ And she had a sister called Mary, who sat at the Lord's feet and listened to his teaching. ⁴⁰ But Martha was distracted with much serving. And she went up to him and said, "Lord, do you not care that my sister has left me to serve alone? Tell her then to help me." ⁴¹ But the Lord answered her, "Martha, Martha, you are anxious and troubled about many things, ⁴² but one thing is necessary. Mary has chosen the good portion, which will not be taken away from her."

Chapter Eleven
The Lord's Prayer

Now Jesus was praying in a certain place, and when he finished, one of his disciples said to him, "Lord, teach us to pray, as John taught his disciples." ² And he said to them, "When you pray, say:

"Father, hallowed be your name.
Your kingdom come.
³ Give us each day our daily bread,
⁴ and forgive us our sins,
for we ourselves forgive

everyone who is indebted to us.
And lead us not into temptation."

⁵ And he said to them, "Which of you who has a friend will go to him at midnight and say to him, 'Friend, lend me three loaves, ⁶ for a friend of mine has arrived on a journey, and I have nothing to set before him'; ⁷ and he will answer from within, 'Do not bother me; the door is now shut, and my children are with me in bed. I cannot get up and give you anything'? ⁸ I tell you, though he will not get up and give him anything because he is his friend, yet because of his impudence he will rise and give him whatever he needs. ⁹ And I tell you, ask, and it will be given to you; seek, and you will find; knock, and it will be opened to you. ¹⁰ For everyone who asks receives, and the one who seeks finds, and to the one who knocks it will be opened. ¹¹ What father among you, if his son asks for a fish, will instead of a fish give him a serpent; ¹² or if he asks for an egg, will give him a scorpion? ¹³ If you then, who are evil, know how to give good gifts to your children, how much more will the heavenly Father give the Holy Spirit to those who ask him!"

Jesus and Beelzebul

¹⁴ Now he was casting out a demon that was mute. When the demon had gone out, the mute man spoke, and the people marvelled. ¹⁵ But some of them said, "He casts out demons by Beelzebul, the prince of demons", ¹⁶ while others, to test him, kept seeking from him a sign from heaven. ¹⁷ But he, knowing their thoughts, said to them, "Every kingdom divided against itself

is laid waste, and a divided household falls. ¹⁸ And if Satan also is divided against himself, how will his kingdom stand? For you say that I cast out demons by Beelzebul. ¹⁹ And if I cast out demons by Beelzebul, by whom do your sons cast them out? Therefore they will be your judges. ²⁰ But if it is by the finger of God that I cast out demons, then the kingdom of God has come upon you. ²¹ When a strong man, fully armed, guards his own palace, his goods are safe; ²² but when one stronger than he attacks him and overcomes him, he takes away his armour in which he trusted and divides his spoil. ²³ Whoever is not with me is against me, and whoever does not gather with me scatters.

Return of an Unclean Spirit

²⁴ "When the unclean spirit has gone out of a person, it passes through waterless places seeking rest, and finding none it says, 'I will return to my house from which I came.' ²⁵ And when it comes, it finds the house swept and put in order. ²⁶ Then it goes and brings seven other spirits more evil than itself, and they enter and dwell there. And the last state of that person is worse than the first."

True Blessedness

²⁷ As he said these things, a woman in the crowd raised her voice and said to him, "Blessed is the womb that bore you, and the breasts at which you nursed!" ²⁸ But he said, "Blessed rather are those who hear the word of God and keep it!"

The Sign of Jonah

²⁹ When the crowds were increasing, he began to say, "This generation is an evil generation. It seeks for a sign, but no sign will be given to it except the sign of Jonah. ³⁰ For as Jonah became a sign to the people of Nineveh, so will the Son of Man be to this generation. ³¹ The queen of the South will rise up at the judgement with the men of this generation and condemn them, for she came from the ends of the earth to hear the wisdom of Solomon, and behold, something greater than Solomon is here. ³² The men of Nineveh will rise up at the judgement with this generation and condemn it, for they repented at the preaching of Jonah, and behold, something greater than Jonah is here.

The Light in You

³³ "No one after lighting a lamp puts it in a cellar or under a basket, but on a stand, so that those who enter may see the light. ³⁴ Your eye is the lamp of your body. When your eye is healthy, your whole body is full of light, but when it is bad, your body is full of darkness. ³⁵ Therefore be careful lest the light in you be darkness. ³⁶ If then your whole body is full of light, having no part dark, it will be wholly bright, as when a lamp with its rays gives you light."

Woes to the Pharisees and Lawyers

³⁷ While Jesus was speaking, a Pharisee asked him to dine with him, so he went in and reclined at table. ³⁸ The Pharisee was astonished to see that he did not first wash before dinner. ³⁹ And the Lord said to him, "Now you Pharisees cleanse the outside of the cup and of the dish, but inside you are full of greed and wickedness. ⁴⁰ You fools! Did not he who made the outside make the inside also? ⁴¹ But give as alms those

things that are within, and behold, everything is clean for you.

⁴²"But woe to you Pharisees! For you tithe mint and rue and every herb, and neglect justice and the love of God. These you ought to have done, without neglecting the others. ⁴³Woe to you Pharisees! For you love the best seat in the synagogues and greetings in the market-places. ⁴⁴Woe to you! For you are like unmarked graves, and people walk over them without knowing it."

⁴⁵ One of the lawyers answered him, "Teacher, in saying these things you insult us also." ⁴⁶ And he said, "Woe to you lawyers also! For you load people with burdens hard to bear, and you yourselves do not touch the burdens with one of your fingers. ⁴⁷Woe to you! For you build the tombs of the prophets whom your fathers killed. ⁴⁸So you are witnesses and you consent to the deeds of your fathers, for they killed them, and you build their tombs. ⁴⁹Therefore also the Wisdom of God said, 'I will send them prophets and apostles, some of whom they will kill and persecute', ⁵⁰so that the blood of all the prophets, shed from the foundation of the world, may be charged against this generation, ⁵¹from the blood of Abel to the blood of Zechariah, who perished between the altar and the sanctuary. Yes, I tell you, it will be required of this generation. ⁵²Woe to you lawyers! For you have taken away the key of knowledge. You did not enter yourselves, and you hindered those who were entering."

⁵³ As he went away from there, the scribes and the Pharisees began to press him hard and to provoke him to speak about many things, ⁵⁴lying in wait for him, to catch him in something he might say.

Chapter Twelve

Beware of the Leaven of the Pharisees

In the meantime, when so many thousands of the people had gathered together that they were trampling one another, he began to say to his disciples first, "Beware of the leaven of the Pharisees, which is hypocrisy. [2]Nothing is covered up that will not be revealed, or hidden that will not be known. [3]Therefore whatever you have said in the dark shall be heard in the light, and what you have whispered in private rooms shall be proclaimed on the housetops.

Have No Fear

[4]"I tell you, my friends, do not fear those who kill the body, and after that have nothing more that they can do.

[5]But I will warn you whom to fear: fear him who, after he has killed, has authority to cast into hell. Yes, I tell you, fear him! [6]Are not five sparrows sold for two pennies? And not one of them is forgotten before God. [7]Why, even the hairs of your head are all numbered. Fear not; you are of more value than many sparrows.

Acknowledge Christ Before Men

[8]"And I tell you, everyone who acknowledges me before men, the Son of Man also will acknowledge before the angels of God, [9]but the one who denies me before men will be denied before the angels of God. [10]And everyone who speaks a word against the Son of Man will be forgiven, but the one who blasphemes against the Holy Spirit will not be forgiven. [11]And when they bring you before the synagogues and the rulers and the authorities, do not be anxious about how you should de-

fend yourself or what you should say, [12]for the Holy Spirit will teach you in that very hour what you ought to say."

The Parable of the Rich Fool

[13]Someone in the crowd said to him, "Teacher, tell my brother to divide the inheritance with me." [14]But he said to him, "Man, who made me a judge or arbitrator over you?" [15]And he said to them, "Take care, and be on your guard against all covetousness, for one's life does not consist in the abundance of one's possessions." [16]And he told them a parable, saying, "The land of a rich man produced plentifully, [17]and he thought to himself, 'What shall I do, for I have nowhere to store my crops?' [18]And he said, 'I will do this: I will tear down my barns and build larger ones, and there I will store all my grain and my goods. [19]And I will say to my soul, "Soul, you have ample goods laid up for many years; relax, eat, drink, be merry."'

AND HE SAID
TO HIS DISCIPLES,
"THEREFORE I
TELL YOU, DO
NOT BE ANXIOUS
ABOUT YOUR
LIFE, WHAT YOU
WILL EAT, NOR
ABOUT YOUR
BODY, WHAT
YOU WILL PUT
ON. FOR LIFE
IS MORE THAN
FOOD, AND
THE BODY
MORE THAN
CLOTHING."

Luke 12:22-23

²⁰But God said to him, 'Fool! This night your soul is required of you, and the things you have prepared, whose will they be?' ²¹So is the one who lays up treasure for himself and is not rich towards God."

Do Not Be Anxious

²²And he said to his disciples, "Therefore I tell you, do not be anxious about your life, what you will eat, nor about your body, what you will put on. ²³For life is more than food, and the body more than clothing. ²⁴Consider the ravens: they neither sow nor reap, they have neither storehouse nor barn, and yet God feeds them. Of how much more value are you than the birds! ²⁵And which of you by being anxious can add a single hour to his span of life? ²⁶If then you are not able to do as small a thing as that, why are you anxious about the rest? ²⁷Consider the lilies, how they grow: they neither toil nor spin, yet I tell you, even Solomon in all his glory was not arrayed like one of these. ²⁸But if God so clothes the grass, which is alive in the field today, and tomorrow is thrown into the oven, how much more will he clothe you, O you of little faith! ²⁹And do not seek what you are to eat and what you are to drink, nor be worried. ³⁰For all the nations of the world seek after these things, and your Father knows that you need them. ³¹Instead, seek his kingdom, and these things will be added to you.

³²"Fear not, little flock, for it is your Father's good pleasure to give you the kingdom. ³³Sell your possessions, and give to the needy. Provide yourselves with money bags that do not grow old, with a treasure in the heavens that does not fail, where no thief approaches and no moth destroys. ³⁴For where your treasure is, there will your heart be also.

You Must Be Ready

³⁵"Stay dressed for action and keep your lamps burning, ³⁶and be like men who are waiting for their master to come home from the wedding feast, so that they may open the door to him at once when he comes and knocks. ³⁷Blessed are those servants whom the master finds awake when he comes. Truly, I say to you, he will dress himself for service and have them recline at table, and he will come and serve them. ³⁸If he comes in the second watch, or in the third, and finds them awake, blessed are those servants! ³⁹But know this, that if the master of the house had known at what hour the thief was coming, he would not have left his house to be broken into. ⁴⁰You also must be ready, for the Son of Man is coming at an hour you do not expect."

⁴¹ Peter said, "Lord, are you telling this parable for us or for all?" ⁴² And the Lord said, "Who then is the faithful and wise manager, whom his master will set over his household, to give them their portion of food at the proper time? ⁴³Blessed is that servant whom his master will find so doing when he comes. ⁴⁴Truly, I say to you, he will set him over all his possessions. ⁴⁵But if that servant says to himself, 'My master is delayed in coming', and begins to beat the male and female servants, and to eat and drink and get drunk, ⁴⁶the master of that servant will come on a day when he does not expect him and at an hour he does not know, and will cut him in pieces and put him with the unfaithful. ⁴⁷And that servant who knew his master's will but did not get ready or act according to his will, will receive a severe beating. ⁴⁸But the one who did not know, and did what deserved a beating, will receive a light beating. Everyone to whom much was given, of him much will be required, and from him to whom they entrusted much, they will demand the more.

Not Peace, but Division

⁴⁹"I came to cast fire on the earth, and would that it were already kindled! ⁵⁰I have a baptism to be baptized with, and how great is my distress until it is accomplished! ⁵¹Do you think that I have come to give peace on earth? No, I tell you, but rather division. ⁵²For from now on in one house there will be five divided, three against two and two against three. ⁵³They will be divided, father against son and son against father, mother against daughter and daughter against mother, mother-in-law against her daughter-in-law and daughter-in-law against mother-in-law."

Interpreting the Time

⁵⁴ He also said to the crowds, "When you see a cloud rising in the west, you say at once, 'A shower is coming.' And so it happens. ⁵⁵And when you see the south wind blowing, you say, 'There will be scorching heat', and it happens. ⁵⁶You hypocrites! You know how to interpret the appearance of earth and sky, but why do you not know how to interpret the present time?

Settle with Your Accuser

⁵⁷"And why do you not judge for yourselves what is right? ⁵⁸As you go with your accuser before the magistrate, make an effort to settle with him on the way, lest he drag you to the judge, and the judge hand you over to the officer, and the officer put you in prison. ⁵⁹I tell you, you will never get out until you have paid the very last penny."

> "BUT KNOW THIS, THAT IF THE MASTER OF THE HOUSE HAD KNOWN AT WHAT HOUR THE THIEF WAS COMING, HE WOULD NOT HAVE LEFT HIS HOUSE TO BE BROKEN INTO. YOU ALSO MUST BE READY, FOR THE SON OF MAN IS COMING AT AN HOUR YOU DO NOT EXPECT."
>
> Luke 12:39-40

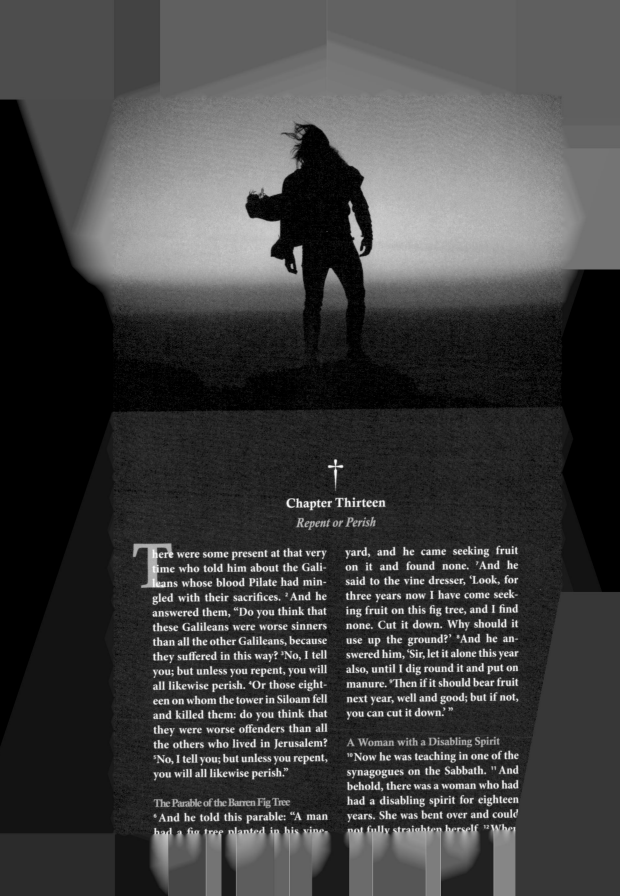

✝

Chapter Thirteen
Repent or Perish

There were some present at that very time who told him about the Galileans whose blood Pilate had mingled with their sacrifices. ² And he answered them, "Do you think that these Galileans were worse sinners than all the other Galileans, because they suffered in this way? ³No, I tell you; but unless you repent, you will all likewise perish. ⁴Or those eighteen on whom the tower in Siloam fell and killed them: do you think that they were worse offenders than all the others who lived in Jerusalem? ⁵No, I tell you; but unless you repent, you will all likewise perish."

The Parable of the Barren Fig Tree
⁶ And he told this parable: "A man had a fig tree planted in his vine-yard, and he came seeking fruit on it and found none. ⁷And he said to the vine dresser, 'Look, for three years now I have come seeking fruit on this fig tree, and I find none. Cut it down. Why should it use up the ground?' ⁸And he answered him, 'Sir, let it alone this year also, until I dig round it and put on manure. ⁹Then if it should bear fruit next year, well and good; but if not, you can cut it down.'"

A Woman with a Disabling Spirit
¹⁰ Now he was teaching in one of the synagogues on the Sabbath. ¹¹ And behold, there was a woman who had had a disabling spirit for eighteen years. She was bent over and could not fully straighten herself. ¹²When

Jesus saw her, he called her over and said to her, "Woman, you are freed from your disability." ¹³ And he laid his hands on her, and immediately she was made straight, and she glorified God. ¹⁴ But the ruler of the synagogue, indignant because Jesus had healed on the Sabbath, said to the people, "There are six days in which work ought to be done. Come on those days and be healed, and not on the Sabbath day." ¹⁵ Then the Lord answered him, "You hypocrites! Does not each of you on the Sabbath untie his ox or his donkey from the manger and lead it away to water it? ¹⁶ And ought not this woman, a daughter of Abraham whom Satan bound for eighteen years, be loosed from this bond on the Sabbath day?" ¹⁷ As he said these things, all his adversaries were put to shame, and all the people rejoiced at all the glorious things that were done by him.

The Mustard Seed and the Leaven
¹⁸ He said therefore, "What is the kingdom of God like? And to what shall I compare it? ¹⁹ It is like a grain of mustard seed that a man took and sowed in his garden, and it grew and became a tree, and the birds of the air made nests in its branches."

²⁰ And again he said, "To what shall I compare the kingdom of God? ²¹ It is like leaven that a woman took and hid in three measures of flour, until it was all leavened."

"AND OUGHT NOT THIS WOMAN, A DAUGHTER OF ABRAHAM WHOM SATAN BOUND FOR EIGHTEEN YEARS, BE LOOSED FROM THIS BOND ON THE SABBATH DAY?" AS HE SAID THESE THINGS, ALL HIS ADVERSARIES WERE PUT TO SHAME, AND ALL THE PEOPLE REJOICED AT ALL THE GLORIOUS THINGS THAT WERE DONE BY HIM.

Luke 13:16-17

The Narrow Door

²² He went on his way through towns and villages, teaching and journeying towards Jerusalem. ²³ And someone said to him, "Lord, will those who are saved be few?" And he said to them, ²⁴"Strive to enter through the narrow door. For many, I tell you, will seek to enter and will not be able. ²⁵When once the master of the house has risen and shut the door, and you begin to stand outside and to knock at the door, saying, 'Lord, open to us', then he will answer you, 'I do not know where you come from.' ²⁶Then you will begin to say, 'We ate and drank in your presence, and you taught in our streets.' ²⁷But he will say, 'I tell you, I do not know where you come from. Depart from me, all you workers of evil!' ²⁸In that place there will be weeping and gnashing of teeth, when you see Abraham and Isaac and Jacob and all the prophets in the kingdom of God but you yourselves cast out. ²⁹And people will come from east and west, and from north and south, and recline at table in the kingdom of God. ³⁰And behold, some are last who will be first, and some are first who will be last."

Lament over Jerusalem

³¹ At that very hour some Pharisees came and said to him, "Get away from here, for Herod wants to kill you." ³² And he said to them, "Go and tell that fox, 'Behold, I cast out demons and perform cures today and tomorrow, and the third day I finish my course. ³³Nevertheless, I must go on my way today and tomorrow and the day following, for it cannot be that a prophet should perish away from Jerusalem.' ³⁴O Jerusalem, Jerusalem, the city that kills the prophets and stones those who are sent to it! How often would I have gathered your children together as a hen gathers her brood under her wings, and you were not willing! ³⁵Behold, your house is forsaken. And I tell you, you will not see me until you say, 'Blessed is he who comes in the name of the Lord!'"

"BUT WHEN YOU ARE

invited, go and sit in the lowest place, so that when your host comes he may say to you, 'Friend, move up higher.' Then you will be honoured in the presence of all who sit at table with you. For everyone who exalts himself will be humbled, and he who humbles himself will be exalted."

Luke 14:10-11

Chapter Fourteen
Healing of a Man on the Sabbath

And he said to them, "Which of you, having a son or an ox that has fallen into a well on a Sabbath day, will not immediately pull him out?"
Luke 14:5

One Sabbath, when he went to dine at the house of a ruler of the Pharisees, they were watching him carefully. ²And behold, there was a man before him who had dropsy. ³And Jesus responded to the lawyers and Pharisees, saying, "Is it lawful to heal on the Sabbath, or not?" ⁴But they remained silent. Then he took him and healed him and sent him away. ⁵And he said to them, "Which of you, having a son or an ox that has fallen into a well on a Sabbath day, will not immediately pull him out?" ⁶And they could not reply to these things.

The Parable of the Wedding Feast
⁷Now he told a parable to those who were invited, when he noticed how they chose the places of honour, saying to them, ⁸"When you are invited by someone to a wedding feast, do not sit down in a place of honour, lest someone more distinguished than you be invited by him, ⁹and he who invited you both will come and say to you, 'Give your place to this person', and then you will begin with shame to take the lowest place. ¹⁰But when you are invited, go and sit in the lowest place, so that when your host comes he may say to you, 'Friend, move up higher.' Then you will be honoured in the presence of all who sit at table with you. ¹¹For everyone who exalts himself will be humbled, and he who humbles himself will be exalted."

The Parable of the Great Banquet
¹²He said also to the man who had invited him, "When you give a dinner or a banquet, do not invite your friends or your brothers or your relatives or rich neighbours, lest they also invite you in return and you be repaid. ¹³But when you give a feast, invite the poor, the crippled, the lame, the blind, ¹⁴and you will be blessed, because they cannot repay you. For you will be repaid at the resurrection of the just."

¹⁵When one of those who reclined at table with him heard these things, he said to him, "Blessed is everyone who will eat bread in the kingdom of God!" ¹⁶But he said to him, "A man once gave a great banquet and invited many. ¹⁷And at the time for the banquet he sent his servant to say to those who had been invited, 'Come, for everything is now ready.' ¹⁸But they all alike began to make excuses. The first said to him, 'I have bought a field, and I must go out and see it. Please excuse me.' ¹⁹And another said, 'I have bought five yoke of oxen, and I am going to examine them. Please excuse me.' ²⁰And another said, 'I have married a wife, and therefore I cannot come.' ²¹So the servant came and reported these things to his master. Then the master of the house became angry and said to his servant, 'Go out quickly to the streets and lanes of the city, and bring in the poor and crippled and blind and lame.' ²²And the servant said, 'Sir, what you commanded has been done, and still there is room.' ²³And the master said to the servant, 'Go out to the highways and hedges and compel people to come in, that my house may be filled. ²⁴For I tell you, none of those men who were invited shall taste my banquet.' "

The Cost of Discipleship
²⁵Now great crowds accompanied him, and he turned and said to them, ²⁶"If anyone comes to me and does not hate his own father and mother and wife and children and brothers and sisters, yes, and even his own life, he cannot be my disciple. ²⁷Whoever does not bear his own cross and come after me cannot be my disciple. ²⁸For which of you, desiring to build a tower, does not first sit down and count the cost, whether he has enough to complete it? ²⁹Otherwise, when he has laid a foundation and is not able to finish, all who see it begin to mock him, ³⁰saying, 'This man began to build and was not able to finish.' ³¹Or what king, going out to encounter another king in war, will not sit down first and deliberate whether he is able with ten thousand to meet him who comes against him with twenty thousand? ³²And if not, while the other is yet a great way off, he sends a delegation and asks for terms of peace. ³³So therefore, any one of you who does not renounce all that he has cannot be my disciple.

Salt Without Taste Is Worthless
³⁴"Salt is good, but if salt has lost its taste, how shall its saltiness be restored? ³⁵It is of no use either for the soil or for the manure pile. It is thrown away. He who has ears to hear, let him hear."

Chapter Fifteen
The Parable of the Lost Sheep

Now the tax collectors and sinners were all drawing near to hear him. ²And the Pharisees and the scribes grumbled, saying, "This man receives sinners and eats with them."

³ So he told them this parable: ⁴"What man of you, having a hundred sheep, if he has lost one of them, does not leave the ninety-nine in the open country, and go after the one that is lost, until he finds it? ⁵And when he has found it, he lays it on his shoulders, rejoicing. ⁶And when he comes home, he calls together his friends and his neighbours, saying to them, 'Rejoice with me, for I have found my sheep that was lost.' ⁷Just so, I tell you, there will be more joy in heaven over one sinner who repents than over ninety-nine righteous persons who need no repentance.

The Parable of the Lost Coin

⁸"Or what woman, having ten silver coins, if she loses one coin, does not light a lamp and sweep the house and seek diligently until she finds it? ⁹And when she has found it, she calls together her friends and neighbours, saying, 'Rejoice with me, for I have found the coin that I had lost.' ¹⁰Just so, I tell you, there is joy before the angels of God over one sinner who repents."

The Parable of the Prodigal Son

¹¹ And he said, "There was a man who had two sons. ¹²And the younger of them said to his father, 'Father, give me the share of property that is coming to me.' And he divided his property between them. ¹³Not many days later, the younger son gathered all he had and took a journey into a far country, and there he squandered his property in reckless living. ¹⁴And when he had spent everything, a severe famine arose in that country, and he began to be in need. ¹⁵So he went and hired himself

out to one of the citizens of that country, who sent him into his fields to feed pigs. [16]And he was longing to be fed with the pods that the pigs ate, and no one gave him anything.

[17]"But when he came to himself, he said, 'How many of my father's hired servants have more than enough bread, but I perish here with hunger! [18]I will arise and go to my father, and I will say to him, "Father, I have sinned against heaven and before you. [19]I am no longer worthy to be called your son. Treat me as one of your hired servants."' [20]And he arose and came to his father. But while he was still a long way off, his father saw him and felt compassion, and ran and embraced him and kissed him. [21]And the son said to him, 'Father, I have sinned against heaven and before you. I am no longer worthy to be called your son.' [22]But the father said to his servants, 'Bring quickly the best robe, and put it on him, and put a ring on his hand, and shoes on his feet. [23]And bring the fattened calf and kill it, and let us eat and celebrate. [24]For this my son was dead, and is alive again; he was lost, and is found.' And they began to celebrate.

[25]"Now his older son was in the field, and as he came and drew near to the house, he heard music and dancing. [26]And he called one of the servants and asked what these things meant. [27]And he said to him, 'Your brother has come, and your father has killed the fattened calf, because he has received him back safe and sound.' [28]But he was angry and refused to go in. His father came out and entreated him, [29]but he answered his father, 'Look, these many years I have served you, and I never disobeyed your command, yet you never gave me a young goat, that I might celebrate with my friends. [30]But when this son of yours came, who has devoured your property with prostitutes, you killed the fattened calf for him!' [31]And he said to him, 'Son, you are always with me, and all that is mine is yours. [32]It was fitting to celebrate and be glad, for this your brother was dead, and is alive; he was lost, and is found.' "

"WHAT MAN OF YOU, HAVING
A HUNDRED SHEEP, IF HE HAS
LOST ONE OF THEM, DOES NOT
LEAVE THE NINETY-NINE IN THE
OPEN COUNTRY, AND GO AFTER
THE ONE THAT IS LOST, UNTIL
HE FINDS IT? AND WHEN HE HAS
FOUND IT, HE LAYS IT ON HIS
SHOULDERS, REJOICING."

Luke 15:4-5

Chapter Sixteen

The Parable of the Dishonest Manager

He also said to the disciples, "There was a rich man who had a manager, and charges were brought to him that this man was wasting his possessions. ²And he called him and said to him, 'What is this that I hear about you? Turn in the account of your management, for you can no longer be manager.' ³And the manager said to himself, 'What shall I do, since my master is taking the management away from me? I am not strong enough to dig, and I am ashamed to beg. ⁴I have decided what to do, so that when I am removed from management, people may receive me into their houses.' ⁵So, summoning his master's debtors one by one, he said to the first, 'How much do you owe my master?' ⁶He said, 'A hundred measures of oil.' He said to him, 'Take your bill, and sit down quickly and write fifty.' ⁷Then he said to another, 'And how much do you owe?' He said, 'A hundred measures of wheat.' He said to him, 'Take your bill, and write eighty.' ⁸The master commended the dishonest manager for his shrewdness. For the sons of this world are more shrewd in dealing with their own generation than the sons of light. ⁹And I tell you, make friends for yourselves by means of unrighteous wealth, so that when it fails they may receive you into the eternal dwellings.

¹⁰"One who is faithful in a very little is also faithful in much, and one who is dishonest in a very little is also dishonest in much. ¹¹If then you have not been faithful with the unrighteous wealth, who will entrust to you the true riches? ¹²And if you have not been faithful with that which is another's, who will give you that which is your own? ¹³No servant can serve two masters, for either he will hate the one and love the other, or he will be devoted to the one and despise the other. You cannot serve God and money."

The Law and the Kingdom of God

¹⁴ The Pharisees, who were lovers of money, heard all these things, and they ridiculed him. ¹⁵ And he said to them, "You are those who justify yourselves before men, but God knows your hearts. For what is exalted among men is an abomination in the sight of God.

¹⁶"The Law and the Prophets were until John; since then the good news of the kingdom of God is preached, and everyone forces his way into it. ¹⁷But it is easier for heaven and earth to pass away than for one dot of the Law to become void.

Divorce and Remarriage

¹⁸"Everyone who divorces his wife and marries another commits adultery, and he who marries a woman divorced from her husband commits adultery.

The Rich Man and Lazarus

¹⁹"There was a rich man who was clothed in purple and fine linen and who feasted sumptuously every day. ²⁰And at his gate was laid a poor man named Lazarus, covered with sores, ²¹who desired to be fed with what fell from the rich man's table. Moreover, even the dogs came and licked his sores. ²²The poor man died and was carried by the angels to Abraham's side. The rich man also died and was buried, ²³and in Hades, being in torment, he lifted up his eyes and saw Abraham far off and Lazarus at his side. ²⁴And he called out, 'Father Abraham, have mercy on me, and send Lazarus to dip the end of his finger in water and cool my tongue, for I am in anguish in this flame.' ²⁵But Abraham said, 'Child, remember that you in your lifetime received your good things, and Lazarus in like manner bad things; but now he is comforted here, and you are in anguish. ²⁶And

besides all this, between us and you a great chasm has been fixed, in order that those who would pass from here to you may not do so, and none may cross from there to us.' ²⁷And he said, 'Then I beg you, father, to send him to my father's house— ²⁸for I have five brothers—so that he may warn them, lest they also come into this place of torment.' ²⁹But Abraham said, 'They have Moses and the Prophets; let them hear them.' ³⁰And he said, 'No, father Abraham, but if someone goes to them from the dead, they will repent.' ³¹He said to him, 'If they do not hear Moses and the Prophets, neither will they be convinced if someone should rise from the dead.' "

Chapter Seventeen
Temptations to Sin

And he said to his disciples, "Temptations to sin are sure to come, but woe to the one through whom they come! ²It would be better for him if a millstone were hung round his neck and he were cast into the sea than that he should cause one of these little ones to sin. ³Pay attention to yourselves! If your brother sins, rebuke him, and if he repents, forgive him, ⁴and if he sins against you seven times in the day, and turns to you seven times, saying, 'I repent', you must forgive him."

Increase Our Faith
⁵ The apostles said to the Lord, "Increase our faith!" ⁶ And the Lord said, "If you had faith like a grain of mustard seed, you could say to this mulberry tree, 'Be uprooted and planted in the sea', and it would obey you.

Unworthy Servants
⁷"Will any one of you who has a servant ploughing or keeping sheep say to him when he has come in from the field,

HE ANSWERED THEM,
"THE KINGDOM OF
GOD IS NOT COMING
IN WAYS THAT CAN
BE OBSERVED, NOR
WILL THEY SAY,
'LOOK, HERE IT IS!'
OR 'THERE!' FOR
BEHOLD, THE
KINGDOM OF GOD
IS IN THE MIDST
OF YOU."

Luke 17:20-21

'Come at once and recline at table'? [8]Will he not rather say to him, 'Prepare supper for me, and dress properly, and serve me while I eat and drink, and afterwards you will eat and drink'? [9]Does he thank the servant because he did what was commanded? [10]So you also, when you have done all that you were commanded, say, 'We are unworthy servants; we have only done what was our duty.' "

Jesus Cleanses Ten Lepers

[11] On the way to Jerusalem he was passing along between Samaria and Galilee. [12] And as he entered a village, he was met by ten lepers, who stood at a distance [13] and lifted up their voices, saying, "Jesus, Master, have mercy on us." [14] When he saw them he said to them, "Go and show yourselves to the priests." And as they went they were cleansed. [15] Then one of them, when he saw that he was healed, turned back, praising God with a loud voice; [16] and he fell on his face at Jesus' feet, giving him thanks. Now he was a Samaritan. [17] Then Jesus answered, "Were not ten cleansed? Where are the nine? [18] Was no one found to return and give praise to God except this foreigner?" [19] And he said to him, "Rise and go your way; your faith has made you well."

The Coming of the Kingdom

[20] Being asked by the Pharisees when the kingdom of God would come, he answered them, "The kingdom of God is not coming in ways that can be observed, [21]nor will they say, 'Look, here it is!' or 'There!' for behold, the kingdom of God is in the midst of you."

[22] And he said to the disciples, "The days are coming when you will desire to see one of the days of the Son of Man, and you will not see it. [23] And they will say to you, 'Look, there!' or 'Look, here!' Do not go out or follow them. [24]For as the lightning flashes and lights up the sky from one side to the other, so will the Son of Man be in his day. [25]But first he must suffer many things and be rejected by this generation. [26]Just as it was in the days of Noah, so will it be in the days of the Son of Man. [27]They were eating and drinking and marrying and being given in marriage, until the day when Noah entered the ark, and the flood came and destroyed them all. [28]Likewise, just as it was in the days of Lot—they were eating and drinking, buying and selling, planting and building, [29]but on the day when Lot went out from Sodom, fire and sulphur rained from heaven and destroyed them all— [30]so will it be on the day when the Son of Man is revealed. [31]On that day, let the one who is on the housetop, with his goods in the house, not come down to take them away, and likewise let the one who is in the field not turn back. [32]Remember Lot's wife. [33]Whoever seeks to preserve his life will lose it, but whoever loses his life will keep it. [34]I tell you, in that night there will be two in one bed. One will be taken and the other left. [35]There will be two women grinding together. One will be taken and the other left." [37] And they said to him, "Where, Lord?" He said to them, "Where the corpse is, there the vultures will gather."

✝

Chapter Eighteen
The Parable of the Persistent Widow

nd he told them a parable to the effect that they ought always to pray and not lose heart. [2] He said, "In a certain city there was a judge who neither feared God nor respected man. [3]And there was a widow in that city who kept coming to him and saying, 'Give me justice against my adversary.' [4]For a while he refused, but afterwards he said to himself, 'Though I neither fear God nor respect man, [5]yet because this widow keeps bothering me, I will give her justice, so that she will not beat me down by her continual coming.' " [6] And the Lord said, "Hear what the unrighteous judge says. [7]And will not God give justice to his elect, who cry to him day and night? Will he delay long over them? [8]I tell you, he will give justice to them speedily. Nevertheless, when the Son of Man comes, will he find faith on earth?"

The Pharisee and the Tax Collector

[9] He also told this parable to some who trusted in themselves that they were righteous, and treated others with contempt: [10]"Two men went up into the temple to pray, one a Pharisee and the other a tax collector. [11]The Pharisee, standing by himself, prayed thus: 'God, I thank you that I am not like other men, extortioners, unjust, adulterers, or even like this tax collector. [12]I fast twice a week; I give tithes of all that I get.' [13]But the tax collector, standing far off, would not even lift up his eyes to heaven, but beat his breast, saying, 'God, be merciful to me, a sinner!' [14]I tell you, this man went down to his house justified, rather than the other. For everyone who exalts himself will be humbled, but the one who humbles himself will be exalted."

Let the Children Come to Me

[15] Now they were bringing even infants to him that he might touch them. And when the disciples saw it, they rebuked them. [16] But Jesus called them to him, saying, "Let the children come to me, and do not hinder them, for to such belongs the kingdom of God. [17]Truly, I say to you, whoever does not receive the kingdom of God like a child shall not enter it."

The Rich Ruler

[18] And a ruler asked him, "Good Teacher, what must I do to inherit eternal life?" [19] And Jesus said to him, "Why do you call me good? No one is good except God alone. [20]You know the commandments: 'Do not commit adultery, Do not murder, Do not steal, Do not

bear false witness, Honour your father and mother.'" ²¹ And he said, "All these I have kept from my youth." ²² When Jesus heard this, he said to him, "One thing you still lack. Sell all that you have and distribute to the poor, and you will have treasure in heaven; and come, follow me." ²³ But when he heard these things, he became very sad, for he was extremely rich. ²⁴ Jesus, seeing that he had become sad, said, "How difficult it is for those who have wealth to enter the kingdom of God! ²⁵For it is easier for a camel to go through the eye of a needle than for a rich person to enter the kingdom of God." ²⁶Those who heard it said, "Then who can be saved?" ²⁷But he said, "What is impossible with man is possible with God." ²⁸And Peter said, "See, we have left our homes and followed you." ²⁹And he said to them, "Truly, I say to you, there is no one who has left house or wife or brothers or parents or children, for the sake of the kingdom of God, ³⁰who will not receive many times more in this time, and in the age to come eternal life."

Jesus Foretells His Death a Third Time
³¹ And taking the twelve, he said to them, "See, we are going up to Jerusalem, and everything that is written about the Son of Man by the prophets will be accomplished. ³²For he will be delivered over to the Gentiles and will be mocked and shamefully treated and spat upon. ³³And after flogging him, they will kill him, and on the third day he will rise." ³⁴But they understood none of these things. This saying was hidden from them, and they did not grasp what was said.

Jesus Heals a Blind Beggar
³⁵ As he drew near to Jericho, a blind man was sitting by the roadside begging. ³⁶ And hearing a crowd going by, he enquired what this meant. ³⁷ They told him, "Jesus of Nazareth is passing by." ³⁸ And he cried out, "Jesus, Son of David, have mercy on me!" ³⁹ And those who were in front rebuked him, telling him to be silent. But he cried out all the more, "Son of David, have mercy on me!" ⁴⁰ And Jesus stopped and commanded him to be brought to him. And when he came near, he asked him, ⁴¹ "What do you want me to do for you?" He said, "Lord, let me recover my sight." ⁴² And Jesus said to him, "Recover your sight; your faith has made you well." ⁴³ And immediately he recovered his sight and followed him, glorifying God. And all the people, when they saw it, gave praise to God.

Chapter Nineteen
Jesus and Zacchaeus

He entered Jericho and was passing through. ² And behold, there was a man named Zacchaeus. He was a chief tax collector and was rich. ³ And he was seeking to see who Jesus was, but on account of the crowd he could not, because he was small in stature. ⁴ So he ran on ahead and climbed up into a sycamore tree to see him, for he was about to pass that way. ⁵ And when Jesus came to the place, he looked up and said to him, "Zacchaeus, hurry and come down, for I must stay at your house today." ⁶ So he hurried and came down and received him joyfully. ⁷ And

when they saw it, they all grumbled, "He has gone in to be the guest of a man who is a sinner." ⁸ And Zacchaeus stood and said to the Lord, "Behold, Lord, half of my goods I give to the poor. And if I have defrauded anyone of anything, I restore it fourfold." ⁹ And Jesus said to him, "Today salvation has come to this house, since he also is a son of Abraham. ¹⁰For the Son of Man came to seek and to save the lost."

The Parable of the Ten Minas

¹¹ As they heard these things, he proceeded to tell a parable, because he was near to Jerusalem, and because they supposed that the kingdom of God was to appear immediately. ¹²He said therefore, "A nobleman went into a far country to receive for himself a kingdom and then return. ¹³Calling ten of his servants, he gave them ten minas, and said to them, 'Engage in business until I come.' ¹⁴But his citizens hated him and sent a delegation after him, saying, 'We do not want this man to reign over us.' ¹⁵When he returned, having received the kingdom, he ordered these servants to whom he had given the money to be called to him, that he might know what they had gained by doing business. ¹⁶The first came before him, saying, 'Lord, your mina has made ten minas more.' ¹⁷And he said to him, 'Well done, good servant! Because you have been faithful in a very little, you shall have authority over ten cities.' ¹⁸And the second came, saying, 'Lord, your mina has made five minas.' ¹⁹And he said to him, 'And you are to be over five cities.' ²⁰Then another came, saying, 'Lord, here is your mina, which I kept laid away in a handkerchief; ²¹for I was afraid of you, because you are a severe man. You take what you did not deposit, and reap what you did not sow.' ²²He said to him, 'I will condemn you with your own words, you wicked servant! You knew that I was a severe man, taking what I did not deposit and reaping what I did

AND AS THEY WERE UNTYING THE COLT, ITS OWNERS SAID
TO THEM, "WHY ARE YOU UNTYING THE COLT?" AND THEY
SAID, "THE LORD HAS NEED OF IT." AND THEY BROUGHT IT
TO JESUS, AND THROWING THEIR CLOAKS ON THE COLT,
THEY SET JESUS ON IT. AND AS HE RODE ALONG, THEY
SPREAD THEIR CLOAKS ON THE ROAD. Luke 19:33-36

not sow? ²³Why then did you not put my money in the bank, and at my coming I might have collected it with interest?' ²⁴And he said to those who stood by, 'Take the mina from him, and give it to the one who has the ten minas.' ²⁵And they said to him, 'Lord, he has ten minas!' ²⁶'I tell you that to everyone who has, more will be given, but from the one who has not, even what he has will be taken away. ²⁷But as for these enemies of mine, who did not want me to reign over them, bring them here and slaughter them before me.' "

The Triumphal Entry

²⁸ And when he had said these things, he went on ahead, going up to Jerusalem. ²⁹ When he drew near to Bethphage and Bethany, at the mount that is called Olivet, he sent two of the disciples, ³⁰ saying, "Go into the village in front of you, where on entering you will find a colt tied, on which no one has ever yet sat. Untie it and bring it here. ³¹If anyone asks you, 'Why are you untying it?' you shall say this: 'The Lord has need of it.' " ³²So those who were sent went away and found it just as he had told them. ³³ And as they were untying the colt, its owners said to them, "Why are you untying the colt?" ³⁴ And they said, "The Lord has need of it." ³⁵ And they brought it to Jesus, and throwing their cloaks on the colt, they set Jesus on it. ³⁶ And as he rode along, they spread their cloaks on the road. ³⁷ As he was drawing near—already on the way down the Mount of Olives—the whole multitude of his disciples began

to rejoice and praise God with a loud voice for all the mighty works that they had seen, ³⁸ saying, "Blessed is the King who comes in the name of the Lord! Peace in heaven and glory in the highest!" ³⁹ And some of the Pharisees in the crowd said to him, "Teacher, rebuke your disciples." ⁴⁰ He answered, "I tell you, if these were silent, the very stones would cry out."

Jesus Weeps over Jerusalem

⁴¹ And when he drew near and saw the city, he wept over it, ⁴² saying, "Would that you, even you, had known on this day the things that make for peace! But now they are hidden from your eyes. ⁴³For the days will come upon you, when your enemies will set up a barricade round you and surround you and hem you in on every side ⁴⁴and tear you down to the ground, you and your children within you. And they will not leave one stone upon another in you, because you did not know the time of your visitation."

Jesus Cleanses the Temple

⁴⁵ And he entered the temple and began to drive out those who sold, ⁴⁶ saying to them, "It is written, 'My house shall be a house of prayer', but you have made it a den of robbers."

⁴⁷ And he was teaching daily in the temple. The chief priests and the scribes and the principal men of the people were seeking to destroy him, ⁴⁸ but they did not find anything they could do, for all the people were hanging on his words.

Chapter Twenty

The Authority of Jesus Challenged

One day, as Jesus was teaching the people in the temple and preaching the gospel, the chief priests and the scribes with the elders came up ²and said to him, "Tell us by what authority you do these things, or who it is that gave you this authority." ³He answered them, "I also will ask you a question. Now tell me, ⁴was the baptism of John from heaven or from man?" ⁵And they discussed it with one another, saying, "If we say, 'From heaven', he will say, 'Why did you not believe him?' ⁶But if we say, 'From man', all the people will stone us to death, for they are convinced that John was a prophet." ⁷So they answered that they did not know where it came from. ⁸And Jesus said to them, "Neither will I tell you by what authority I do these things."

The Parable of the Wicked Tenants

⁹And he began to tell the people this parable: "A man planted a vineyard and let it out to tenants and went into another country for a long while. ¹⁰When the time came, he sent a servant to the tenants, so that they would give him some of the fruit of the vineyard. But the tenants beat him and sent him away empty-handed. ¹¹And he sent another servant. But they also beat and treated him shamefully, and sent him away empty-handed. ¹²And he sent yet a third. This one also they wounded and cast out. ¹³Then the owner of the vineyard said, 'What shall I do? I will send my beloved son; perhaps they will respect him.' ¹⁴But when the tenants saw him, they said to themselves, 'This is the heir. Let us kill him, so that the inheritance may be ours.' ¹⁵And they threw him out of the vineyard and killed him. What then will the owner of the vineyard do to them? ¹⁶He will come and destroy those tenants and

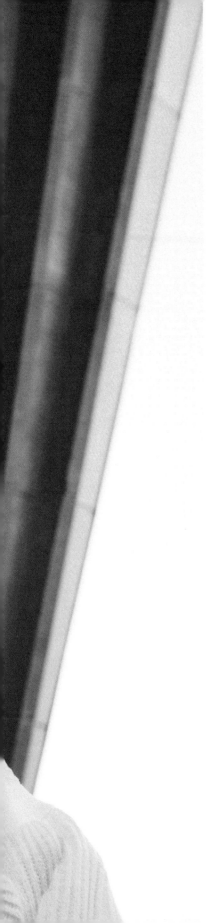

give the vineyard to others." When they heard this, they said, "Surely not!" [17] But he looked directly at them and said, "What then is this that is written:

" 'The stone that the builders rejected
has become the corner stone'?

[18]Everyone who falls on that stone will be broken to pieces, and when it falls on anyone, it will crush him."

Paying Taxes to Caesar

[19] The scribes and the chief priests sought to lay hands on him at that very hour, for they perceived that he had told this parable against them, but they feared the people. [20] So they watched him and sent spies, who pretended to be sincere, that they might catch him in something he said, so as to deliver him up to the authority and jurisdiction of the governor. [21] So they asked him, "Teacher, we know that you speak and teach rightly, and show no partiality, but truly teach the way of God. [22] Is it lawful for us to give tribute to Caesar, or not?" [23] But he perceived their craftiness, and said to them, [24]"Show me a denarius. Whose likeness and inscription does it have?" They said, "Caesar's." [25] He said to them, "Then render to Caesar the things that are Caesar's, and to God the things that are God's." [26] And they were not able in the presence of the people to catch him in what he said, but marvelling at his answer they became silent.

Sadducees Ask About the Resurrection

[27] There came to him some Sadducees, those who deny that there is a resurrection, [28] and they asked him a question, saying, "Teacher, Moses wrote for us that if a man's brother dies, having a wife but no children, the man must take the widow and raise up offspring for his brother. [29] Now there were seven brothers. The first took a wife, and died without children. [30] And the second [31] and the third took her, and likewise all seven left no children and died. [32] Afterwards the woman also died. [33] In the resurrection, therefore, whose wife will the woman be? For the seven had her as wife."

[34] And Jesus said to them, "The sons of this age marry and are given in marriage, [35]but those who are considered worthy to attain to that age and to the resurrection from the dead neither marry nor are given in marriage, [36]for they cannot die any more, because they are equal to angels and are sons of God, being sons of the resurrection. [37]But that the dead are raised, even Moses showed, in the passage about the bush, where he calls the Lord the God of Abraham and the God of Isaac and the God of Jacob. [38]Now he is not God of the dead, but of the living, for all live to him." [39] Then some of the scribes answered, "Teacher, you have spoken well." [40] For they no longer dared to ask him any question.

Whose Son Is the Christ?

[41] But he said to them, "How can they say that the Christ is David's son? [42]For David himself says in the Book of Psalms,

" 'The Lord said to my Lord,
"Sit at my right hand,
[43]   until I make your enemies
your footstool."'

[44]David thus calls him Lord, so how is he his son?"

Beware of the Scribes

[45] And in the hearing of all the people he said to his disciples, [46]"Beware of the scribes, who like to walk around in long robes, and love greetings in the market-places and the best seats in the synagogues and the places of honour at feasts, [47]who devour widows' houses and for a pretence make long prayers. They will receive the greater condemnation.

✝

Chapter Twenty-One
The Widow's Offering

**And he saw a poor widow put in two small copper coins.
And he said, "Truly, I tell you, this poor widow has put in more than all of them."**

Luke 21:2-3

Jesus looked up and saw the rich putting their gifts into the offering box, [2] and he saw a poor widow put in two small copper coins. [3] And he said, "Truly, I tell you, this poor widow has put in more than all of them. [4] For they all contributed out of their abundance, but she out of her poverty put in all she had to live on."

Jesus Foretells Destruction of the Temple

[5] And while some were speaking of the temple, how it was adorned with noble stones and offerings, he said, [6] "As for these things that you see, the days will come when there will not be left here one stone upon another that will not be thrown down." [7] And they asked him, "Teacher, when will these things be, and what will be the sign when these things are about to take place?" [8] And he said, "See that you are not led astray. For many will come in my name, saying, 'I am he!' and, 'The time is at hand!' Do not go after them. [9] And when you hear of wars and tumults, do not be terrified, for these things must first take place, but the end will not be at once."

Jesus Foretells Wars and Persecution

[10] Then he said to them, "Nation will rise against nation, and kingdom against kingdom. [11] There will be great earthquakes, and in various places famines and pestilences. And there will be terrors and great signs from heaven. [12] But before all this they will lay their hands on you and persecute you, delivering you up to the synagogues and prisons, and you will be brought before kings and governors for my name's sake. [13] This will be your opportunity to bear witness. [14] Settle it therefore in your minds not to meditate beforehand how to answer, [15] for I will give you a mouth and wisdom, which none of your adversaries will be able to withstand or contradict. [16] You will be delivered up even by parents and brothers and relatives and friends, and some of you they will put to death. [17] You will be hated by all for my name's sake. [18] But not a hair of your head will perish. [19] By your endurance you will gain your lives.

Jesus Foretells Destruction of Jerusalem

[20] "But when you see Jerusalem surrounded by armies, then know that its desolation has come near. [21] Then let those who are in Judea flee to the mountains, and let those who are inside the city depart, and let not those who are out in the country enter it, [22] for these are days of vengeance, to fulfil all that is written. [23] Alas for women who are pregnant and for those who are nursing infants in those days! For there will be great distress upon the earth and wrath against this people. [24] They will fall by the edge of the sword and be led captive among all nations, and Jerusalem will be trampled underfoot by the Gentiles, until the times of the Gentiles are fulfilled.

The Coming of the Son of Man

[25] "And there will be signs in sun and moon and stars, and on the earth distress of nations in perplexity because of the roaring of the sea and the waves, [26] people fainting with fear and with foreboding of what is coming on the world. For the powers of the heavens will be shaken. [27] And then they will see the Son of Man coming in a cloud with power and great glory. [28] Now when these things begin to take place, straighten up and raise your heads, because your redemption is drawing near."

The Lesson of the Fig Tree

[29] And he told them a parable: "Look at the fig tree, and all the trees. [30] As soon as they come out in leaf, you see for yourselves and know that the summer is already near. [31] So also, when you see these things taking place, you know that the kingdom of God is near. [32] Truly, I say to you, this generation will not pass away until all has taken place. [33] Heaven and earth will pass away, but my words will not pass away.

Watch Yourselves

[34] "But watch yourselves lest your hearts be weighed down with dissipation and drunkenness and cares of this life, and that day come upon you suddenly like a trap. [35] For it will come upon all who dwell on the face of the whole earth. [36] But stay awake at all times, praying that you may have strength to escape all these things that are going to take place, and to stand before the Son of Man."

[37] And every day he was teaching in the temple, but at night he went out and lodged on the mount called Olivet. [38] And early in the morning all the people came to him in the temple to hear him.

✝

Chapter Twenty-Two
The Plot to Kill Jesus

Now the Feast of Unleavened Bread drew near, which is called the Passover. ²And the chief priests and the scribes were seeking how to put him to death, for they feared the people.

Judas to Betray Jesus
³Then Satan entered into Judas called Iscariot, who was of the number of the twelve. ⁴He went away and conferred with the chief priests and officers how he might betray him to them. ⁵And they were glad, and agreed to give him money. ⁶So he consented and sought an opportunity to betray him to them in the absence of a crowd.

The Passover with the Disciples
⁷Then came the day of Unleavened Bread, on which the Passover lamb had to be sacrificed. ⁸So Jesus sent Peter and John, saying, "Go and prepare the Passover for us, that we may eat it." ⁹They said to him, "Where would you have us prepare it?" ¹⁰He said to them, "Behold, when you have entered the city, a man carrying a jar of water will meet you. Follow him into the house that he enters ¹¹and tell the master of the house, 'The Teacher says to you, Where is the guest room, where I may eat the Passover with my disciples?' ¹²And he will show you a large upper room furnished; prepare it there." ¹³And they went and found it just as he had told them, and they prepared the Passover.

Institution of the Lord's Supper
¹⁴And when the hour came, he reclined at table, and the apostles with him. ¹⁵And he said to them, "I have earnestly desired to eat this Passover with you before I suffer. ¹⁶For I tell you I will not eat it until it is fulfilled in the kingdom of God." ¹⁷And he took a cup, and when he had given thanks he said, "Take this, and divide it among yourselves. ¹⁸For I tell you that from now on I will not drink of the fruit of the vine until

the kingdom of God comes." ¹⁹ And he took bread, and when he had given thanks, he broke it and gave it to them, saying, "This is my body, which is given for you. Do this in remembrance of me." ²⁰ And likewise the cup after they had eaten, saying, "This cup that is poured out for you is the new covenant in my blood. ²¹ But behold, the hand of him who betrays me is with me on the table. ²² For the Son of Man goes as it has been determined, but woe to that man by whom he is betrayed!" ²³ And they began to question one another, which of them it could be who was going to do this.

Who Is the Greatest?

²⁴ A dispute also arose among them, as to which of them was to be regarded as the greatest. ²⁵ And he said to them, "The kings of the Gentiles exercise lordship over them, and those in authority over them are called benefactors. ²⁶ But not so with you. Rather, let the greatest among you become as the youngest, and the leader as one who serves. ²⁷ For who is the greater, one who reclines at table or one who serves? Is it not the one who reclines at table? But I am among you as the one who serves.

²⁸ "You are those who have stayed with me in my trials, ²⁹ and I assign to you, as my Father assigned to me, a kingdom, ³⁰ that you may eat and drink at my table in my kingdom and sit on thrones judging the twelve tribes of Israel.

Jesus Foretells Peter's Denial

³¹ "Simon, Simon, behold, Satan demanded to have you, that he might sift you like wheat, ³² but I have prayed for you that your faith may not fail. And when you have turned again, strengthen your brothers." ³³ Peter said to him, "Lord, I am ready to go with you both to prison and to death." ³⁴ Jesus said, "I tell you, Peter, the cock will not crow this day, until you deny three times that you know me."

Scripture Must Be Fulfilled in Jesus

³⁵ And he said to them, "When I sent you out with no money bag or knapsack or sandals, did you lack anything?" They said, "Nothing." ³⁶ He said to them, "But now let the one who has a money bag take it, and likewise a knapsack. And let the one who has no sword sell his cloak and buy one. ³⁷ For I tell you that this Scripture must be fulfilled in me: 'And he was numbered with the transgressors.' For what is written about me has its fulfilment." ³⁸ And they said, "Look, Lord, here are two swords." And he said to them, "It is enough."

Jesus Prays on the Mount of Olives

³⁹ And he came out and went, as was his custom, to the Mount of Olives, and the disciples followed him. ⁴⁰ And when he came to the place, he said to them, "Pray that you may not enter into temptation." ⁴¹ And he withdrew from them about a stone's throw, and knelt down and prayed, ⁴² saying, "Father, if you are willing, remove this cup from me. Nevertheless, not my will, but yours, be done." ⁴³ And there appeared to him an angel from heaven, strengthening him. ⁴⁴ And being in agony he prayed more earnestly; and his sweat became like great drops of blood falling down to the ground. ⁴⁵ And when he rose from prayer, he came to the disciples and found them sleeping for sorrow, ⁴⁶ and he

said to them, "Why are you sleeping? Rise and pray that you may not enter into temptation."

Betrayal and Arrest of Jesus

[47] While he was still speaking, there came a crowd, and the man called Judas, one of the twelve, was leading them. He drew near to Jesus to kiss him, [48] but Jesus said to him, "Judas, would you betray the Son of Man with a kiss?" [49] And when those who were around him saw what would follow, they said, "Lord, shall we strike with the sword?" [50] And one of them struck the servant of the high priest and cut off his right ear. [51] But Jesus said, "No more of this!" And he touched his ear and healed him. [52] Then Jesus said to the chief priests and officers of the temple and elders, who had come out against him, "Have you come out as against a robber, with swords and clubs? [53] When I was with you day after day in the temple, you did not lay hands on me. But this is your hour, and the power of darkness."

Peter Denies Jesus

[54] Then they seized him and led him away, bringing him into the high priest's house, and Peter was following at a distance. [55] And when they had kindled a fire in the middle of the courtyard and sat down together, Peter sat down among them. [56] Then a servant girl, seeing him as he sat in the light and looking closely at him, said, "This man also was with him." [57] But he denied it, saying, "Woman, I do not know him." [58] And a little later someone else saw him and said, "You also are one of them." But Peter said, "Man, I am not." [59] And after an interval of about an hour still another insisted, saying, "Certainly this man also was with him, for he too is a Galilean." [60] But Peter said, "Man, I do not know what you are talking about." And immediately, while he was still speaking, the cock crowed. [61] And the Lord turned and looked at Peter. And Peter remembered the saying of the Lord, how he had said to him, "Before the cock crows today, you will deny me three times." [62] And he went out and wept bitterly.

Jesus Is Mocked

[63] Now the men who were holding Jesus in custody were mocking him as they beat him. [64] They also blindfolded him and kept asking him, "Prophesy! Who is it that struck you?" [65] And they said many other things against him, blaspheming him.

Jesus Before the Council

[66] When day came, the assembly of the elders of the people gathered together, both chief priests and scribes. And they led him away to their council, and they said, [67] "If you are the Christ, tell us." But he said to them, "If I tell you, you will not believe, [68] and if I ask you, you will not answer. [69] But from now on the Son of Man shall be seated at the right hand of the power of God." [70] So they all said, "Are you the Son of God, then?" And he said to them, "You say that I am." [71] Then they said, "What further testimony do we need? We have heard it ourselves from his own lips."

AND ONE OF THEM STRUCK THE SERVANT OF THE HIGH PRIEST AND CUT OFF HIS RIGHT EAR. BUT JESUS SAID, "NO MORE OF THIS!" AND HE TOUCHED HIS EAR AND HEALED HIM. Luke 22:50-51

Chapter Twenty-Three
Jesus Before Pilate

Then the whole company of them arose and brought him before Pilate. ² And they began to accuse him, saying, "We found this man misleading our nation and forbidding us to give tribute to Caesar, and saying that he himself is Christ, a king." ³ And Pilate asked him, "Are you the King of the Jews?" And he answered him, "You have said so." ⁴ Then Pilate said to the chief priests and the crowds, "I find no guilt in this man." ⁵ But they were urgent, saying, "He stirs up the people, teaching throughout all Judea, from Galilee even to this place."

Jesus Before Herod
⁶ When Pilate heard this, he asked whether the man was a Galilean. ⁷ And when he learned that he belonged to Herod's jurisdiction, he sent him over to Herod, who was himself in Jerusalem at that time. ⁸ When Herod saw Jesus, he was very glad, for he had long desired to see him, because he had heard about him, and he was hoping to see some sign done by him. ⁹ So he questioned him at some length, but he made no answer. ¹⁰ The chief priests and the scribes stood by, vehemently accusing him. ¹¹ And Herod with his soldiers treated him with contempt and mocked him. Then, arraying him in splendid clothing, he sent him back to Pilate. ¹² And Herod and Pilate became friends with each other that very day, for before this they had been at enmity with each other.

¹³ Pilate then called together the chief priests and the rulers and the people, ¹⁴ and said to them, "You brought me this man as one who was misleading

THEN PILATE SAID TO THE CHIEF PRIESTS AND THE CROWDS, "I FIND NO GUILT IN THIS MAN."

Luke 23:4

the people. And after examining him before you, behold, I did not find this man guilty of any of your charges against him. ¹⁵ Neither did Herod, for he sent him back to us. Look, nothing deserving death has been done by him. ¹⁶ I will therefore punish and release him."

Pilate Delivers Jesus to Be Crucified

¹⁸ But they all cried out together, "Away with this man, and release to us Barabbas"— ¹⁹ a man who had been thrown into prison for an insurrection started in the city and for murder. ²⁰ Pilate addressed them once more, desiring to release Jesus, ²¹ but they kept shouting, "Crucify, crucify him!" ²² A third time he said to them, "Why? What evil has he done? I have found in him no guilt deserving death. I will therefore punish and release him." ²³ But they were urgent, demanding with loud cries that he should be crucified. And their voices prevailed. ²⁴ So Pilate decided that their demand should be granted. ²⁵ He released the man who had been thrown into prison for insurrection and murder, for whom they asked, but he delivered Jesus over to their will.

The Crucifixion

²⁶ And as they led him away, they seized one Simon of Cyrene, who was coming in from the country, and laid on him the cross, to carry it behind Jesus. ²⁷ And there followed him a great multitude of the people and of women who were mourning and lamenting for him. ²⁸ But turning to them Jesus said, "Daughters of Jerusalem, do not weep for me, but weep for yourselves and for your children. ²⁹ For behold, the days are coming when they will say, 'Blessed are the barren and the wombs that never bore and the breasts that never nursed!' ³⁰ Then they will begin to say to the mountains, 'Fall on us,' and to the hills, 'Cover us.' ³¹ For if they do these things when the wood is green, what will happen when it is dry?"

WHILE THE SUN'S LIGHT FAILED AND THE CURTAIN OF THE TEMPLE WAS TORN IN TWO. THEN JESUS, CALLING OUT WITH A LOUD VOICE SAID, "FATHER, INTO YOUR HANDS I COMMIT MY SPIRIT." AND HAVING SAID THIS HE BREATHED HIS LAST.

Luke 23:45-46

³² Two others, who were criminals, were led away to be put to death with him. ³³ And when they came to the place that is called The Skull, there they crucified him, and the criminals, one on his right and one on his left. ³⁴ And Jesus said, "Father, forgive them, for they know not what they do." And they cast lots to divide his garments. ³⁵ And the people stood by, watching, but the rulers scoffed at him, saying, "He saved others; let him save himself, if he is the Christ of God, his Chosen One!" ³⁶ The soldiers also mocked him, coming up and offering him sour wine ³⁷ and saying, "If you are the King of the Jews, save yourself!" ³⁸ There was also an inscription over him, "This is the King of the Jews."

³⁹ One of the criminals who were hanged railed at him, saying, "Are you not the Christ? Save yourself and us!" ⁴⁰ But the other rebuked him, saying, "Do you not fear God, since you are under the same sentence of condemnation? ⁴¹ And we indeed justly, for we are receiving the due reward of our deeds; but this man has done nothing wrong." ⁴² And he said, "Jesus, remember me when you come into your kingdom." ⁴³ And he said to him, "Truly, I say to you, today you will be with me in paradise."

The Death of Jesus

⁴⁴ It was now about the sixth hour, and there was darkness over the whole land until the ninth hour, ⁴⁵ while the sun's light failed. And the curtain of the temple was torn in two. ⁴⁶ Then Jesus, calling out with a loud voice, said, "Father, into your hands I commit my spirit!" And having said this he breathed his last. ⁴⁷ Now when the centurion saw what had taken place, he praised God, saying, "Certainly this man was innocent!" ⁴⁸ And all the crowds that had assembled for this spectacle, when they saw what had taken place, returned home beating their breasts. ⁴⁹ And all his acquaintances and the women who had followed him from Galilee stood at a distance watching these things.

Jesus Is Buried

⁵⁰ Now there was a man named Joseph, from the Jewish town of Arimathea. He was a member of the council, a good and righteous man, ⁵¹ who had not consented to their decision and action; and he was looking for the kingdom of God. ⁵² This man went to Pilate and asked for the body of Jesus. ⁵³ Then he took it down and wrapped it in a linen shroud and laid him in a tomb cut in stone, where no one had ever yet been laid. ⁵⁴ It was the day of Preparation, and the Sabbath was beginning. ⁵⁵ The women who had come with him from Galilee followed and saw the tomb and how his body was laid. ⁵⁶ Then they returned and prepared spices and ointments.

On the Sabbath they rested according to the commandment.

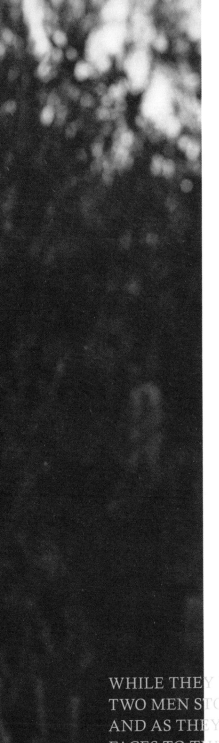

Chapter Twenty-Four

The Resurrection

But on the first day of the week, at early dawn, they went to the tomb, taking the spices they had prepared. ²And they found the stone rolled away from the tomb, ³but when they went in they did not find the body of the Lord Jesus. ⁴While they were perplexed about this, behold, two men stood by them in dazzling apparel. ⁵And as they were frightened and bowed their faces to the ground, the men said to them, "Why do you seek the living among the dead? ⁶He is not here, but has risen. Remember how he told you, while he was still in Galilee, ⁷that the Son of Man must be delivered into the hands of sinful men and be crucified and on the third day rise." ⁸And they remembered his words, ⁹and returning from the tomb they told all these things to the eleven and to all the rest. ¹⁰Now it was Mary Magdalene and Joanna and Mary the mother of James and the other women with them who told these things to the apostles, ¹¹but these words seemed to them an idle tale, and they did not believe them. ¹²But Peter rose and ran to the tomb; stooping and looking in, he saw the linen cloths by themselves; and he went home marvelling at what had happened.

On the Road to Emmaus

¹³That very day two of them were going to a village named Emmaus, about seven miles from Jerusalem, ¹⁴and they were talking with each other about all these things that had happened. ¹⁵While they were talking and discussing together, Jesus himself drew near and went with them. ¹⁶But their eyes were kept from recognizing him. ¹⁷And he said to them, "What is this conversation that you are holding with each other as you walk?" And they stood still, looking sad. ¹⁸Then one of them, named Cleopas, answered him, "Are you the only visitor to Jerusalem who does not know the things that have happened there in these days?" ¹⁹And he said to them, "What things?" And they said to him, "Concerning Jesus of Nazareth, a man who was a prophet mighty in deed and word before God and all the people, ²⁰and how our chief priests and rulers delivered him up to be condemned to death, and crucified him. ²¹But we had hoped that he was the one to redeem Israel. Yes, and besides all this, it is now the third day since these things happened. ²²Moreover, some women of our company amazed us. They were at the tomb early in the

WHILE THEY WERE PERPLEXED ABOUT THIS, BEHOLD,
TWO MEN STOOD BY THEM IN DAZZLING APPAREL.
AND AS THEY WERE FRIGHTENED AND BOWED THEIR
FACES TO THE GROUND, THE MEN SAID TO THEM,
"WHY DO YOU SEEK THE LIVING AMONG THE DEAD?"

Luke 24:4-5

morning, [23] and when they did not find his body, they came back saying that they had even seen a vision of angels, who said that he was alive. [24] Some of those who were with us went to the tomb and found it just as the women had said, but him they did not see." [25] And he said to them, "O foolish ones, and slow of heart to believe all that the prophets have spoken! [26] Was it not necessary that the Christ should suffer these things and enter into his glory?" [27] And beginning with Moses and all the Prophets, he interpreted to them in all the Scriptures the things concerning himself.

[28] So they drew near to the village to which they were going. He acted as if he were going farther, [29] but they urged him strongly, saying, "Stay with us, for it is towards evening and the day is now far spent." So he went in to stay with them. [30] When he was at table with them, he took the bread and blessed and broke it and gave it to them. [31] And their eyes were opened, and they recognized him. And he vanished from their sight. [32] They said to each other, "Did not our hearts burn within us while he talked to us on the road, while he opened to us the Scriptures?" [33] And they rose that same hour and returned to Jerusalem. And they found the eleven and those who were with them gathered together, [34] saying, "The Lord has risen indeed, and has appeared to Simon!" [35] Then they told what had happened on the road, and how he was known to them in the breaking of the bread.

Jesus Appears to His Disciples

[36] As they were talking about these things, Jesus himself stood among them, and said to them, "Peace to you!" [37] But they were startled and frightened and thought they saw a spirit. [38] And he said to them, "Why are you troubled, and why do doubts arise in your hearts? [39] See my hands and my feet, that it is I myself. Touch me, and see. For a spirit

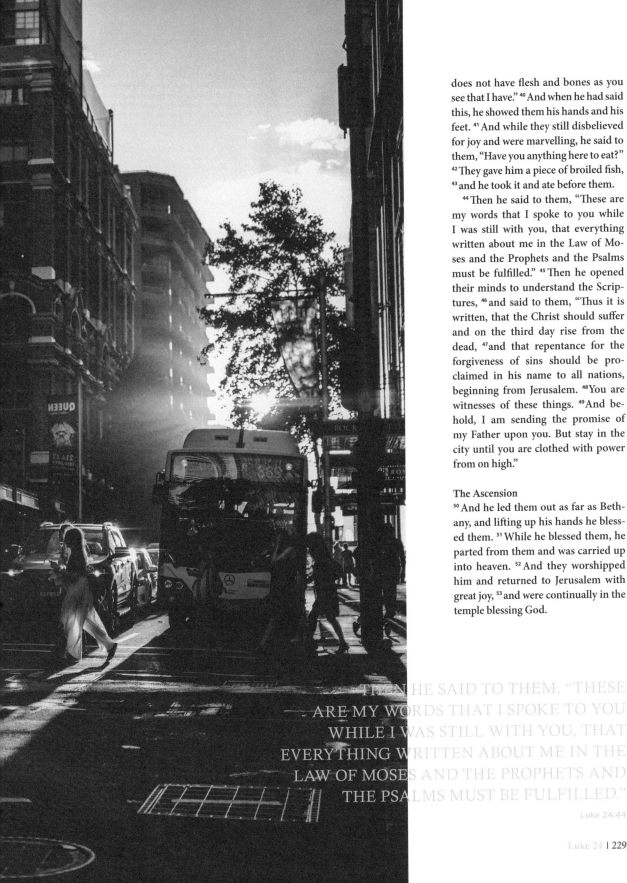

does not have flesh and bones as you see that I have." ⁴⁰ And when he had said this, he showed them his hands and his feet. ⁴¹ And while they still disbelieved for joy and were marvelling, he said to them, "Have you anything here to eat?" ⁴² They gave him a piece of broiled fish, ⁴³ and he took it and ate before them.

⁴⁴ Then he said to them, "These are my words that I spoke to you while I was still with you, that everything written about me in the Law of Moses and the Prophets and the Psalms must be fulfilled." ⁴⁵ Then he opened their minds to understand the Scriptures, ⁴⁶ and said to them, "Thus it is written, that the Christ should suffer and on the third day rise from the dead, ⁴⁷ and that repentance for the forgiveness of sins should be proclaimed in his name to all nations, beginning from Jerusalem. ⁴⁸ You are witnesses of these things. ⁴⁹ And behold, I am sending the promise of my Father upon you. But stay in the city until you are clothed with power from on high."

The Ascension

⁵⁰ And he led them out as far as Bethany, and lifting up his hands he blessed them. ⁵¹ While he blessed them, he parted from them and was carried up into heaven. ⁵² And they worshipped him and returned to Jerusalem with great joy, ⁵³ and were continually in the temple blessing God.

THEN HE SAID TO THEM, "THESE ARE MY WORDS THAT I SPOKE TO YOU WHILE I WAS STILL WITH YOU, THAT EVERYTHING WRITTEN ABOUT ME IN THE LAW OF MOSES AND THE PROPHETS AND THE PSALMS MUST BE FULFILLED."

Luke 24:44

Inspired by the Holy Spirit

EXPERIENCE LUKE

JESUS IS THE PINNACLE OF SALVATION HISTORY

AND JESUS SAID TO HIM, "TODAY SALVATION HAS COME TO THIS HOUSE, SINCE HE ALSO IS A SON OF ABRAHAM. FOR THE SON OF MAN CAME TO SEEK AND TO SAVE THE LOST."
Luke 19:9-10

HOW LUKE FITS INTO GOD'S STORY AND MY STORY
God acts in history and his actions aren't myth or legend, but verifiable history.
As Jesus lived and breathed in the flesh, so also his life empowers the way I live now.

KEY CHARACTERS
Jesus, Mary the mother of Jesus, John the Baptist, Mary Magdalene, Peter, Scribes and Pharisees, Zacchaeus

LUKE IS A BIOGRAPHY OF JESUS FROM THE PERSPECTIVE OF HIS FOLLOWERS.

KEY WORD IN LUKE: HISTORY

Greek: διήγησις, *diēgēsis*, narrative, account

At the very beginning of Luke's Gospel he calls his work an "orderly account". This is a technical term in the ancient world signalling that the author is interested in a particular type of history. The type of history that Luke is interested in is a combination of ancient Jewish history (with its focus on God's work and salvation) and Graeco-Roman history (along with stylistic features from ancient novels, etc.). History in the ancient world was not like what we think of history today (dates, numbers, "facts" and so on). It was based on important witnesses and events, but it was not concerned with a comprehensive exhaustive snapshot of a person's life. Luke is a biography of Jesus from the perspective of his followers. It is a construction of his life to the best of the author's ability. The reason why history is so important for Luke is because of God's salvation plan since Abraham to bring salvation to Israel and then to all the nations. Jesus is the fulfilment of this history and therefore deserves special attention.

LUKE: QUICK FACTS

• Luke is actually the first part of a single work. The second part of Luke is the Book of Acts. The two are companion volumes and should be read as such. • Probably written by a Jewish Christian who had an advanced education and a profound knowledge of the Hebrew Bible. • Written sometime near the end of the first century. • By the time Luke was written it is likely that the Gospels were intended for wide circulation around the Mediterranean. • While Jesus is the main character (the protagonist) in Luke's Gospel, in Acts some argue that the Holy Spirit replaces Jesus at the protagonist of the story. • Luke's narrative is shaped by a long journey to Jerusalem (about 10 chapters), filled with teaching and parables.

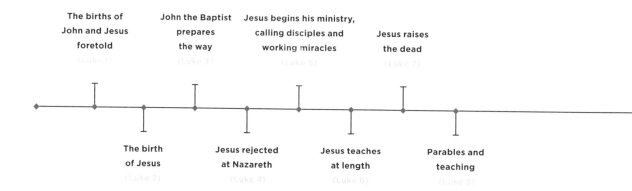

The births of John and Jesus foretold (Luke 1)

John the Baptist prepares the way (Luke 3)

Jesus begins his ministry, calling disciples and working miracles (Luke 5)

Jesus raises the dead (Luke 7)

The birth of Jesus (Luke 2)

Jesus rejected at Nazareth (Luke 4)

Jesus teaches at length (Luke 6)

Parables and teaching (Luke 8)

UNIQUE PATTERN: THE ROLE OF WOMEN IN JESUS' MINISTRY

Out of all the other Gospel writers, Luke spends the most amount of time including women in his story. Some of the unique material that Luke has are his stories of women. They are not always presented in a positive light. However, those that are presented positively show how valuable women were to Jesus' ministry. Mary, Jesus' mother, is shown to trust God faithfully (Luke 1-2). She is also, more significantly, an important treasurer of memories about Jesus' teaching and life. In Luke 8:1-3, Luke refers to a number of different women who are named (the majority of women in other Gospels go unnamed). Mary Magdalene, Joanna, Chuza, Susanna and others—all are named as benefactors (people who supply material and financial means) for Jesus' ministry. Lastly, two women named Martha and Mary are able to sit at Jesus' feet and to learn (Luke 10:38-42). Women rarely had a formal education in the ancient world, especially Jewish women (their education mostly consisted of learning at home or at the synagogue). To sit and learn at a rabbi's feet was socially progressive and unusual for the time. Such women had a special role in Jesus' ministry and in establishing the early tradition about his life. Without such women Luke's rich and beautiful history of Jesus would not have been the same.

WOMEN RARELY HAD A FORMAL EDUCATION
IN THE ANCIENT WORLD, ESPECIALLY JEWISH
WOMEN (THEIR EDUCATION MOSTLY CONSISTED
OF LEARNING AT HOME OR AT THE SYNAGOGUE).
TO SIT AND LEARN AT A RABBI'S FEET WAS
SOCIALLY PROGRESSIVE AND UNUSUAL FOR THE
TIME. SUCH WOMEN HAD A SPECIAL ROLE IN
JESUS' MINISTRY AND IN ESTABLISHING THE
EARLY TRADITION ABOUT HIS LIFE.

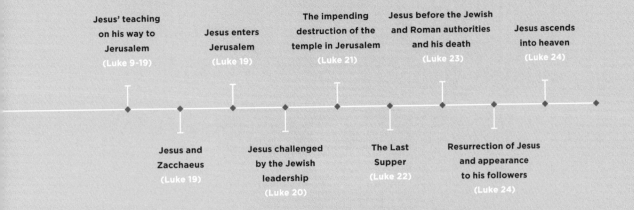

Jesus' teaching on his way to Jerusalem (Luke 9-19)

Jesus enters Jerusalem (Luke 19)

The impending destruction of the temple in Jerusalem (Luke 21)

Jesus before the Jewish and Roman authorities and his death (Luke 23)

Jesus ascends into heaven (Luke 24)

Jesus and Zacchaeus (Luke 19)

Jesus challenged by the Jewish leadership (Luke 20)

The Last Supper (Luke 22)

Resurrection of Jesus and appearance to his followers (Luke 24)

KEY THEME: WITNESSES AND TESTIMONY

Since Luke is interested in history he relies upon both earlier traditions (Mark's Gospel, oral tradition) and eyewitness testimony. Mary, Jesus' mother, was a treasurer of Jesus memories. In Acts, the companion volume to Luke's Gospel, the disciples (the main leaders of the early Christian movement) were chosen because they had been eyewitnesses to Jesus' ministry from John the Baptist until his resurrection (Acts 1:21-22). The importance of eyewitnesses is obvious. Jesus did a lot of unexplainable things, things that even the natural sciences today struggle to accept. Of course, they cannot be confirmed in the same way that we can look into a microscope today. We rely on the testimony of ancient witnesses. The early Christians were careful about what information passed along in tradition was "true" and what was "fictional". For the Gospel material, their content was accepted as authoritative very early on (within 50-100 years of Jesus' death). The reliability of the Gospel tradition was established by those who were in contact with Jesus himself or by those who knew those who were in contact with Jesus.

JOHN

THE NEW TESTAMENT EXPERIENCE

JESUS IS GOD

WRITTEN BY JOHN THE EVANGELIST

THERE WAS A MAN SENT FROM GOD, WHOSE NAME WAS JOHN. HE CAME AS A WITNESS,
TO BEAR WITNESS ABOUT THE LIGHT, THAT ALL MIGHT BELIEVE THROUGH HIM. HE WAS NOT THE LIGHT,
BUT CAME TO BEAR WITNESS ABOUT THE LIGHT. John 1:6-8

IMPORTANT STORIES IN JOHN

The Testimony of John the Baptist: John 1:19-23 **Jesus and the Woman of Samaria:** John 4:7-42
Jesus Feeds the Five Thousand: John 6:5-14 **The Women Caught in Adultery:** John 8:3-11 **The Death of Lazarus:** John 11:1-44
Jesus Washes the Disciples' Feet: John 13:4-17 **The High Priestly Prayer:** John 17:1-26 **The Crucifixion:** John 19:16-30
Jesus Appears to Mary Magdalene: John 20:11-18 **Jesus and the Beloved Apostle:** John 21:20-25

INTRODUCTION
TO JOHN

BOGOTÁ, COLOMBIA

AUTHOR, DATE AND AUDIENCE

John the son of Zebedee wrote this Gospel. He was a Palestinian Jew, one of the twelve disciples, and a member of Jesus' inner apostolic circle. He was referred to as the disciple "whom Jesus loved" (13:23). John also wrote 1–3 John and Revelation. He probably wrote his Gospel account between AD 70 (the date of the destruction of the temple) and AD 100 (the reputed end of John's life). It was probably written from Ephesus in Asia Minor (modern-day Turkey), one of the most important cities of the Roman Empire at the time. His original audience consisted of Jews and non-Jewish Christians living in the larger Greco-Roman world in Ephesus and beyond, towards the close of the first century AD.

THEME AND PURPOSE

The theme of John's Gospel is that Jesus is the long-awaited, promised Messiah and Son of God. By believing in Jesus, people have eternal life (see 20:30–31).

As evidence that Jesus is the Messiah, John relies on several selected messianic signs performed by Jesus and a series of witnesses to Jesus. These include the Scriptures, John the Baptist, Jesus himself, God the Father, Jesus' miraculous works, the Holy Spirit and John himself.

THE WOMAN SAID TO HIM,
"I KNOW THAT MESSIAH IS COMING (HE WHO
IS CALLED CHRIST). WHEN HE COMES, HE
WILL TELL US ALL THINGS." JESUS SAID TO
HER, "I WHO SPEAK TO YOU AM HE."

John 4:25-26

Chapter One
The Word Became Flesh

In the beginning was the Word, and the Word was with God, and the Word was God. [2] He was in the beginning with God. [3] All things were made through him, and without him was not any thing made that was made. [4] In him was life, and the life was the light of men. [5] The light shines in the darkness, and the darkness has not overcome it.

[6] There was a man sent from God, whose name was John. [7] He came as a witness, to bear witness about the light, that all might believe through him. [8] He was not the light, but came to bear witness about the light.

[9] The true light, which gives light to everyone, was coming into the world. [10] He was in the world, and the world was made through him, yet the world did not know him. [11] He came to his own, and his own people did not receive

him. ¹²But to all who did receive him, who believed in his name, he gave the right to become children of God, ¹³who were born, not of blood nor of the will of the flesh nor of the will of man, but of God.

¹⁴And the Word became flesh and dwelt among us, and we have seen his glory, glory as of the only Son from the Father, full of grace and truth. ¹⁵(John bore witness about him, and cried out, "This was he of whom I said, 'He who comes after me ranks before me, because he was before me.'") ¹⁶For from his fullness we have all received, grace upon grace. ¹⁷For the law was given through Moses; grace and truth came through Jesus Christ. ¹⁸No one has ever seen God; the only God, who is at the Father's side, he has made him known.

THE ONLY SON
FROM THE FATHER

THE WORD BECAME FLESH AND DWELT AMONG US, AND WE HAVE SEEN HIS GLORY, GLORY AS OF THE ONLY SON FROM THE FATHER, FULL OF GRACE AND TRUTH.

John 1:14

THE NEXT DAY HE SAW JESUS COMING TOWARDS HIM, AND SAID, "BEHOLD, THE LAMB OF GOD, WHO TAKES AWAY THE SIN OF THE WORLD! THIS IS HE OF WHOM I SAID, 'AFTER ME COMES A MAN WHO RANKS BEFORE ME, BECAUSE HE WAS BEFORE ME.' I MYSELF DID NOT KNOW HIM, BUT FOR THIS PURPOSE I CAME BAPTIZING WITH WATER, THAT HE MIGHT BE REVEALED TO ISRAEL." John 1:29-31

The Testimony of John the Baptist

¹⁹And this is the testimony of John, when the Jews sent priests and Levites from Jerusalem to ask him, "Who are you?" ²⁰He confessed, and did not deny, but confessed, "I am not the Christ." ²¹And they asked him, "What then? Are you Elijah?" He said, "I am not." "Are you the Prophet?" And he answered, "No." ²²So they said to him, "Who are you? We need to give an answer to those who sent us. What do you say about yourself?" ²³He said, "I am the voice of one crying out in the wilderness, 'Make straight the way of the Lord', as the prophet Isaiah said."

²⁴(Now they had been sent from the Pharisees.) ²⁵They asked him, "Then why are you baptizing, if you are neither the Christ, nor Elijah, nor the Prophet?" ²⁶John answered them, "I baptize with water, but among you stands one you do not know, ²⁷even he who comes after me, the strap of whose sandal I am not worthy to untie." ²⁸These things took place in Bethany across the Jordan, where John was baptizing.

Behold, the Lamb of God

²⁹The next day he saw Jesus coming towards him, and said, "Behold, the Lamb of God, who takes away the sin of the world! ³⁰This is he of whom I said, 'After me comes a man who ranks

before me, because he was before me.' [31] I myself did not know him, but for this purpose I came baptizing with water, that he might be revealed to Israel." [32] And John bore witness: "I saw the Spirit descend from heaven like a dove, and it remained on him. [33] I myself did not know him, but he who sent me to baptize with water said to me, 'He on whom you see the Spirit descend and remain, this is he who baptizes with the Holy Spirit.' [34] And I have seen and have borne witness that this is the Son of God."

Jesus Calls the First Disciples

[35] The next day again John was standing with two of his disciples, [36] and he looked at Jesus as he walked by and said, "Behold, the Lamb of God!" [37] The two disciples heard him say this, and they followed Jesus. [38] Jesus turned and saw them following and said to them, "What are you seeking?" And they said to him, "Rabbi" (which means Teacher), "where are you staying?" [39] He said to them, "Come and you will see." So they came and saw where he was staying, and they stayed with him that day, for it was about the tenth hour. [40] One of the two who heard John speak and followed Jesus was

Andrew, Simon Peter's brother. ⁴¹ He first found his own brother Simon and said to him, "We have found the Messiah" (which means Christ). ⁴² He brought him to Jesus. Jesus looked at him and said, "You are Simon the son of John. You shall be called Cephas" (which means Peter).

Jesus Calls Philip and Nathanael

⁴³ The next day Jesus decided to go to Galilee. He found Philip and said to him, "Follow me." ⁴⁴ Now Philip was from Bethsaida, the city of Andrew and Peter. ⁴⁵ Philip found Nathanael and said to him, "We have found him of whom Moses in the Law and also the prophets wrote, Jesus of Nazareth, the son of Joseph." ⁴⁶ Nathanael said to him, "Can anything good come out of Nazareth?" Philip said to him, "Come and see." ⁴⁷ Jesus saw Nathanael coming towards him and said of him, "Behold, an Israelite indeed, in whom there is no deceit!" ⁴⁸ Nathanael said to him, "How do you know me?" Jesus answered him, "Before Philip called you, when you were under the fig tree, I saw you." ⁴⁹ Nathanael answered him, "Rabbi, you are the Son of God! You are the King of Israel!" ⁵⁰ Jesus answered him, "Because I said to you, 'I saw you under the fig tree', do you believe? You will see greater things than these." ⁵¹ And he said to him, "Truly, truly, I say to you, you will see heaven opened, and the angels of God ascending and descending on the Son of Man."

"I MYSELF DID NOT KNOW HIM, BUT HE WHO SENT ME TO BAPTIZE WITH WATER SAID TO ME, 'HE ON WHOM YOU SEE THE SPIRIT DESCEND AND REMAIN, THIS IS HE WHO BAPTIZES WITH THE HOLY SPIRIT.' AND I HAVE SEEN AND HAVE BORNE WITNESS THAT THIS IS THE SON OF GOD."

John 1:33-34

Chapter Two
The Wedding at Cana

This, the first of his signs, Jesus did at Cana in Galilee, and manifested his glory. And his disciples believed in him.
John 2:11

On the third day there was a wedding at Cana in Galilee, and the mother of Jesus was there. ² Jesus also was invited to the wedding with his disciples. ³ When the wine ran out, the mother of Jesus said to him, "They have no wine." ⁴ And Jesus said to her, "Woman, what does this have to do with me? My hour has not yet come." ⁵ His mother said to the servants, "Do whatever he tells you."

⁶ Now there were six stone water jars there for the Jewish rites of purification, each holding twenty or thirty gallons. ⁷ Jesus said to the servants, "Fill the jars with water." And they filled them up to the brim. ⁸ And he said to them, "Now draw some out and take it to the master of the feast." So they took it. ⁹ When the master of the feast tasted the water now become wine, and did not know where it came from (though the servants who had drawn the water knew), the master of the feast called the bridegroom ¹⁰ and said to him, "Everyone serves the good wine first, and when people have drunk freely, then the poor wine. But you have kept the good wine until now." ¹¹ This, the first of his signs, Jesus did at Cana in Galilee, and manifested his glory. And his disciples believed in him.

¹² After this he went down to Capernaum, with his mother and his brothers and his disciples, and they stayed there for a few days.

Jesus Cleanses the Temple
¹³ The Passover of the Jews was at hand, and Jesus went up to Jerusalem. ¹⁴ In the temple he found those who were selling oxen and sheep and pigeons, and the money-changers sitting there. ¹⁵ And making a whip of cords, he drove them all out of the temple, with the sheep and oxen. And he poured out the coins of the money-changers and overturned their tables. ¹⁶ And he told those who sold the pigeons, "Take these things away; do not make my Father's house a house of trade." ¹⁷ His disciples remembered that it was written, "Zeal for your house will consume me."

¹⁸ So the Jews said to him, "What sign do you show us for doing these things?" ¹⁹ Jesus answered them, "Destroy this temple, and in three days I will raise it up." ²⁰ The Jews then said, "It has taken forty-six years to build this temple, and will you raise it up in three days?" ²¹ But he was speaking about the temple of his body. ²² When therefore he was raised from the dead, his disciples remembered that he had said this, and they believed the Scripture and the word that Jesus had spoken.

Jesus Knows What Is in Man
²³ Now when he was in Jerusalem at the Passover Feast, many believed in his name when they saw the signs that he was doing. ²⁴ But Jesus on his part did not entrust himself to them, because he knew all people ²⁵ and needed no one to bear witness about man, for he himself knew what was in man.

THE BIBLE

GOD-BREATHED

In the world of literature, no book has sold more copies and been translated into more languages than the Bible. The Bible has been quoted in some of the most significant speeches of history, it's commonly referenced in popular culture and it has formed the basis of many of the laws and customs of the western world. It is an inspiration for many, whether Christian or not, yet it has historically been greatly misunderstood.

For some, the Bible is just an inspirational book; a useful guide for navigating life. Perhaps you picked up this Bible with curiosity, not sure quite what you make of it or what to think of it. Or perhaps you picked up a copy wanting to understand more of what the Bible is and teaches.

As Christians, we believe the Bible is the "word of God". That doesn't mean that God himself wrote the Bible out in its entirety, as the Bible was written by

different people of different occupations, in different countries, in different languages, across different genres of literature. So, the Bible is not God-written, but it is God-breathed, as 2 Timothy 3:16 tells us when it says "all Scripture is breathed out by God and profitable for teaching, for reproof, for correction, and for training in righteousness". What this means is that God worked through people to produce the Bible: an eclectic mix of history, letters, poetry, wisdom literature and prophecy weaved together by the Spirit of God to produce a coherent message which spans all 66 books. There is no parallel for the literary consistency of such a diverse collection of works, which was written over a staggering 1500 years!

The Bible is a library of books, which is divided into two sections; the Old Testament, which was compiled before Jesus was born, and the New Testament, which was compiled after Jesus died and rose again. The Old Testament tells the story of God creating the world, the introduction of sin, humanity's rebellion against God and God's actions of entering into the world to give his people of Israel a way of living life through the law. The New Testament tells the story of Jesus' life, death, resurrection and the beginning of the church.

The enduring message of the Bible is that God is calling each of us to himself and that he desires a relationship with each and every one of us. It is from the Bible that we discover who God is, who we are and what we are here on earth to do. Whether we read Genesis, the first book of the Bible, or Revelation, the last book of the Bible, the whole Bible tells the same story of God's love and his pursuit of humanity. He desires to redeem all of creation back to himself, which he made possible through the pinnacle moment of Jesus' death and resurrection.

The fact that the Bible is God's Word truly makes it the most valuable object in the world. Surely no object on earth could compare to the fact that we have the words of the creator God available to us on a daily basis! The amazing thing is that we can access the Bible at any time and in any place, knowing that God can speak into our lives through his written Word.

There is an incredible depth and amount of wisdom in the Bible, and for that reason people can often be unsure of where to start when it comes to reading the Bible. One good way to begin is by using the 'SOAP' structure. It's a memorable structure that you can apply to your Bible reading, whatever it is that you decide to read:

SCRIPTURE
Start with a passage from the Bible. You can start anywhere, but if it's your first time opening the Bible, a great place to start is in the Gospels, which are in this book. The Gospels tell the story of Jesus' life, ministry, death and resurrection. Read the passage of Scripture, whether it is a verse, a chapter or a book, to begin your time with God. You can download the 'YouVersion' app to get the Bible on your mobile or tablet.

OBSERVATION
Consider what you notice about that passage that you read. As you read through the text, what is it that stands out and what grabs your attention? Ponder what comes to mind.

APPLICATION
Think about how that observation applies to your daily life. Why has that thought grabbed you and how can you apply it to your day that is ahead of you?

PRAYER
Begin to pray that God will help you to understand what you have read and apply it to your life. Ask God for his guidance and wisdom as you continue your day.

The Bible is the living word of God, which means that it is as relevant to us today as it was for the first people who read it. As you read through the Bible, it can be helpful to use the 'SOAP' structure to get the most out of your Bible reading. But remember that, ultimately, the point of the Bible is that we use it to grow in our relationship with God. The great thing about a relationship with God is that God is available at any time and in any place. We don't need to be in church or be with other Christians; if we want to hear from God, we can open the Bible and receive from him whenever we want to.

THE BIBLE IS THE LIVING WORD OF GOD, WHICH MEANS THAT IT IS AS RELEVANT TO US TODAY AS IT WAS FOR THE FIRST PEOPLE WHO READ IT.

Chapter Three

You Must be Born Again

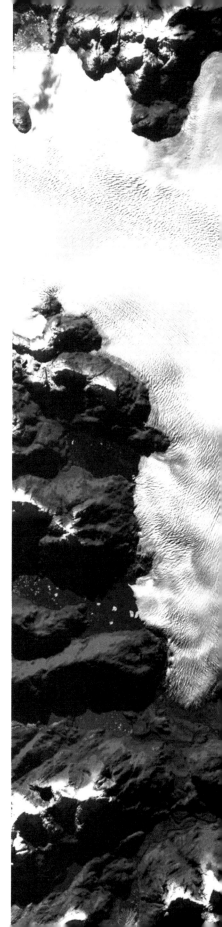

ow there was a man of the Pharisees named Nicodemus, a ruler of the Jews. [2] This man came to Jesus by night and said to him, "Rabbi, we know that you are a teacher come from God, for no one can do these signs that you do unless God is with him." [3] Jesus answered him, "Truly, truly, I say to you, unless one is born again he cannot see the kingdom of God." [4] Nicodemus said to him, "How can a man be born when he is old? Can he enter a second time into his mother's womb and be born?" [5] Jesus answered, "Truly, truly, I say to you, unless one is born of water and the Spirit, he cannot enter the kingdom of God. [6] That which is born of the flesh is flesh, and that which is born of the Spirit is spirit. [7] Do not marvel that I said to you, 'You must be born again.' [8] The wind blows where it wishes, and you hear its sound, but you do not know where it comes from or where it goes. So it is with everyone who is born of the Spirit."

[9] Nicodemus said to him, "How can these things be?" [10] Jesus answered him, "Are you the teacher of Israel and yet you do not understand these things? [11] Truly, truly, I say to you, we speak of what we know, and bear witness to what we have seen, but you do not receive our testimony. [12] If I have told you earthly things and you do not believe, how can you believe if I tell you heavenly things? [13] No one has ascended into heaven except he who descended from heaven, the Son of Man. [14] And as Moses lifted up the serpent in the wilderness, so must the Son of Man be lifted up, [15] that whoever believes in him may have eternal life.

For God So Loved the World

[16] "For God so loved the world, that he gave his only Son, that whoever believes in him should not perish but have eternal life. [17] For God did not send his Son into the world to condemn the world, but in order that the world might be saved through him. [18] Whoever believes in him is not condemned, but whoever does not believe is condemned already, because he has not believed in the name of the only Son of God. [19] And this is the judgement: the light has come into the world, and people loved the darkness rather than the light because their works were evil. [20] For everyone who does wicked things hates the light and does not come to the light, lest his works should be exposed. [21] But whoever does what is true comes to the light, so that it may be clearly seen that his works have been carried out in God."

John the Baptist Exalts Christ

[22] After this Jesus and his disciples went into the Judean countryside, and he remained there with them and was baptizing. [23] John also was baptizing at Aenon near Salim, because water was plentiful there, and people were coming and being baptized [24] (for John had not yet been put in prison).

[25] Now a discussion arose between some of John's disciples and a Jew over purification. [26] And they came to John and said to him, "Rabbi, he who was with you across the Jordan, to whom you bore witness—look, he is baptizing, and all are going to him." [27] John answered, "A person cannot receive even one thing unless it is given him from heaven. [28] You yourselves bear me witness, that I said, 'I am not the Christ, but I have been sent before him.' [29] The one who has the bride is the bridegroom. The friend of the bridegroom, who stands and hears him, re-

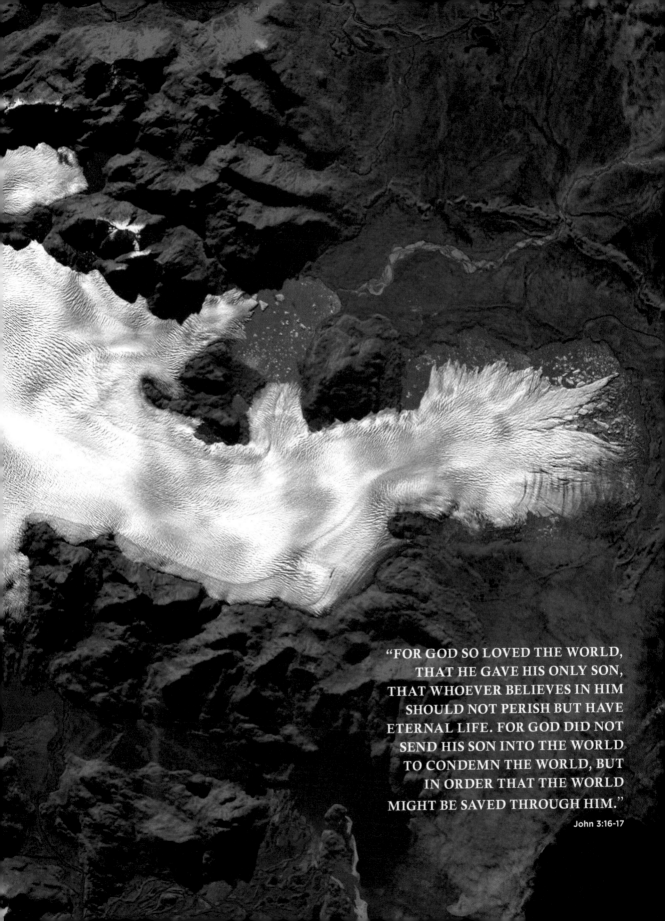

"FOR GOD SO LOVED THE WORLD,
THAT HE GAVE HIS ONLY SON,
THAT WHOEVER BELIEVES IN HIM
SHOULD NOT PERISH BUT HAVE
ETERNAL LIFE. FOR GOD DID NOT
SEND HIS SON INTO THE WORLD
TO CONDEMN THE WORLD, BUT
IN ORDER THAT THE WORLD
MIGHT BE SAVED THROUGH HIM."

John 3:16-17

JOHN ANSWERED,
"A PERSON CANNOT
RECEIVE EVEN ONE
THING UNLESS IT IS
GIVEN HIM FROM
HEAVEN. YOU
YOURSELVES BEAR
WITNESS, THAT I SAID,
'I AM NOT THE CHRIST,
BUT I HAVE BEEN
SENT BEFORE HIM."

John 3:27-28

joices greatly at the bridegroom's voice. Therefore this joy of mine is now complete. ³⁰ He must increase, but I must decrease."

³¹ He who comes from above is above all. He who is of the earth belongs to the earth and speaks in an earthly way. He who comes from heaven is above all. ³² He bears witness to what he has seen and heard, yet no one receives his testimony. ³³ Whoever receives his testimony sets his seal to this, that God is true. ³⁴ For he whom God has sent utters the words of God, for he gives the Spirit without measure. ³⁵ The Father loves the Son and has given all things into his hand. ³⁶ Whoever believes in the Son has eternal life; whoever does not obey the Son shall not see life, but the wrath of God remains on him.

Chapter Four

Jesus and the Woman of Samaria

Now when Jesus learned that the Pharisees had heard that Jesus was making and baptizing more disciples than John ² (although Jesus himself did not baptize, but only his disciples), ³ he left Judea and departed again for Galilee. ⁴ And he had to pass through Samaria. ⁵ So he came to a town of Samaria called Sychar, near the field that Jacob had given to his son Joseph. ⁶ Jacob's well was there; so Jesus, wearied as he was from his journey, was sitting beside the well. It was about the sixth hour.

⁷ A woman from Samaria came to draw water. Jesus said to her, "Give me a drink." ⁸ (For his disciples had gone away into the city to buy food.) ⁹ The Samaritan woman said to him, "How is it that you, a Jew, ask for a drink from me, a woman of Samaria?" (For Jews have no dealings with Samaritans.) ¹⁰ Jesus answered her, "If you knew the gift of God, and who it is that is saying to you, 'Give me a drink', you would have asked him, and he would have given you living water." ¹¹ The woman said to him, "Sir, you have nothing to draw water with, and the well is deep. Where do you get that living water? ¹² Are you greater than our father Jacob? He gave us the well and drank from it himself, as did his sons and his livestock." ¹³ Jesus said to her, "Everyone who drinks of this water will be thirsty again, ¹⁴ but whoever drinks of the water that I will give him will never be thirsty again. The water that I will give him will become in him a spring of water welling up to eternal life." ¹⁵ The woman said to him, "Sir, give me this water, so that I will not be thirsty or have to come here to draw water."

¹⁶ Jesus said to her, "Go, call your husband, and come here." ¹⁷ The woman answered him, "I have no husband." Jesus said to her, "You are right in saying, 'I have no husband'; ¹⁸ for you have had five husbands, and the one you now have is not your husband. What you have said is true." ¹⁹ The woman said to him, "Sir, I perceive that you are a prophet. ²⁰ Our fathers worshipped on this mountain, but you say that in Jerusalem is the place where people ought to worship." ²¹ Jesus said to her, "Woman, believe me, the hour is coming when neither on this mountain nor in Jerusalem will you worship the Father. ²² You worship what you do not know; we worship what we know, for salvation is from the Jews. ²³ But the hour is coming, and is now here, when the true worshippers will worship the Father in spirit and truth, for the Father is seeking such people to worship him. ²⁴ God is spirit,

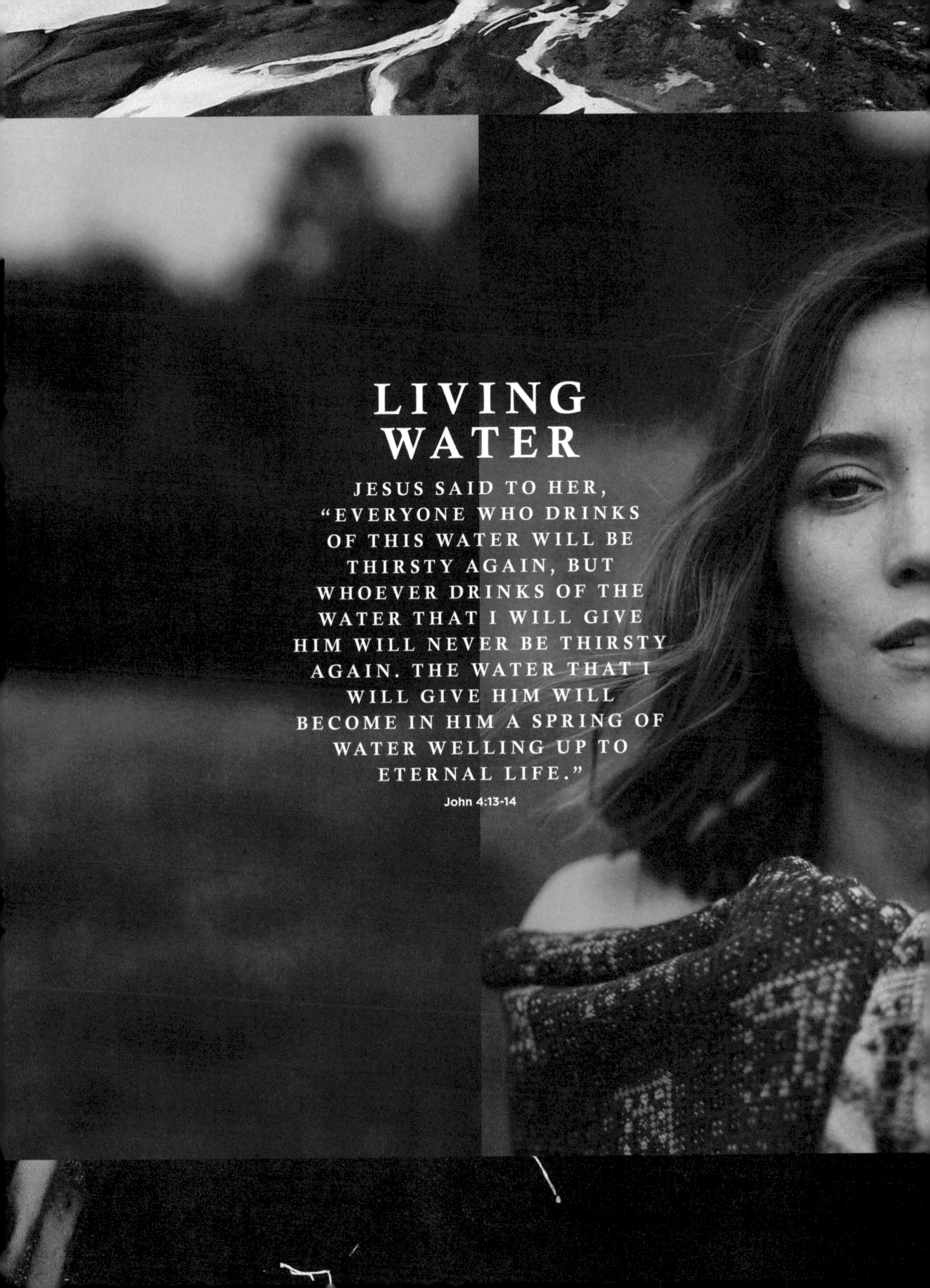

LIVING WATER

JESUS SAID TO HER,
"EVERYONE WHO DRINKS
OF THIS WATER WILL BE
THIRSTY AGAIN, BUT
WHOEVER DRINKS OF THE
WATER THAT I WILL GIVE
HIM WILL NEVER BE THIRSTY
AGAIN. THE WATER THAT I
WILL GIVE HIM WILL
BECOME IN HIM A SPRING OF
WATER WELLING UP TO
ETERNAL LIFE."

John 4:13-14

and those who worship him must worship in spirit and truth." ²⁵ The woman said to him, "I know that Messiah is coming (he who is called Christ). When he comes, he will tell us all things." ²⁶ Jesus said to her, "I who speak to you am he."

²⁷ Just then his disciples came back. They marvelled that he was talking with a woman, but no one said, "What do you seek?" or, "Why are you talking with her?" ²⁸ So the woman left her water jar and went away into town and said to the people, ²⁹ "Come, see a man who told me all that I ever did. Can this be the Christ?" ³⁰ They went out of the town and were coming to him.

³¹ Meanwhile the disciples were urging him, saying, "Rabbi, eat." ³² But he said to them, "I have food to eat that you do not know about." ³³ So the disciples said to one another, "Has anyone brought him something to eat?" ³⁴ Jesus said to them, "My food is to do the will of him who sent me and to accomplish his work. ³⁵ Do you not say, 'There are yet four months, then comes the harvest'? Look, I tell you, lift up your eyes, and see that the fields are white for harvest. ³⁶ Already the one who reaps is receiving wages and gathering fruit for eternal life, so that sower and reaper may rejoice together. ³⁷ For here the saying holds true, 'One sows and another reaps.' ³⁸ I sent you to reap that for which you did not labour. Others have laboured, and you have entered into their labour."

³⁹ Many Samaritans from that town believed in him because of the woman's testimony, "He told me all that I ever did." ⁴⁰ So when the Samaritans came to him, they asked him to stay with them, and he stayed there two days. ⁴¹ And many more believed because of his word. ⁴² They said to the woman, "It is no longer because of what you said that we believe, for we have heard for ourselves, and we know that this is indeed the Saviour of the world."

⁴³ After the two days he departed for Galilee. ⁴⁴ (For Jesus himself had testified that a prophet has no honour in his own home town.) ⁴⁵ So when he came to Galilee, the Galileans welcomed him, having seen all that he had done in Jerusalem at the feast. For they too had gone to the feast.

Jesus Heals an Official's Son

⁴⁶ So he came again to Cana in Galilee, where he had made the water wine. And at Capernaum there was an official whose son was ill. ⁴⁷ When this man heard that Jesus had come from Judea to Galilee, he went to him and asked him to come down and heal his son, for he was at the point of death. ⁴⁸ So Jesus said to him, "Unless you see signs and wonders you will not believe." ⁴⁹ The official said to him, "Sir, come down before my child dies." ⁵⁰ Jesus said to him, "Go; your son will live." The man believed the word that Jesus spoke to him and went on his way. ⁵¹ As he was going down, his servants met him and told him that his son was recovering. ⁵² So he asked them the hour when he began to get better, and they said to him, "Yesterday at the seventh hour the fever left him." ⁵³ The father knew that was the hour when Jesus had said to him, "Your son will live." And he himself believed, and all his household. ⁵⁴ This was now the second sign that Jesus did when he had come from Judea to Galilee.

Chapter Five

The Healing at the Pool on the Sabbath

Jesus said to him, "Get up, take up your bed, and walk." And at once the man was healed, and he took up his bed and walked. Now that day was the Sabbath.

John 5:8-9

After this there was a feast of the Jews, and Jesus went up to Jerusalem.

²Now there is in Jerusalem by the Sheep Gate a pool, in Aramaic called Bethesda, which has five roofed colonnades. ³In these lay a multitude of invalids—blind, lame, and paralysed. ⁵One man was there who had been an invalid for thirty-eight years. ⁶When Jesus saw him lying there and knew that he had already been there a long time, he said to him, "Do you want to be healed?" ⁷The sick man answered him, "Sir, I have no one to put me into the pool when the water is stirred up, and while I am going another steps down before me." ⁸Jesus said to him, "Get up, take up your bed, and walk." ⁹And at once the man was healed, and he took up his bed and walked.

Now that day was the Sabbath. ¹⁰So the Jews said to the man who had been healed, "It is the Sabbath, and it is not lawful for you to take up your bed." ¹¹But he answered them, "The man who healed me, that man said to me, 'Take up your bed, and walk.'" ¹²They asked him, "Who is the man who said to you, 'Take up your bed and walk'?" ¹³Now the man who had been healed did not know who it was, for Jesus had withdrawn, as there was a crowd in the place. ¹⁴Afterwards Jesus found him in the temple and said to him, "See, you are well! Sin no more, that nothing worse may happen to you." ¹⁵The man went away and told the Jews that it was Jesus who had healed him. ¹⁶And this was why the Jews were persecuting Jesus, because he was doing these things on the Sabbath. ¹⁷But Jesus answered them, "My Father is working until now, and I am working."

Jesus Is Equal with God

¹⁸This was why the Jews were seeking all the more to kill him, because not only was he breaking the Sabbath, but he was even calling God his own Father, making himself equal with God.

The Authority of the Son

¹⁹So Jesus said to them, "Truly, truly, I say to you, the Son can do nothing of his own accord, but only what he sees the Father doing. For whatever the Father does, that the Son does likewise. ²⁰For the Father loves the Son and shows him all that he himself is doing. And greater works than these will he show him, so that you may marvel. ²¹For as the Father raises the dead and gives them life, so also the Son gives life to whom he will. ²²For the Father judges no one, but has given all judgement to the Son, ²³that all may honour the Son, just as they honour the Father. Whoever does not honour the Son does not honour the Father who sent him. ²⁴Truly, truly, I say to you, whoever hears my word and believes him who sent me has eternal life. He does not come into judgement, but has passed from death to life. ²⁵"Truly, truly, I say to you, an hour is coming, and is now here, when the dead will hear the voice of the Son of God, and those who hear will live. ²⁶For as the Father has life in himself, so he has granted the Son also to have life in himself. ²⁷And he has given him authority to execute judgement, because he is the Son of Man. ²⁸Do not marvel at this, for an hour is coming when all who are in the tombs will hear his voice ²⁹and come out, those who have done good to the resurrection of life, and those who have done evil to the resurrection of judgement.

Witnesses to Jesus

³⁰"I can do nothing on my own. As I hear, I judge, and my judgement is just, because I seek not my own will but the will of him who sent me. ³¹If I alone bear witness about myself, my testimony is not true. ³²There is another who bears witness about me, and I know that the testimony that he bears about me is true. ³³You sent to John,

and he has borne witness to the truth. [34]Not that the testimony that I receive is from man, but I say these things so that you may be saved. [35]He was a burning and shining lamp, and you were willing to rejoice for a while in his light. [36]But the testimony that I have is greater than that of John. For the works that the Father has given me to accomplish, the very works that I am doing, bear witness about me that the Father has sent me. [37]And the Father who sent me has himself borne witness about me. His voice you have never heard, his form you have never seen, [38]and you do not have his word abiding in you, for you do not believe the one whom he has sent. [39]You search the Scriptures because you think that in them you have eternal life; and it is they that bear witness about me, [40]yet you refuse to come to me that you may have life. [41]I do not receive glory from people. [42]But I know that you do not have the love of God within you. [43]I have come in my Father's name, and you do not receive me. If another comes in his own name, you will receive him. [44]How can you believe, when you receive glory from one another and do not seek the glory that comes from the only God? [45]Do not think that I will accuse you to the Father. There is one who accuses you: Moses, on whom you have set your hope. [46]For if you believed Moses, you would believe me; for he wrote of me. [47]But if you do not believe his writings, how will you believe my words?"

Chapter Six

Jesus Feeds the Five Thousand

After this Jesus went away to the other side of the Sea of Galilee, which is the Sea of Tiberias. [2]And a large crowd was following him, because they saw the signs that he was doing on the sick. [3]Jesus went up on the mountain, and there he sat down with his disciples. [4]Now the Passover, the feast of the Jews, was at hand. [5]Lifting up his eyes, then, and seeing that a large crowd was coming towards him, Jesus said to Philip, "Where are we to buy bread, so that these people may eat?" [6]He said this to test him, for he himself knew what he would do. [7]Philip answered him, "Two hundred denarii worth of bread would not be enough for each of them to get a little." [8]One of his disciples, Andrew, Simon Peter's brother, said to him, [9]"There is a boy here who has five barley loaves and two fish, but what are they for so many?" [10]Jesus said, "Make the people sit down." Now there was much grass in the place. So the men sat down, about five thousand in number. [11]Jesus then took the loaves, and when he had given thanks, he distributed them to those who were seated. So also the fish, as much as they wanted. [12]And when they had eaten their fill, he told

his disciples, "Gather up the leftover fragments, that nothing may be lost." [13] So they gathered them up and filled twelve baskets with fragments from the five barley loaves left by those who had eaten. [14] When the people saw the sign that he had done, they said, "This is indeed the Prophet who is to come into the world!"

[15] Perceiving then that they were about to come and take him by force to make him king, Jesus withdrew again to the mountain by himself.

Jesus Walks on Water

[16] When evening came, his disciples went down to the lake, [17] got into a boat, and started across the lake to Capernaum. It was now dark, and Jesus had not yet come to them. [18] The lake became rough because a strong wind was blowing. [19] When they had rowed about three or four miles, they saw Jesus walking on the lake and coming near the boat, and they were frightened. [20] But he said to them, "It is I; do not be afraid." [21] Then they were glad to take him into the boat, and immediately the boat was at the land to which they were going.

I Am the Bread of Life

[22] On the next day the crowd that remained on the other side of the lake saw that there had been only one boat there, and that Jesus had not entered the boat with his disciples, but that his disciples had gone away alone. [23] Other boats from Tiberias came near the place where they had eaten the bread after the Lord had given thanks. [24] So when the crowd saw that Jesus was not there, nor his disciples, they themselves got into the boats and went to Capernaum, seeking Jesus.

[25] When they found him on the other side of the sea, they said to him, "Rabbi, when did you come here?" [26] Jesus answered them, "Truly, truly, I say to you, you are seeking me, not because you saw signs, but because you ate your

ONE OF HIS DISCIPLES, ANDREW, SIMON PETER'S BROTHER, SAID TO HIM, "THERE IS A BOY HERE WHO HAS FIVE BARLEY LOAVES AND TWO FISH, BUT WHAT ARE THEY FOR SO MANY?"

John 6:8-9

THE TRUE BREAD FROM HEAVEN

"OUR FATHERS ATE THE MANNA IN THE WILDERNESS; AS IT IS WRITTEN, 'HE GAVE THEM BREAD FROM HEAVEN TO EAT.'" JESUS THEN SAID TO THEM, "TRULY, TRULY, I SAY TO YOU, IT WAS NOT MOSES WHO GAVE YOU THE BREAD FROM HEAVEN, BUT MY FATHER GIVES YOU THE TRUE BREAD FROM HEAVEN. FOR THE BREAD OF GOD IS HE WHO COMES DOWN FROM HEAVEN AND GIVES LIFE TO THE WORLD." THEY SAID TO HIM, "SIR, GIVE US THIS BREAD ALWAYS."

John 6:31-34

fill of the loaves. ²⁷Do not work for the food that perishes, but for the food that endures to eternal life, which the Son of Man will give to you. For on him God the Father has set his seal." ²⁸Then they said to him, "What must we do, to be doing the works of God?" ²⁹Jesus answered them, "This is the work of God, that you believe in him whom he has sent." ³⁰So they said to him, "Then what sign do you do, that we may see and believe you? What work do you perform? ³¹Our fathers ate the manna in the wilderness; as it is written, 'He gave them bread from heaven to eat.'" ³²Jesus then said to them, "Truly, truly, I say to you, it was not Moses who gave you the bread from heaven, but my Father gives you the true bread from heaven. ³³For the bread of God is he who comes down from heaven and gives life to the world." ³⁴They said to him, "Sir, give us this bread always."

³⁵Jesus said to them, "I am the bread of life; whoever comes to me shall not hunger, and whoever believes in me shall never thirst. ³⁶But I said to you that you have seen me and yet do not believe. ³⁷All that the Father gives me will come to me, and whoever comes to me I will never cast out. ³⁸For I have come down from heaven, not to do my own will but the will of him who sent me. ³⁹And this is the will of him who sent me, that I should lose nothing of all that he has given me, but raise it up on the last day. ⁴⁰For this is the will of my Father, that everyone who looks on the Son and believes in him should have eternal life, and I will raise him up on the last day."

⁴¹So the Jews grumbled about him, because he said, "I am the bread that came down from heaven." ⁴²They said, "Is not this Jesus, the son of Joseph, whose father and mother we know? How does he now say, 'I have come down from heaven'?" ⁴³Jesus answered them, "Do not grumble among yourselves. ⁴⁴No one can come to me unless the Father who sent me draws him. And I will raise him up on the last day. ⁴⁵It is written in the Prophets, 'And they will all be taught by God.' Everyone who has heard and learned from the Father comes to me— ⁴⁶not that anyone has seen the Father except he who is from God; he has seen the Father. ⁴⁷Truly, truly, I say to you, whoever believes has eternal life. ⁴⁸I am the bread of life. ⁴⁹Your fathers ate the manna in the wilderness, and they died. ⁵⁰This is the bread that comes down from heaven, so that one may eat of it and not die. ⁵¹I am the living bread that came down from heaven. If anyone eats of this bread, he will live for ever. And the bread that I will give for the life of the world is my flesh."

⁵²The Jews then disputed among themselves, saying, "How can this man give us his flesh to eat?" ⁵³So Jesus said to them, "Truly, truly, I say to you, unless you eat the flesh of the Son of Man and drink his blood, you have

SO JESUS SAID
TO THE TWELVE,
"DO YOU WANT
TO GO AWAY
AS WELL?"
SIMON PETER
ANSWERED
HIM, "LORD, TO
WHOM SHALL
WE GO? YOU
HAVE THE
WORDS OF
ETERNAL LIFE,
AND WE HAVE
BELIEVED, AND
HAVE COME
TO KNOW, THAT
YOU ARE THE
HOLY ONE
OF GOD."

John 6:67-69

no life in you. ⁵⁴Whoever feeds on my flesh and drinks my blood has eternal life, and I will raise him up on the last day. ⁵⁵For my flesh is true food, and my blood is true drink. ⁵⁶Whoever feeds on my flesh and drinks my blood abides in me, and I in him. ⁵⁷As the living Father sent me, and I live because of the Father, so whoever feeds on me, he also will live because of me. ⁵⁸This is the bread that came down from heaven, not like the bread the fathers ate, and died. Whoever feeds on this bread will live for ever." ⁵⁹ Jesus said these things in the synagogue, as he taught at Capernaum.

The Words of Eternal Life

⁶⁰ When many of his disciples heard it, they said, "This is a hard saying; who can listen to it?" ⁶¹ But Jesus, knowing in himself that his disciples were grumbling about this, said to them, "Do you take offence at this? ⁶²Then what if you were to see the Son of Man ascending to where he was before? ⁶³It is the Spirit who gives life; the flesh is no help at all. The words that I have spoken to you are spirit and life. ⁶⁴But there are some of you who do not believe." (For Jesus knew from the beginning who those were who did not believe, and who it was who would betray him.) ⁶⁵And he said, "This is why I told you that no one can come to me unless it is granted him by the Father."

⁶⁶After this many of his disciples turned back and no longer walked with him. ⁶⁷ So Jesus said to the twelve, "Do you want to go away as well?" ⁶⁸ Simon Peter answered him, "Lord, to whom shall we go? You have the words of eternal life, ⁶⁹ and we have believed, and have come to know, that you are the Holy One of God." ⁷⁰Jesus answered them, "Did I not choose you, the twelve? And yet one of you is a devil." ⁷¹ He spoke of Judas the son of Simon Iscariot, for he, one of the twelve, was going to betray him.

Chapter Seven
Jesus at the Feast of Booths

"Whoever believes in me, as the Scripture has said, 'Out of his heart will flow rivers of living water.'"

John 7:38

After this Jesus went about in Galilee. He would not go about in Judea, because the Jews were seeking to kill him. ²Now the Jews' Feast of Booths was at hand. ³So his brothers said to him, "Leave here and go to Judea, that your disciples also may see the works you are doing. ⁴For no one works in secret if he seeks to be known openly. If you do these things, show yourself to the world." ⁵For not even his brothers believed in him. ⁶Jesus said to them, "My time has not yet come, but your time is always here. ⁷The world cannot hate you, but it hates me because I testify about it that its works are evil. ⁸You go up to the feast. I am not going up to this feast, for my time has not yet fully come." ⁹After saying this, he remained in Galilee.

¹⁰But after his brothers had gone up to the feast, then he also went up, not publicly but in private. ¹¹The Jews were looking for him at the feast, and saying, "Where is he?" ¹²And there was much muttering about him among the people. While some said, "He is a good man", others said, "No, he is leading the people astray." ¹³Yet for fear of the Jews no one spoke openly of him.

¹⁴About the middle of the feast Jesus went up into the temple and began teaching. ¹⁵The Jews therefore marvelled, saying, "How is it that this man has learning, when he has never studied?" ¹⁶So Jesus answered them, "My teaching is not mine, but his who sent me. ¹⁷If anyone's will is to do God's will, he will know whether the teaching is from God or whether I am speaking on my own authority. ¹⁸The one who speaks on his own authority seeks his own glory; but the one who seeks the glory of him who sent him is true, and in him there is no falsehood. ¹⁹Has not Moses given you the law? Yet none of you keeps the law. Why do you seek to kill me?" ²⁰The crowd answered, "You have a demon! Who is seeking to kill you?" ²¹Jesus answered them, "I did one work, and you all marvel at it. ²²Moses gave you circumcision (not that it is from Moses, but from the fathers), and you circumcise a man on the Sabbath. ²³If on the Sabbath a man receives circumcision, so that the law of Moses may not be broken, are you angry with me because on the Sabbath I made a man's whole body well? ²⁴Do not judge by appearances, but judge with right judgement."

Can This Be the Christ?
²⁵Some of the people of Jerusalem therefore said, "Is not this the man whom they seek to kill? ²⁶And here he is, speaking openly, and they say nothing to him! Can it be that the authorities really know that this is the Christ? ²⁷But we know where this man comes from, and when the Christ appears, no one will know where he comes from." ²⁸So Jesus proclaimed, as he taught in the temple, "You know me, and you know where I come from. But I have not come of my own accord. He who sent me is true, and him you do not know. ²⁹I know him, for I come from him, and he sent me." ³⁰So they were seeking to arrest him, but no one laid a hand on him, because his hour had not yet come. ³¹Yet many of the people believed in him. They said, "When the Christ appears, will he do more signs than this man has done?"

Officers Sent to Arrest Jesus
³²The Pharisees heard the crowd muttering these things about him, and the chief priests and Pharisees sent officers to arrest him. ³³Jesus then said, "I will be with you a little longer, and then I am going to him who sent me. ³⁴You will seek me and you will not find me. Where I am you cannot come." ³⁵The Jews said to one another, "Where does this man intend to go that we will not find him? Does he intend to go to the Dispersion among the Greeks and

teach the Greeks? **³⁶** What does he mean by saying, 'You will seek me and you will not find me', and, 'Where I am you cannot come'?"

Rivers of Living Water

³⁷ On the last day of the feast, the great day, Jesus stood up and cried out, "If anyone thirsts, let him come to me and drink. **³⁸** Whoever believes in me, as the Scripture has said, 'Out of his heart will flow rivers of living water.'" **³⁹** Now this he said about the Spirit, whom those who believed in him were to receive, for as yet the Spirit had not been given, because Jesus was not yet glorified.

Division Among the People

⁴⁰ When they heard these words, some of the people said, "This really is the Prophet." **⁴¹** Others said, "This is the Christ." But some said, "Is the Christ to come from Galilee? **⁴²** Has not the Scripture said that the Christ comes from the offspring of David, and comes from Bethlehem, the village where David was?" **⁴³** So there was a division among the people over him. **⁴⁴** Some of them wanted to arrest him, but no one laid hands on him.

⁴⁵ The officers then came to the chief priests and Pharisees, who said to them, "Why did you not bring him?" **⁴⁶** The officers answered, "No one ever spoke like this man!" **⁴⁷** The Phar-

isees answered them, "Have you also been deceived? **⁴⁸** Have any of the authorities or the Pharisees believed in him? **⁴⁹** But this crowd that does not know the law is accursed." **⁵⁰** Nicodemus, who had gone to him before, and who was one of them, said to them, **⁵¹** "Does our law judge a man without first giving him a hearing and learning what he does?" **⁵²** They replied, "Are you from Galilee too? Search and see that no prophet arises from Galilee."

[The earliest manuscripts do not include 7:53–8:11.]

Chapter Eight

The Women Caught in Adultery

⁵³ [[They went each to his own house, **¹** but Jesus went to the Mount of Olives. **²** Early in the morning he came again to the temple. All the people came to him, and he sat down and taught them. **³** The scribes and the Pharisees brought a woman who had been caught in adultery, and placing her in the midst **⁴** they said to him, "Teacher, this woman has been caught in the act of adultery. **⁵** Now in the Law, Moses commanded us to stone such women. So what do you say?" **⁶** This they said to test him, that they might have some charge to bring

against him. Jesus bent down and wrote with his finger on the ground. [7] And as they continued to ask him, he stood up and said to them, "Let him who is without sin among you be the first to throw a stone at her." [8] And once more he bent down and wrote on the ground. [9] But when they heard it, they went away one by one, beginning with the older ones, and Jesus was left alone with the woman standing before him. [10] Jesus stood up and said to her, "Woman, where are they? Has no one condemned you?" [11] She said, "No one, Lord." And Jesus said, "Neither do I condemn you; go, and from now on sin no more."]]

I Am the Light of the World

[12] Again Jesus spoke to them, saying, "I am the light of the world. Whoever follows me will not walk in darkness, but will have the light of life." [13] So the Pharisees said to him, "You are bearing witness about yourself; your testimony is not true." [14] Jesus answered, "Even if I do bear witness about myself, my testimony is true, for I know where I came from and where I am going, but you do not know where I come from or where I am going. [15] You judge according to the flesh; I judge no one. [16] Yet even if I do judge, my judgement is true, for it is not I alone who judge, but I and the Father who sent me. [17] In your Law it is written that the testimony of two people is true. [18] I am the one who bears witness about myself, and the Father who sent me bears witness about me." [19] They said to him therefore, "Where is your Father?" Jesus answered, "You know neither me nor my Father. If you knew me, you would know my Father also." [20] These words he spoke in the treasury, as he taught in the temple; but no one arrested him, because his hour had not yet come.

²¹ So he said to them again, "I am going away, and you will seek me, and you will die in your sin. Where I am going, you cannot come." ²² So the Jews said, "Will he kill himself, since he says, 'Where I am going, you cannot come'?" ²³ He said to them, "You are from below; I am from above. You are of this world; I am not of this world. ²⁴ I told you that you would die in your sins, for unless you believe that I am he you will die in your sins." ²⁵ So they said to him, "Who are you?" Jesus said to them, "Just what I have been telling you from the beginning. ²⁶ I have much to say about you and much to judge, but he who sent me is true, and I declare to the world what I have heard from him." ²⁷ They did not understand that he had been speaking to them about the Father. ²⁸ So Jesus said to them, "When you have lifted up the Son of Man, then you will know that I am he, and that I do nothing on my own authority, but speak just as the Father taught me. ²⁹ And he who sent me is with me. He has not left me alone, for I always do the things that are pleasing to him." ³⁰ As he was saying these things, many believed in him.

The Truth Will Set You Free

³¹ So Jesus said to the Jews who had believed him, "If you abide in my word, you are truly my disciples, ³² and you will know the truth, and the truth will set you free." ³³ They answered him, "We are offspring of Abraham and have never been enslaved to anyone. How is it that you say, 'You will become free'?"

³⁴ Jesus answered them, "Truly, truly, I say to you, everyone who practises sin is a slave to sin. ³⁵ The slave does not remain in the house for ever; the son remains for ever. ³⁶ So if the Son sets you free, you will be free indeed. ³⁷ I know that you are offspring of Abraham; yet you seek to kill me because my word finds no place in you.

[38] I speak of what I have seen with my Father, and you do what you have heard from your father."

You Are of Your Father the Devil

[39] They answered him, "Abraham is our father." Jesus said to them, "If you were Abraham's children, you would be doing the works Abraham did, [40] but now you seek to kill me, a man who has told you the truth that I heard from God. This is not what Abraham did. [41] You are doing the works your father did." They said to him, "We were not born of sexual immorality. We have one Father—even God." [42] Jesus said to them, "If God were your Father, you would love me, for I came from God and I am here. I came not of my own accord, but he sent me. [43] Why do you not understand what I say? It is because you cannot bear to hear my word. [44] You are of your father the devil, and your will is to do your father's desires. He was a murderer from the beginning, and does not stand in the truth, because there is no truth in him. When he lies, he speaks out of his own character, for he is a liar and the father of lies. [45] But because I tell the truth, you do not believe me. [46] Which one of you convicts me of sin? If I tell the truth, why do you not believe me? [47] Whoever is of God hears the words of God. The reason why you do not hear them is that you are not of God."

Before Abraham Was, I Am

[48] The Jews answered him, "Are we not right in saying that you are a Samaritan and have a demon?" [49] Jesus answered, "I do not have a demon, but I honour my Father, and you dishonour me. [50] Yet I do not seek my own glory; there is One who seeks it, and he is the judge. [51] Truly, truly, I say to you, if anyone keeps my word, he will never see death." [52] The Jews said to him, "Now we know that you have a demon! Abraham died, as did the prophets, yet you say, 'If anyone keeps my word, he will never taste death.' [53] Are you greater than our father Abraham, who died? And the prophets died! Who do you make yourself out to be?" [54] Jesus answered, "If I glorify myself, my glory is nothing. It is my Father who glorifies me, of whom you say, 'He is our God.' [55] But you have not known him. I know him. If I were to say that I do not know him, I would be a liar like you, but I do know him and I keep his word. [56] Your father Abraham rejoiced that he would see my day. He saw it and was glad." [57] So the Jews said to him, "You are not yet fifty years old, and have you seen Abraham?" [58] Jesus said to them, "Truly, truly, I say to you, before Abraham was, I am." [59] So they picked up stones to throw at him, but Jesus hid himself and went out of the temple.

JESUS SAID TO THEM, "IF GOD WERE YOUR FATHER, YOU WOULD LOVE ME, FOR I CAME FROM GOD AND I AM HERE. I CAME NOT OF MY OWN ACCORD, BUT HE SENT ME. WHY DO YOU NOT UNDERSTAND WHAT I SAY? IT IS BECAUSE YOU CANNOT BEAR TO HEAR MY WORD." John 8:42-43

Chapter Nine
Jesus Heals a Man Born Blind

He answered, "The man called Jesus made mud and anointed my eyes and said to me, 'Go to Siloam and wash.' So I went and washed and received my sight."

John 9:11

s he passed by, he saw a man blind from birth. ²And his disciples asked him, "Rabbi, who sinned, this man or his parents, that he was born blind?" ³Jesus answered, "It was not that this man sinned, or his parents, but that the works of God might be displayed in him. ⁴We must work the works of him who sent me while it is day; night is coming, when no one can work. ⁵As long as I am in the world, I am the light of the world." ⁶Having said these things, he spat on the ground and made mud with the saliva. Then he anointed the man's eyes with the mud ⁷and said to him, "Go, wash in the pool of Siloam" (which means Sent). So he went and washed and came back seeing.

⁸The neighbours and those who had seen him before as a beggar were saying, "Is this not the man who used to sit and beg?" ⁹Some said, "It is he." Others said, "No, but he is like him." He kept saying, "I am the man." ¹⁰So they said to him, "Then how were your eyes opened?" ¹¹He answered, "The man called Jesus made mud and anointed my eyes and said to me, 'Go to Siloam and wash.' So I went and washed and received my sight." ¹²They said to him, "Where is he?" He said, "I do not know."

¹³They brought to the Pharisees the man who had formerly been blind. ¹⁴Now it was a Sabbath day when Jesus made the mud and opened his eyes. ¹⁵So the Pharisees again asked him how he had received his sight. And he said to them, "He put mud on my eyes, and I washed, and I see." ¹⁶Some of the Pharisees said, "This man is not from God, for he does not keep the Sabbath." But others said, "How can a man who is a sinner do such signs?" And there was a division among them. ¹⁷So they said again to the blind man, "What do you say about him, since he has opened your eyes?" He said, "He is a prophet."

¹⁸The Jews did not believe that he had been blind and had received his sight, until they called the parents of the man who had received his sight ¹⁹and asked them, "Is this your son, who you say was born blind? How then does he now see?" ²⁰His parents answered, "We know that this is our son and that he was born blind. ²¹But how he now sees we do not know, nor do we know who opened his eyes. Ask him; he is of age. He will speak for himself." ²²(His parents said these things because they feared the Jews, for the Jews had already agreed that if anyone should confess Jesus to be Christ, he was to be put out of the synagogue.) ²³Therefore his parents said, "He is of age; ask him."

²⁴So for the second time they called the man who had been blind and said to him, "Give glory to God. We know that this man is a sinner." ²⁵He answered, "Whether he is a sinner I do not know. One thing I do know, that though I was blind, now I see." ²⁶They said to him, "What did he do to you? How did he open your eyes?" ²⁷He answered them, "I have told you already, and you would not listen. Why do you want to hear it again? Do you also want to become his disciples?" ²⁸And they reviled him, saying, "You are his disciple, but we are disciples of Moses. ²⁹We know that God has spoken to Moses, but as for this man, we do not know where he comes from." ³⁰The man answered, "Why, this is an amazing thing! You do not know where he comes from, and yet he opened my eyes. ³¹We know that God does not listen to sinners, but if anyone is a worshipper of God and does his will, God listens to him. ³²Never since the world began has it been heard that anyone opened the eyes of a man born blind. ³³If this man were not from God, he could do nothing." ³⁴They answered him, "You were born in utter sin, and would you teach us?" And they cast him out.

³⁵Jesus heard that they had cast him out, and having found him he said, "Do you believe in the Son of Man?" ³⁶He answered, "And who is he, sir, that I may believe in him?" ³⁷Jesus said to him, "You have seen him, and it is he who is speaking to you." ³⁸He said, "Lord, I believe", and he worshipped him. ³⁹Jesus said, "For judgement I came into this world, that those who do not see may see, and those who see may become blind." ⁴⁰Some of the Pharisees near him heard these things, and said to him, "Are we also blind?" ⁴¹Jesus said to them, "If you were blind, you would have no guilt; but now that you say, 'We see', your guilt remains.

Chapter Ten

I Am the Good Shepherd

"Truly, truly, I say to you, he who does not enter the sheepfold by the door but climbs in by another way, that man is a thief and a robber. ²But he who enters by the door is the shepherd of the sheep. ³To him the gatekeeper opens. The sheep hear his voice, and he calls his own sheep by name and leads them out. ⁴When he has brought out all his own, he goes before them, and the sheep follow him, for they know his voice. ⁵A stranger they will not follow, but they will flee from him, for they do not know the voice of strangers." ⁶This figure of speech Jesus used with them, but they did not understand what he was saying to them.

⁷So Jesus again said to them, "Truly, truly, I say to you, I am the door of the sheep. ⁸All who came before me are thieves and robbers, but the sheep did not listen to them. ⁹I am the door. If anyone enters by me, he will be saved and will go in and out and find pasture. ¹⁰The thief comes only to steal and kill and destroy. I came that they may have life and have it abundantly. ¹¹I am the good shepherd. The good shepherd lays down his life for the sheep. ¹²He who is a hired hand and not a shepherd, who does not own the sheep, sees the wolf coming and leaves the sheep and flees, and the wolf snatches them and scatters them. ¹³He flees because he is a hired hand and cares nothing for the sheep. ¹⁴I am the good shepherd. I know my own and my own know me, ¹⁵just as the Father knows me and I know the Father; and I lay down my life for the sheep. ¹⁶And I have other

"THE THIEF COMES ONLY TO
STEAL AND KILL AND DESTROY."

sheep that are not of this fold. I must bring them also, and they will listen to my voice. So there will be one flock, one shepherd. [17]For this reason the Father loves me, because I lay down my life that I may take it up again. [18]No one takes it from me, but I lay it down of my own accord. I have authority to lay it down, and I have authority to take it up again. This charge I have received from my Father."

[19]There was again a division among the Jews because of these words. [20]Many of them said, "He has a demon, and is insane; why listen to him?" [21]Others said, "These are not the words of one who is oppressed by a demon. Can a demon open the eyes of the blind?"

I and the Father Are One
[22]At that time the Feast of Dedication took place at Jerusalem. It was winter, [23]and Jesus was walking in the temple, in the colonnade of Solomon. [24]So the Jews gathered around him and said to him, "How long will you keep us in suspense? If you are the Christ, tell us plainly." [25]Jesus answered them, "I told you, and you do not believe. The works that I do in my Father's name bear witness about me, [26]but you do not believe because you are not among my sheep. [27]My sheep hear my voice, and I know them, and they follow me. [28]I give them eternal life, and they will never perish, and no one will snatch them out of my hand. [29]My Father, who has given them to me, is greater than all, and no one is able to snatch them out of the Father's hand. [30]I and the Father are one."

[31]The Jews picked up stones again to stone him. [32]Jesus answered them, "I have shown you many good works from the Father; for which of them are you going to stone me?" [33]The Jews answered him, "It is not for a good work that we are going to stone you but for blasphemy, because you, being a man, make yourself God." [34]Jesus answered them, "Is it not written in your Law, 'I said, you are gods'? [35]If he called them gods to whom the word of God came— and Scripture cannot be broken— [36]do you say of him whom the Father consecrated and sent into the world, 'You are blaspheming', because I said, 'I am the Son of God'? [37]If I am not doing the works of my Father, then do not believe me; [38]but if I do them, even though you do not believe me, believe the works, that you may know and understand that the Father is in me and I am in the Father." [39]Again they sought to arrest him, but he escaped from their hands.

[40]He went away again across the Jordan to the place where John had been baptizing at first, and there he remained. [41]And many came to him. And they said, "John did no sign, but everything that John said about this man was true." [42]And many believed in him there.

"I CAME THAT THEY MAY HAVE LIFE
AND HAVE IT ABUNDANTLY."

John 10:10

SO THE SISTERS
SENT TO HIM,
SAYING,
"LORD, HE
WHOM YOU
LOVE IS ILL."
BUT WHEN
JESUS HEARD
IT HE SAID,
"THIS ILLNESS
DOES NOT LEAD
TO DEATH. IT
IS FOR THE
GLORY OF GOD,
SO THAT THE
SON OF
GOD MAY BE
GLORIFIED
THROUGH IT."

John 11:3-4

Chapter Eleven

The Death of Lazarus

Now a certain man was ill, Lazarus of Bethany, the village of Mary and her sister Martha. ² It was Mary who anointed the Lord with ointment and wiped his feet with her hair, whose brother Lazarus was ill. ³ So the sisters sent to him, saying, "Lord, he whom you love is ill." ⁴ But when Jesus heard it he said, "This illness does not lead to death. It is for the glory of God, so that the Son of God may be glorified through it."

⁵ Now Jesus loved Martha and her sister and Lazarus. ⁶ So, when he heard that Lazarus was ill, he stayed two days longer in the place where he was. ⁷ Then after this he said to the disciples, "Let us go to Judea again." ⁸ The disciples said to him, "Rabbi, the Jews were just now seeking to stone you, and are you going there again?" ⁹ Jesus answered, "Are there not twelve hours in the day? If anyone walks in the day, he does not stumble, because he sees the light of this world. ¹⁰ But if anyone walks in the night, he stumbles, because the light is not in him." ¹¹ After saying these things, he said to them, "Our friend Lazarus has fallen asleep, but I go to awaken him." ¹² The disciples said to him, "Lord, if he has fallen asleep, he will recover." ¹³ Now Jesus had spoken of his death, but they thought that he meant taking rest in sleep. ¹⁴ Then Jesus told them plainly, "Lazarus has died, ¹⁵ and for your sake I am glad that I was not there, so that you may believe. But let us go to him." ¹⁶ So Thomas, called the Twin, said to his fellow disciples, "Let us also go, that we may die with him."

I Am the Resurrection and the Life

¹⁷ Now when Jesus came, he found that Lazarus had already been in the tomb four days. ¹⁸ Bethany was near Jerusalem, about two miles off, ¹⁹ and many of the Jews had come to Martha and Mary to console them concerning their brother. ²⁰ So when Martha heard that Jesus was coming, she went and met him, but Mary remained seated in the house. ²¹ Martha said to Jesus, "Lord, if you had been here, my brother would not have died. ²² But even now I know that whatever you ask from God, God will give you." ²³ Jesus said to her, "Your brother will rise again." ²⁴ Martha said to him, "I know that he will rise again in the resurrection on the last day." ²⁵ Jesus said to her, "I am the resurrection and the life. Whoever believes in me, though he die, yet shall he live, ²⁶ and everyone who lives and believes in me shall never die. Do you believe this?" ²⁷ She said to him, "Yes, Lord; I believe that you are the Christ, the Son of God, who is coming into the world."

Jesus Weeps

²⁸ When she had said this, she went and called her sister Mary, saying in private, "The Teacher is here and is calling for you." ²⁹ And when she heard it, she rose quickly and went to him. ³⁰ Now Jesus had not yet come into the village, but

JESUS SAID, "TAKE AWAY THE STONE."
MARTHA, THE SISTER OF THE DEAD MAN, SAID
TO HIM, "LORD, BY THIS TIME THERE WILL BE
AN ODOUR, FOR HE HAS BEEN DEAD FOUR
DAYS." JESUS SAID TO HER, "DID I NOT TELL YOU
THAT IF YOU BELIEVED YOU WOULD SEE
THE GLORY OF GOD?"

John 11:39-40

was still in the place where Martha had met him. [31] When the Jews who were with her in the house, consoling her, saw Mary rise quickly and go out, they followed her, supposing that she was going to the tomb to weep there. [32] Now when Mary came to where Jesus was and saw him, she fell at his feet, saying to him, "Lord, if you had been here, my brother would not have died." [33] When Jesus saw her weeping, and the Jews who had come with her also weeping, he was deeply moved in his spirit and greatly troubled. [34] And he said, "Where have you laid him?" They said to him, "Lord, come and see." [35] Jesus wept. [36] So the Jews said, "See how he loved him!" [37] But some of them said, "Could not he who opened the eyes of the blind man also have kept this man from dying?"

Jesus Raises Lazarus

[38] Then Jesus, deeply moved again, came to the tomb. It was a cave, and a stone lay against it. [39] Jesus said, "Take away the stone." Martha, the sister of the dead man, said to him, "Lord, by this time there will be an odour, for he has been dead four days." [40] Jesus said

to her, "Did I not tell you that if you believed you would see the glory of God?" [41] So they took away the stone. And Jesus lifted up his eyes and said, "Father, I thank you that you have heard me. [42] I knew that you always hear me, but I said this on account of the people standing around, that they may believe that you sent me." [43] When he had said these things, he cried out with a loud voice, "Lazarus, come out." [44] The man who had died came out, his hands and feet bound with linen strips, and his face wrapped with a cloth. Jesus said to them, "Unbind him, and let him go."

The Plot to Kill Jesus

[45] Many of the Jews therefore, who had come with Mary and had seen what he did, believed in him, [46] but some of them went to the Pharisees and told them what Jesus had done. [47] So the chief priests and the Pharisees gathered the council and said, "What are we to do? For this man performs many signs. [48] If we let him go on like this, everyone will believe in him, and the Romans will come and take away both our place and our nation." [49] But one of them,

Caiaphas, who was high priest that year, said to them, "You know nothing at all. [50] Nor do you understand that it is better for you that one man should die for the people, not that the whole nation should perish." [51] He did not say this of his own accord, but being high priest that year he prophesied that Jesus would die for the nation, [52] and not for the nation only, but also to gather into one the children of God who are scattered abroad. [53] So from that day on they made plans to put him to death.

[54] Jesus therefore no longer walked openly among the Jews, but went from there to the region near the wilderness, to a town called Ephraim, and there he stayed with the disciples.

[55] Now the Passover of the Jews was at hand, and many went up from the country to Jerusalem before the Passover to purify themselves. [56] They were looking for Jesus and saying to one another as they stood in the temple, "What do you think? That he will not come to the feast at all?" [57] Now the chief priests and the Pharisees had given orders that if anyone knew where he was, he should let them know, so that they might arrest him.

ANOINTED

MARY THEREFORE TOOK A POUND
OF EXPENSIVE OINTMENT MADE FROM
PURE NARD, AND ANOINTED THE FEET
OF JESUS AND WIPED HIS FEET WITH
HER HAIR. THE HOUSE WAS FILLED
WITH THE FRAGRANCE OF
THE PERFUME.

John 12:3

Chapter Twelve

Mary Anoints Jesus at Bethany

Six days before the Passover, Jesus therefore came to Bethany, where Lazarus was, whom Jesus had raised from the dead. ² So they gave a dinner for him there. Martha served, and Lazarus was one of those reclining with him at table. ³ Mary therefore took a pound of expensive ointment made from pure nard, and anointed the feet of Jesus and wiped his feet with her hair. The house was filled with the fragrance of the perfume. ⁴ But Judas Iscariot, one of his disciples (he who was about to betray him), said, ⁵ "Why was this ointment not sold for three hundred denarii and given to the poor?" ⁶ He said this, not because he cared about the poor, but because he was a thief, and having charge of the money bag he used to help himself to what was put into it. ⁷ Jesus said, "Leave her alone, so that she may keep it for the day of my burial. ⁸ For the poor you always have with you, but you do not always have me."

The Plot to Kill Lazarus

⁹ When the large crowd of the Jews learned that Jesus was there, they came, not only on account of him but also to see Lazarus, whom he had raised from the dead. ¹⁰ So the chief priests made plans to put Lazarus to death as well, ¹¹ because on account of him many of the Jews were going away and believing in Jesus.

The Triumphal Entry

¹² The next day the large crowd that had come to the feast heard that Jesus was coming to Jerusalem. ¹³ So they took branches of palm trees and went out to meet him, crying out, "Hosanna! Blessed is he who comes in the name of the Lord, even the King of Israel!" ¹⁴ And Jesus found a young donkey and sat on it, just as it is written,

¹⁵ "Fear not, daughter of Zion;
  behold, your king is coming,
    sitting on a donkey's colt!"

¹⁶ His disciples did not understand these things at first, but when Jesus was glorified, then they remembered that these things had been written about him and had been done to him. ¹⁷ The crowd that had been with him when he called Lazarus out of the tomb and raised him from the dead continued to bear witness. ¹⁸ The reason why the crowd went to meet him was that they heard he had done this sign. ¹⁹ So the Pharisees said to one another, "You see that you are gaining nothing. Look, the world has gone after him."

Some Greeks Seek Jesus

²⁰ Now among those who went up to worship at the feast were some Greeks. ²¹ So these came to Philip, who was from Bethsaida in Galilee, and asked him, "Sir, we wish to see Jesus." ²² Philip went and told Andrew; Andrew and Philip went and told Jesus. ²³ And Jesus answered them, "The hour has come for the Son of Man to be glorified. ²⁴ Truly, truly, I say to you, unless a grain of wheat falls into the earth and dies, it remains alone; but if it dies, it

"...I HAVE COME INTO THE WORLD AS LIGHT, SO THAT WHOEVER BELIEVES IN ME MAY NOT REMAIN IN DARKNESS. IF ANYONE HEARS MY WORDS AND DOES NOT KEEP THEM, I DO NOT JUDGE HIM; FOR I DID NOT COME TO JUDGE THE WORLD BUT TO SAVE THE WORLD."

John 12:46-47

bears much fruit. ²⁵ Whoever loves his life loses it, and whoever hates his life in this world will keep it for eternal life. ²⁶ If anyone serves me, he must follow me; and where I am, there will my servant be also. If anyone serves me, the Father will honour him.

The Son of Man Must Be Lifted Up

²⁷ "Now is my soul troubled. And what shall I say? 'Father, save me from this hour'? But for this purpose I have come to this hour. ²⁸ Father, glorify your name." Then a voice came from heaven: "I have glorified it, and I will glorify it again." ²⁹ The crowd that stood there and heard it said that it had thundered. Others said, "An angel has spoken to him." ³⁰ Jesus answered, "This voice has come for your sake, not mine. ³¹ Now is the judgement of this world; now will the ruler of this world be cast out. ³² And I, when I am lifted up from the earth, will draw all people to myself." ³³ He said this to show by what kind of death he was going to die. ³⁴ So the crowd answered him, "We have heard from the Law that the Christ remains for ever. How can you say that the Son of Man must be lifted up? Who is this Son of Man?" ³⁵ So Jesus said to them, "The light is among you for a little while longer. Walk while you have the light, lest darkness overtake you. The one who walks in the darkness does not know where he is going. ³⁶ While you have the light, believe in the light, that you may become sons of light."

The Unbelief of the People

When Jesus had said these things, he departed and hid himself from them. ³⁷ Though he had done so many signs before them, they still did not believe in him, ³⁸ so that the word spoken by the prophet Isaiah might be fulfilled:

"Lord, who has believed what he
    heard from us,
  and to whom has the arm of the
    Lord been revealed?"

³⁹ Therefore they could not believe. For again Isaiah said,

⁴⁰   "He has blinded their eyes
      and hardened their heart,
  lest they see with their eyes,
    and understand with their
      heart, and turn,
    and I would heal them."

⁴¹ Isaiah said these things because he saw his glory and spoke of him. ⁴² Nevertheless, many even of the authorities believed in him, but for fear of the Pharisees they did not confess it, so that they would not be put out of the synagogue; ⁴³ for they loved the glory that comes from man more than the glory that comes from God.

Jesus Came to Save the World

⁴⁴ And Jesus cried out and said, "Whoever believes in me, believes not in me but in him who sent me. ⁴⁵ And whoever sees me sees him who sent me. ⁴⁶ I have come into the world as light, so that whoever believes in me may not remain in darkness. ⁴⁷ If anyone hears my words and does not keep them, I do not judge him; for I did not come to judge the world but to save the world. ⁴⁸ The one who rejects me and does not receive my words has a judge; the word that I have spoken will judge him on the last day. ⁴⁹ For I have not spoken on my own authority, but the Father who sent me has himself given me a commandment—what to say and what to speak. ⁵⁰ And I know that his commandment is eternal life. What I say, therefore, I say as the Father has told me."

Chapter Thirteen
Jesus Washes the Disciples' Feet

Now before the Feast of the Passover, when Jesus knew that his hour had come to depart out of this world to the Father, having loved his own who were in the world, he loved them to the end. ² During supper, when the devil had already put it into the heart of Judas Iscariot, Simon's son, to betray him, ³ Jesus, knowing that the Father had given all things into his hands, and that he had come from God and was going back to God, ⁴ rose from supper. He laid aside his outer garments, and taking a towel, tied it round his waist. ⁵ Then he poured water into a basin and began to wash the disciples' feet and to wipe them with the towel that was wrapped round him. ⁶ He came to Simon Peter, who said to him, "Lord, do you wash my feet?" ⁷ Jesus answered him, "What I am doing you do not understand now, but afterwards you will understand." ⁸ Peter said to him, "You shall never wash my feet." Jesus answered him, "If I do not wash you, you have no share with me." ⁹ Simon Peter said to him, "Lord, not my feet only but also my hands and my head!" ¹⁰ Jesus said to him, "The one who has bathed does not need to wash, except for his feet, but is completely clean. And you are clean, but not every one of you." ¹¹ For he knew who was to betray him; that was why he said, "Not all of you are clean."

¹² When he had washed their feet and put on his outer garments and resumed his place, he said to them, "Do you understand what I have done to you? ¹³ You call me Teacher and Lord, and you are right, for so I am. ¹⁴ If I then,

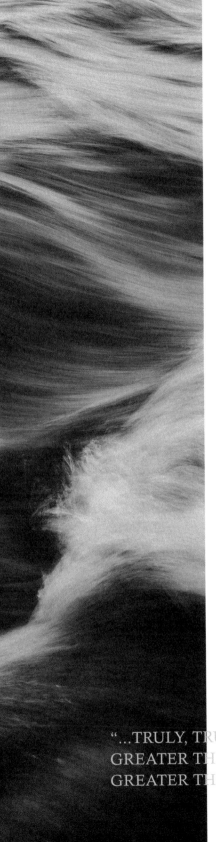

your Lord and Teacher, have washed your feet, you also ought to wash one another's feet. ¹⁵For I have given you an example, that you also should do just as I have done to you. ¹⁶Truly, truly, I say to you, a servant is not greater than his master, nor is a messenger greater than the one who sent him. ¹⁷If you know these things, blessed are you if you do them. ¹⁸I am not speaking of all of you; I know whom I have chosen. But the Scripture will be fulfilled, 'He who ate my bread has lifted his heel against me.' ¹⁹I am telling you this now, before it takes place, that when it does take place you may believe that I am he. ²⁰Truly, truly, I say to you, whoever receives the one I send receives me, and whoever receives me receives the one who sent me."

One of You Will Betray Me

²¹After saying these things, Jesus was troubled in his spirit, and testified, "Truly, truly, I say to you, one of you will betray me." ²²The disciples looked at one another, uncertain of whom he spoke. ²³One of his disciples, whom Jesus loved, was reclining at table at Jesus' side, ²⁴so Simon Peter motioned to him to ask Jesus of whom he was speaking. ²⁵So that disciple, leaning back against Jesus, said to him, "Lord, who is it?" ²⁶Jesus answered, "It is he to whom I will give this morsel of bread when I have dipped it." So when he had dipped the morsel, he gave it to Judas, the son of Simon Iscariot. ²⁷Then after he had taken the morsel, Satan entered into him. Jesus said to him, "What you are going to do, do quickly." ²⁸Now no one at the table knew why he said this to him. ²⁹Some thought that, because Judas had the money bag, Jesus was telling him, "Buy what we need for the feast", or that he should give something to the poor. ³⁰So, after receiving the morsel of bread, he immediately went out. And it was night.

A New Commandment

³¹When he had gone out, Jesus said, "Now is the Son of Man glorified, and God is glorified in him. ³²If God is glorified in him, God will also glorify him in himself, and glorify him at once. ³³Little children, yet a little while I am with you. You will seek me, and just as I said to the Jews, so now I also say to you, 'Where I am going you cannot come.' ³⁴A new commandment I give to you, that you love one another: just as I have loved you, you also are to love one another. ³⁵By this all people will know that you are my disciples, if you have love for one another."

Jesus Foretells Peter's Denial

³⁶Simon Peter said to him, "Lord, where are you going?" Jesus answered him, "Where I am going you cannot follow me now, but you will follow afterwards." ³⁷Peter said to him, "Lord, why can I not follow you now? I will lay down my life for you." ³⁸Jesus answered, "Will you lay down your life for me? Truly, truly, I say to you, the cock will not crow till you have denied me three times.

"...TRULY, TRULY, I SAY TO YOU, A SERVANT IS NOT GREATER THAN HIS MASTER, NOR IS A MESSENGER GREATER THAN THE ONE WHO SENT HIM." John 13:16

Chapter Fourteen
I Am the Way, and the Truth, and the Life

"Let not your hearts be troubled. Believe in God; believe also in me. ²In my Father's house are many rooms. If it were not so, would I have told you that I go to prepare a place for you? ³And if I go and prepare a place for you, I will come again and will take you to myself, that where I am you may be also. ⁴And you know the way to where I am going." ⁵Thomas said to him, "Lord, we do not know where you are going. How can we know the way?" ⁶Jesus said to him, "I am the way, and the truth, and the life. No one comes to the Father except through me. ⁷If you had known me, you would have known my Father also. From now on you do know him and have seen him."

⁸Philip said to him, "Lord, show us the Father, and it is enough for us." ⁹Je-sus said to him, "Have I been with you so long, and you still do not know me, Philip? Whoever has seen me has seen the Father. How can you say, 'Show us the Father'? ¹⁰Do you not believe that I am in the Father and the Father is in me? The words that I say to you I do not speak on my own authority, but the Father who dwells in me does his works. ¹¹Believe me that I am in the Father and the Father is in me, or else believe on account of the works themselves.

¹²"Truly, truly, I say to you, whoever believes in me will also do the works that I do; and greater works than these will he do, because I am going to the Father. ¹³Whatever you ask in my name, this I will do, that the Father may be glorified in the Son. ¹⁴If you ask me for anything in my name, I will do it.

Jesus Promises the Holy Spirit

[15]"If you love me, you will keep my commandments. [16]And I will ask the Father, and he will give you another Helper, to be with you for ever, [17]even the Spirit of truth, whom the world cannot receive, because it neither sees him nor knows him. You know him, for he dwells with you and will be in you.

[18]"I will not leave you as orphans; I will come to you. [19]Yet a little while and the world will see me no more, but you will see me. Because I live, you also will live. [20]In that day you will know that I am in my Father, and you in me, and I in you. [21]Whoever has my commandments and keeps them, he it is who loves me. And he who loves me will be loved by my Father, and I will love him and manifest myself to him." [22]Judas (not Iscariot) said to him, "Lord, how is it that you will manifest yourself to us, and not to the world?" [23]Jesus answered him, "If anyone loves me, he will keep my word, and my Father will love him, and we will come to him and make our home with him.

[24]Whoever does not love me does not keep my words. And the word that you hear is not mine but the Father's who sent me.

[25]"These things I have spoken to you while I am still with you. [26]But the Helper, the Holy Spirit, whom the Father will send in my name, he will teach you all things and bring to your remembrance all that I have said to you. [27]Peace I leave with you; my peace I give to you. Not as the world gives do I give to you. Let not your hearts be troubled, neither let them be afraid. [28]You heard me say to you, 'I am going away, and I will come to you.' If you loved me, you would have rejoiced, because I am going to the Father, for the Father is greater than I. [29]And now I have told you before it takes place, so that when it does take place you may believe. [30]I will no longer talk much with you, for the ruler of this world is coming. He has no claim on me, [31]but I do as the Father has commanded me, so that the world may know that I love the Father. Rise, let us go from here.

> "I WILL NOT LEAVE YOU AS ORPHANS; I WILL COME TO YOU. YET A LITTLE WHILE AND THE WORLD WILL SEE ME NO MORE, BUT YOU WILL SEE ME. BECAUSE I LIVE, YOU ALSO WILL LIVE. IN THAT DAY YOU WILL KNOW THAT I AM IN MY FATHER, AND YOU IN ME, AND I IN YOU."
>
> Luke 14:18-20

"AS THE FATHER HAS LOVED ME, SO HAVE I LOVED YOU. ABIDE IN MY LOVE. IF YOU KEEP MY COMMANDMENTS, YOU WILL ABIDE IN MY LOVE, JUST AS I HAVE KEPT MY FATHER'S COMMANDMENTS AND ABIDE IN HIS LOVE."

John 15:9-10

Chapter Fifteen
I Am the True Vine

I am the true vine, and my Father is the vine dresser. [2]Every branch in me that does not bear fruit he takes away, and every branch that does bear fruit he prunes, that it may bear more fruit. [3]Already you are clean because of the word that I have spoken to you. [4]Abide in me, and I in you. As the branch cannot bear fruit by witself, unless it abides in the vine, neither can you, unless you abide in me. [5]I am the vine; you are the branches. Whoever abides in me and I in him, he it is that bears much fruit, for apart from me you can do nothing. [6]If anyone does not abide in me he is thrown away like a branch and withers; and the branches are gathered, thrown into the fire, and burned. [7]If you abide in me, and my words abide in you, ask whatever you wish, and it will be done for you. [8]By this my Father is glorified, that you bear much fruit and so prove to be my disciples. [9]As the Father has loved me, so have I loved you. Abide in my love. [10]If you keep my commandments, you will abide in my love, just as I have kept my Father's commandments and abide in his love. [11]These things I have spoken to you, that my joy may be in you, and that your joy may be full.

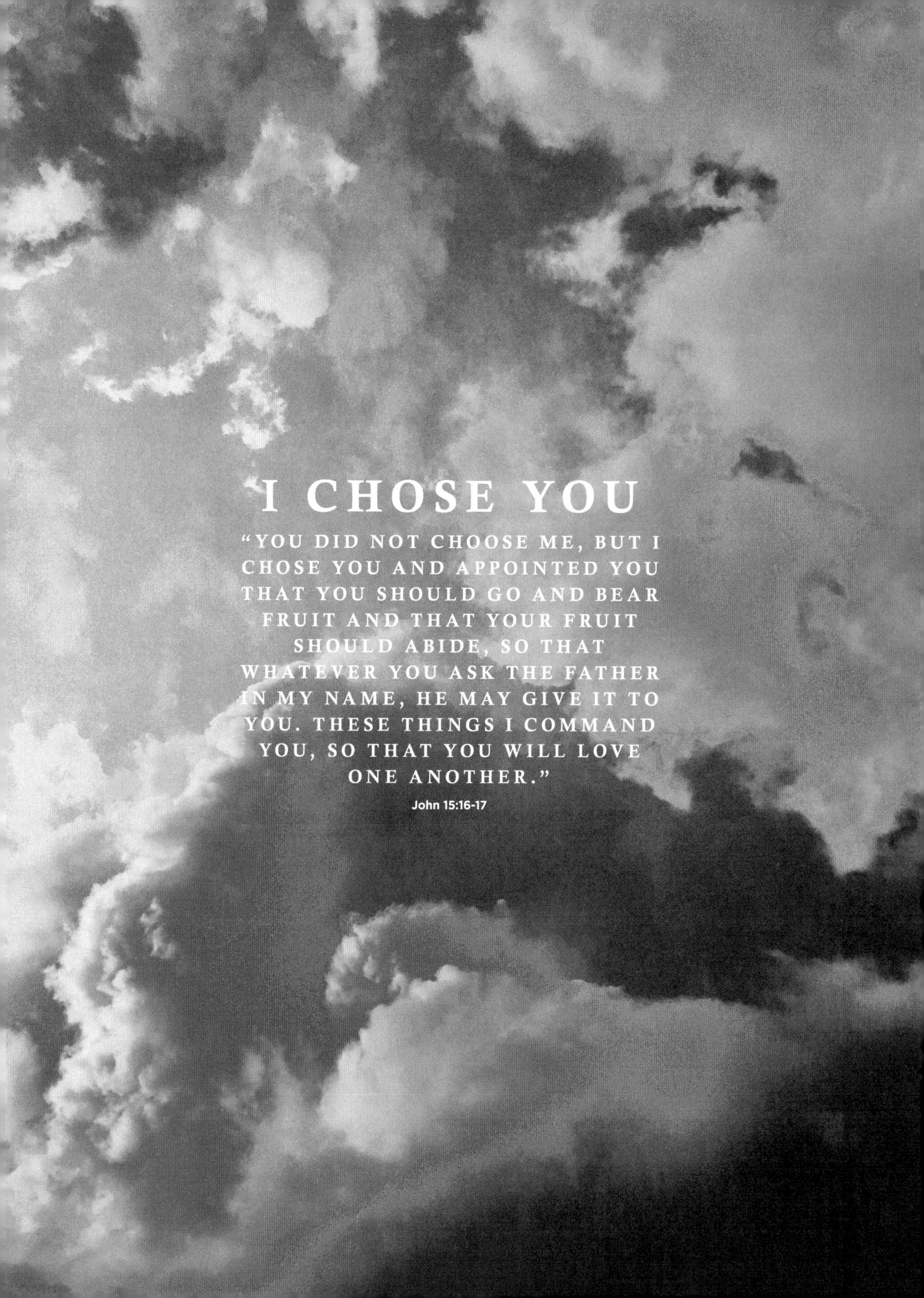

I CHOSE YOU

"YOU DID NOT CHOOSE ME, BUT I
CHOSE YOU AND APPOINTED YOU
THAT YOU SHOULD GO AND BEAR
FRUIT AND THAT YOUR FRUIT
SHOULD ABIDE, SO THAT
WHATEVER YOU ASK THE FATHER
IN MY NAME, HE MAY GIVE IT TO
YOU. THESE THINGS I COMMAND
YOU, SO THAT YOU WILL LOVE
ONE ANOTHER."

John 15:16-17

¹²"This is my commandment, that you love one another as I have loved you. ¹³Greater love has no one than this, that someone lay down his life for his friends. ¹⁴You are my friends if you do what I command you.

¹⁵No longer do I call you servants, for the servant does not know what his master is doing; but I have called you friends, for all that I have heard from my Father I have made known to you. ¹⁶You did not choose me, but I chose you and appointed you that you should go and bear fruit and that your fruit should abide, so that whatever you ask the Father in my name, he may give it to you. ¹⁷These things I command you, so that you will love one another.

The Hatred of the World

¹⁸"If the world hates you, know that it has hated me before it hated you. ¹⁹If you were of the world, the world would love you as its own; but because you are not of the world, but I chose you out of the world, therefore the world hates you. ²⁰Remember the word that I said to you: 'A servant is not greater than his master.' If they persecuted me, they will also persecute you. If they kept my word, they will also keep yours. ²¹But all these things they will do to you on account of my name, because they do not know him who sent me. ²²If I had not come and spoken to them, they would not have been guilty of sin, but now they have no excuse for their sin. ²³Whoever hates me hates my Father also. ²⁴If I had not done among them the works that no one else did, they would not be guilty of sin, but now they have seen and hated both me and my Father. ²⁵But the word that is written in their Law must be fulfilled: 'They hated me without a cause.'

²⁶"But when the Helper comes, whom I will send to you from the Father, the Spirit of truth, who proceeds from the Father, he will bear witness about me. ²⁷And you also will bear witness, because you have been with me from the beginning.

Chapter Sixteen

"I have said all these things to you to keep you from falling away. ²They will put you out of the synagogues. Indeed, the hour is coming when whoever kills you will think he is offering service to God. ³And they will do these things because they have not known the Father, nor me. ⁴But I have said these things to you, that when their hour comes you may remember that I told them to you.

The Work of the Holy Spirit

"I did not say these things to you from the beginning, because I was with you. ⁵But now I am going to him who sent me, and none of you asks me, 'Where are you going?' ⁶But because I have said these things to you, sorrow has filled your heart. ⁷Nevertheless, I tell you the truth: it is to your advantage that I go away, for if I do not go away, the Helper will not come to you. But if I go, I will send him to you. ⁸And when he comes, he will convict the world concerning sin and righteousness and judgement: ⁹concerning sin, because they do not believe in me; ¹⁰concerning righteousness, because I go to the Father, and you will see me no longer; [11]concerning judgement, because the ruler of this world is judged.

[12]"I still have many things to say to you, but you cannot bear them now. [13]When the Spirit of truth comes, he will guide you into all the truth, for he will not speak on his own authority, but whatever he hears he will speak, and he will declare to you the things that are to come. [14]He will glorify me, for he will take what is mine and declare it to you. [15]All that the Father has is mine; therefore I said that he will take what is mine and declare it to you.

Your Sorrow Will Turn into Joy

[16]"A little while, and you will see me no longer; and again a little while, and you will see me." [17]So some of his disciples said to one another, "What is this that he says to us, 'A little while, and you will not see me, and again a little while, and you will see me'; and, 'because I am going to the Father'?" [18]So they were saying, "What does he mean by 'a little while'? We do not know what he is talking about." [19]Jesus knew that they wanted to ask him, so he said to them, "Is this what you are asking yourselves, what I meant by saying, 'A little while and you will not see me, and again a little while and you will see me'? [20]Truly, truly, I say to you, you will weep and lament, but the world will rejoice. You will be sorrowful, but your sorrow will turn into joy. [21]When a woman is giving birth, she has sorrow because her hour has come, but when she has delivered the baby, she no longer remembers the anguish, for joy that a human being has been born into the world. [22]So also you have sorrow now, but I will see you again, and your hearts will rejoice, and no one will take your joy from you. [23]In that day you will ask nothing of me. Truly, truly, I say to you, what- ever you ask of the Father in my name, he will give it to you. [24]Until now you have asked nothing in my name. Ask, and you will receive, that your joy may be full.

I Have Overcome the World

[25]"I have said these things to you in figures of speech. The hour is coming when I will no longer speak to you in figures of speech but will tell you plainly about the Father. [26]In that day you will ask in my name, and I do not say to you that I will ask the Father on your behalf; [27]for the Father himself loves you, because you have loved me and have believed that I came from God. [28]I came from the Father and have come into the world, and now I am leaving the world and going to the Father."

[29]His disciples said, "Ah, now you are speaking plainly and not using figurative speech! [30]Now we know that you know all things and do not need anyone to question you; this is why we believe that you came from God." [31]Jesus answered them, "Do you now believe? [32]Behold, the hour is coming, indeed it has come, when you will be scattered, each to his own home, and will leave me alone. Yet I am not alone, for the Father is with me. [33]I have said these things to you, that in me you may have peace. In the world you will have tribulation. But take heart; I have overcome the world."

Chapter Seventeen
The High Priestly Prayer

When Jesus had spoken these words, he lifted up his eyes to heaven, and said, "Father, the hour has come; glorify your Son that the Son may glorify you, ²since you have given him authority over all flesh, to give eternal life to all whom you have given him. ³And this is eternal life, that they know you, the only true God, and Jesus Christ whom you have sent. ⁴I glorified you on earth, having accomplished the work that you gave me to do. ⁵And now, Father, glorify me in your own presence with the glory that I had with you before the world existed.

⁶"I have manifested your name to the people whom you gave me out of the world. Yours they were, and you gave them to me, and they have kept your word. ⁷Now they know that everything that you have given me is from you. ⁸For I have given them the words that you gave me, and they have received them and have come to know in truth that I came from you; and they have believed that you sent me. ⁹I am praying for them. I am not praying for the world but for those whom you have given me, for they are yours. ¹⁰All mine are yours, and yours are mine, and I am glorified in them. ¹¹And I am no longer in the world, but they are in the world, and I am coming to you. Holy Father, keep them in your name, which you have given me, that they may be one, even as we are one. ¹²While I was with them, I kept them in your name, which you have given me. I have guarded them, and not one of them has been lost except the son of destruction, that the Scripture might be fulfilled.

¹³But now I am coming to you, and these things I speak in the world, that they may have my joy fulfilled in themselves. ¹⁴I have given them your word, and the world has hated them because they are not of the world, just as I am not of the world. ¹⁵I do not ask that you take them out of the world, but that you keep them from the evil one. ¹⁶They are not of the world, just as I am not of the world. ¹⁷Sanctify them in the truth; your word is truth. ¹⁸As you sent me into the world, so I have sent them into the world. ¹⁹And for their sake I consecrate myself, that they also may be sanctified in truth.

²⁰"I do not ask for these only, but also for those who will believe in me through their word, ²¹that they may all be one, just as you, Father, are in me, and I in you, that they also may be in us, so that the world may believe that you have sent me. ²²The glory that you have given me I have given to them, that they may be one even as we are one, ²³I in them and you in me, that they may become perfectly one, so that the world may know that you sent me and loved them even as you loved me. ²⁴Father, I desire that they also, whom you have given me, may be with me where I am, to see my glory that you have given me because you loved me before the foundation of the world. ²⁵O righteous Father, even though the world does not know you, I know you, and these know that you have sent me. ²⁶I made known to them your name, and I will continue to make it known, that the love with which you have loved me may be in them, and I in them."

ONE OF THE SERVANTS OF THE HIGH PRIEST, A RELATIVE OF THE MAN WHOSE EAR PETER HAD CUT OFF, ASKED, "DID I NOT SEE YOU IN THE GARDEN WITH HIM?" PETER AGAIN DENIED IT, AND AT ONCE A COCK CROWED.

John 18:26-27

Chapter Eighteen

Betrayal and Arrest of Jesus

When Jesus had spoken these words, he went out with his disciples across the brook Kidron, where there was a garden, which he and his disciples entered. ² Now Judas, who betrayed him, also knew the place, for Jesus often met there with his disciples. ³ So Judas, having procured a band of soldiers and some officers from the chief priests and the Pharisees, went there with lanterns and torches and weapons. ⁴ Then Jesus, knowing all that would happen to him, came forward and said to them, "Whom do you seek?" ⁵ They answered him, "Jesus of Nazareth." Jesus said to them, "I am he." Judas, who betrayed him, was standing with them. ⁶ When Jesus said to them, "I am he", they drew back and fell to the ground. ⁷ So he asked them again, "Whom do you seek?" And they said, "Jesus of Nazareth." ⁸ Jesus answered, "I told you that I am he. So, if you seek me, let these men go." ⁹ This was to fulfil the word that he had spoken: "Of those whom you gave me I have lost not one." ¹⁰ Then Simon Peter, having a sword, drew it and struck the high priest's servant and cut off his right ear. (The servant's name was Malchus.) ¹¹ So Jesus said to Peter, "Put your sword into its sheath; shall I not drink the cup that the Father has given me?"

Jesus Faces Annas and Caiaphas

¹² So the band of soldiers and their captain and the officers of the Jews arrested Jesus and bound him. ¹³ First they led him to Annas, for he was the father-in-law of Caiaphas, who was high priest that year. ¹⁴ It was Caiaphas who had advised the Jews that it would be expedient that one man should die for the people.

Peter Denies Jesus

¹⁵ Simon Peter followed Jesus, and so did another disciple. Since that disciple was known to the high priest, he entered with Jesus into the courtyard of the high priest, ¹⁶ but Peter stood outside at the door. So the other disciple, who was known to the high priest, went out and spoke to the servant girl who kept watch at the door, and brought Peter in. ¹⁷ The servant girl at the door said to Peter, "You also are not one of this man's disciples, are you?" He said, "I am not." ¹⁸ Now the servants and officers had made a charcoal fire, because it was cold, and they were standing and warming themselves. Peter also was with them, standing and warming himself.

The High Priest Questions Jesus

¹⁹ The high priest then questioned Jesus about his disciples and his teaching. ²⁰ Jesus answered him, "I have spoken openly to the world. I have always taught in synagogues and in the temple, where all Jews come together. I have said nothing in secret. ²¹ Why do you ask me? Ask those who have heard me what I said to them; they know

what I said." 22 When he had said these things, one of the officers standing by struck Jesus with his hand, saying, "Is that how you answer the high priest?" 23 Jesus answered him, "If what I said is wrong, bear witness about the wrong; but if what I said is right, why do you strike me?" 24 Annas then sent him bound to Caiaphas the high priest.

Peter Denies Jesus Again

25 Now Simon Peter was standing and warming himself. So they said to him, "You also are not one of his disciples, are you?" He denied it and said, "I am not." 26 One of the servants of the high priest, a relative of the man whose ear Peter had cut off, asked, "Did I not see you in the garden with him?" 27 Peter again denied it, and at once a cock crowed.

Jesus Before Pilate

28 Then they led Jesus from the house of Caiaphas to the governor's headquarters. It was early morning. They themselves did not enter the governor's headquarters, so that they would not be defiled, but could eat the Passover. 29 So Pilate went outside to them and said, "What accusation do you bring against this man?" 30 They answered him, "If this man were not doing evil, we would not have delivered him over to you." 31 Pilate said to them, "Take him yourselves and judge him by your own law." The Jews said to him,

"It is not lawful for us to put anyone to death." 32 This was to fulfil the word that Jesus had spoken to show by what kind of death he was going to die.

My Kingdom Is Not of This World

33 So Pilate entered his headquarters again and called Jesus and said to him, "Are you the King of the Jews?" 34 Jesus answered, "Do you say this of your own accord, or did others say it to you about me?" 35 Pilate answered, "Am I a Jew? Your own nation and the chief priests have delivered you over to me. What have you done?" 36 Jesus answered, "My kingdom is not of this world. If my kingdom were of this world, my servants would have been fighting, that I might not be delivered over to the Jews. But my kingdom is not from the world." 37 Then Pilate said to him, "So you are a king?" Jesus answered, "You say that I am a king. For this purpose I was born and for this purpose I have come into the world—to bear witness to the truth. Everyone who is of the truth listens to my voice." 38 Pilate said to him, "What is truth?"

After he had said this, he went back outside to the Jews and told them, "I find no guilt in him. 39 But you have a custom that I should release one man for you at the Passover. So do you want me to release to you the King of the Jews?" 40 They cried out again, "Not this man, but Barabbas!" Now Barabbas was a robber.

THEN PILATE SAID TO HIM, "SO YOU ARE A KING?" JESUS ANSWERED, "YOU SAY THAT I AM A KING. FOR THIS PURPOSE I WAS BORN AND FOR THIS PURPOSE I HAVE COME INTO THE WORLD—TO BEAR WITNESS TO THE TRUTH. EVERYONE WHO IS OF THE TRUTH LISTENS TO MY VOICE."

John 18:37

Chapter Nineteen
Jesus Delivered to Be Crucified

Then Pilate took Jesus and flogged him. ² And the soldiers twisted together a crown of thorns and put it on his head and arrayed him in a purple robe. ³ They came up to him, saying, "Hail, King of the Jews!" and struck him with their hands. ⁴ Pilate went out again and said to them, "See, I am bringing him out to you that you may know that I find no guilt in him." ⁵ So Jesus came out, wearing the crown of thorns and the purple robe. Pilate said to them, "Behold the man!" ⁶ When the chief priests and the officers saw him, they cried out, "Crucify him, crucify him!" Pilate said to them, "Take him yourselves and crucify him, for I find no guilt in him." ⁷ The Jews answered him, "We have a law, and according to that law he ought to die because he has made himself the Son of God." ⁸ When Pilate heard this statement, he was even more afraid. ⁹ He entered his headquarters again and said to Jesus, "Where are you from?" But Jesus gave him no answer. ¹⁰ So Pilate said to him, "You will not speak to me? Do you not know that I have authority to release you and authority to crucify you?" ¹¹ Jesus answered him, "You would have no authority over me at all unless it had been given you from above. Therefore

he who delivered me over to you has the greater sin."

¹² From then on Pilate sought to release him, but the Jews cried out, "If you release this man, you are not Caesar's friend. Everyone who makes himself a king opposes Caesar." ¹³ So when Pilate heard these words, he brought Jesus out and sat down on the judgement seat at a place called The Stone Pavement, and in Aramaic Gabbatha. ¹⁴ Now it was the day of Preparation of the Passover. It was about the sixth hour. He said to the Jews, "Behold your King!" ¹⁵ They cried out, "Away with him, away with him, crucify him!" Pilate said to them, "Shall I crucify your King?" The chief priests answered, "We have no king but Caesar." ¹⁶ So he delivered him over to them to be crucified.

The Crucifixion
So they took Jesus, ¹⁷ and he went out, bearing his own cross, to the place called The Place of a Skull, which in Aramaic is called Golgotha. ¹⁸ There they crucified him, and with him two others, one on either side, and Jesus between them. ¹⁹ Pilate also wrote an inscription and put it on the cross. It read, "Jesus of Nazareth, the King of the Jews." ²⁰ Many of the Jews read this

inscription, for the place where Jesus was crucified was near the city, and it was written in Aramaic, in Latin, and in Greek. [21] So the chief priests of the Jews said to Pilate, "Do not write, 'The King of the Jews', but rather, 'This man said, I am King of the Jews.'" [22] Pilate answered, "What I have written I have written."

[23] When the soldiers had crucified Jesus, they took his garments and divided them into four parts, one part for each soldier; also his tunic. But the tunic was seamless, woven in one piece from top to bottom, [24] so they said to one another, "Let us not tear it, but cast lots for it to see whose it shall be." This was to fulfil the Scripture which says,

"They divided my garments among
        them,
    and for my clothing they cast
        lots."

So the soldiers did these things, [25] but standing by the cross of Jesus were his mother and his mother's sister, Mary the wife of Clopas, and Mary Magdalene. [26] When Jesus saw his mother and the disciple whom he loved standing nearby, he said to his mother, "Woman, behold, your son!" [27] Then he said to the disciple, "Behold, your mother!" And from that hour the disciple took her to his own home.

The Death of Jesus

[28] After this, Jesus, knowing that all was now finished, said (to fulfil the Scripture), "I thirst." [29] A jar full of sour wine stood there, so they put a sponge full of the sour wine on a hyssop branch and held it to his mouth. [30] When Jesus had received the sour wine, he said, "It is finished", and he bowed his head and gave up his spirit.

Jesus' Side Is Pierced

[31] Since it was the day of Preparation, and so that the bodies would not remain on the cross on the Sabbath (for that Sabbath was a high day), the Jews asked Pilate that their legs might be broken and that they might be taken away. [32] So the soldiers came and broke the legs of the first, and of the other who had been crucified with him. [33] But when they came to Jesus and saw that he was already dead, they did not break his legs. [34] But one of the soldiers pierced his side with a spear, and at once there came out blood and water. [35] He who saw it has borne witness—his testimony is true, and he knows that he is telling the truth—that you also may believe. [36] For these things took place that the Scripture might be fulfilled: "Not one of his bones will be broken." [37] And again another Scripture says, "They will look on him whom they have pierced."

Jesus Is Buried

[38] After these things Joseph of Arimathea, who was a disciple of Jesus, but secretly for fear of the Jews, asked Pilate that he might take away the body of Jesus, and Pilate gave him permission. So he came and took away his body. [39] Nicodemus also, who earlier had come to Jesus by night, came bringing a mixture of myrrh and aloes, about seventy-five pounds in weight. [40] So they took the body of Jesus and bound it in linen cloths with the spices, as is the burial custom of the Jews. [41] Now in the place where he was crucified there was a garden, and in the garden a new tomb in which no one had yet been laid. [42] So because of the Jewish day of Preparation, since the tomb was close at hand, they laid Jesus there.

WHEN JESUS HAD
RECEIVED THE SOUR WINE, HE SAID,

"IT IS FINISHED"

AND HE BOWED HIS HEAD AND
GAVE UP HIS SPIRIT.

John 19:30

GRACE

THE GIFT

Here, at the end of John 19, we arrive at a point in John's narrative where Jesus' body is buried. Jesus has been humiliated, tortured and crucified, and then he is laid to rest in a tomb. John's description of how Jesus is killed is incredibly detailed, it leaves very little to the imagination, and one would think that with only two chapters remaining in his account of the life of Jesus, there is very little

opportunity for Jesus to come out of this situation well.

If you have heard of the story of Jesus before, you may know what is to come in the last two chapters of John's Gospel, but for the people who were there at the time, Jesus being laid in a tomb must have looked like the end of the road. Imagine the disciples' confusion—these people had been following Jesus around for the last three years, convinced that he was

God, that he was going to lead them to victory and that he would offer the redemption that they needed. Yet after all the miracles, the healings and the promises of victory, it all ends up with Jesus lying dead in a tomb. It can't have made any sense to them at all.

If John's Gospel were to end at this point, it undoubtedly wouldn't be a book of good news. But in the next chapter we read about Jesus rising from the dead. At the point where it seems like all hope is lost, and it appears that Jesus has been defeated, he defies the very nature of death by rising from the grave in bodily form. Although the tomb looked like the end, it didn't have the final word, as Jesus rose victorious over death itself.

For the Gospel writers, the death and resurrection of Jesus are the climax of their accounts. Matthew, Mark, Luke and John all wrote their Gospels building up to this event. It's one of the few narrative parts of the life of Jesus that is shared by all four of the Gospel writers.

The reason for this is that it is at the cross that we see the greatest act of grace that the world has ever seen. Jesus, the Son of God, was crucified as an innocent sacrifice for humanity. Jesus, the innocent one, was judged in our place, so that we, the guilty party, could walk free.

We read in the book of Genesis, the first book of the Bible, that God created humanity to live in perfect relationship with him. From the first few chapters of the Bible we are given an image of humanity flourishing in their relationships with each other and their relationship with God. Yet as a result of humanity turning its back on God, a relational separation is introduced between God and humanity. When humanity chose to be its own king, God didn't want to force us to be in a relationship with him, so he gave us the choice of who to live for—ourselves or him.

One of the biggest myths that people often believe is that humans need to behave to a certain standard to fix this separation and come back into relationship with God. But the truth is that there is nothing we can do; there is no way we can bridge that divide in our own strength. The apostle Paul says in his letter to the Romans that "all ... fall short of the glory of God (3:23). By turning our backs on God we forfeited the relationship we had, and there is no way that we can bridge that divide on our own.

The good news, though, is that Jesus paid the price we should have paid and bridged the divide that we initiated. Jesus demonstrated grace for us so that we could come to know our Saviour. He died for us before we even were able to accept this gift; while we were still turning our backs on him, he came to embrace us. Grace is neither an idea nor a religious concept—grace is a person, and his name is Jesus.

Grace is the unmerited favour of God. We haven't earned the grace that God gives us and we don't deserve it, yet nonetheless God pours out his favour towards us. It is of course at the cross that God poured out his grace towards us, but every day that we live as Christians, we live in the grace of God. Jesus lives in us and he empowers us to live the life he created us to live. How amazing is that!

The incredible thing is that grace is not forced upon us, but it is actually a gift. God will never force anyone to come into relationship with him, and each person has a choice of how to respond. The nature of any gift is that it is unconditional, yet we get to choose how we respond to it. If you haven't yet decided to accept God's gift of grace, why not make that decision today? It is truly the greatest decision you could ever make.

GRACE IS NEITHER AN IDEA NOR A RELIGIOUS CONCEPT, GRACE IS A PERSON, AND HIS NAME IS JESUS. GRACE IS THE UNMERITED FAVOUR OF GOD. WE HAVEN'T EARNED THE GRACE THAT GOD GIVES US AND WE DON'T DESERVE IT, YET NONETHELESS GOD POURS OUT HIS FAVOUR TOWARDS US.

Chapter Twenty
The Resurrection

ow on the first day of the week Mary Magdalene came to the tomb early, while it was still dark, and saw that the stone had been taken away from the tomb. ²So she ran and went to Simon Peter and the other disciple, the one whom Jesus loved, and said to them, "They have taken the Lord out of the tomb, and we do not know where they have laid him." ³So Peter went out with the other disciple, and they were going towards the tomb. ⁴Both of them were running together, but the other disciple outran Peter and reached the tomb first. ⁵And stooping to look in, he saw the linen cloths lying there, but he did not go in. ⁶Then Simon Peter came, following him, and went into the tomb. He saw the linen cloths lying there, ⁷and the face cloth, which had been on Jesus' head, not lying with the linen cloths but folded up in a place by itself. ⁸Then the other disciple, who had reached the tomb first, also went in, and he saw and believed; ⁹for as yet they did not

JESUS SAID TO HER,
"WOMAN, WHY ARE
YOU WEEPING? WHOM
ARE YOU SEEKING?"
SUPPOSING HIM TO
BE THE GARDENER,
SHE SAID TO HIM,
"SIR, IF YOU HAVE
CARRIED HIM AWAY,
TELL ME WHERE
YOU HAVE LAID HIM,
AND I WILL TAKE
HIM AWAY." JESUS
SAID TO HER, "MARY."
SHE TURNED AND
SAID TO HIM IN
ARAMAIC, "RABBONI!"
(WHICH MEANS
TEACHER).

John 20:15-16

understand the Scripture, that he must rise from the dead. ¹⁰ Then the disciples went back to their homes.

Jesus Appears to Mary Magdalene

¹¹ But Mary stood weeping outside the tomb, and as she wept she stooped to look into the tomb. ¹²And she saw two angels in white, sitting where the body of Jesus had lain, one at the head and one at the feet. ¹³ They said to her, "Woman, why are you weeping?" She said to them, "They have taken away my Lord, and I do not know where they have laid him." ¹⁴ Having said this, she turned round and saw Jesus standing, but she did not know that it was Jesus. ¹⁵ Jesus said to her, "Woman, why are you weeping? Whom are you seeking?" Supposing him to be the gardener, she said to him, "Sir, if you have carried him away, tell me where you have laid him, and I will take him away." ¹⁶ Jesus said to her, "Mary." She turned and said to him in Aramaic, "Rabboni!" (which means Teacher). ¹⁷ Jesus said to her, "Do not cling to me, for I have not yet ascended to the Father; but go to my brothers and say to them, 'I am ascending to my Father and your Father, to my God and your God.'" ¹⁸ Mary Magdalene went and announced to the disciples, "I have seen the Lord"—and that he had said these things to her.

Jesus Appears to the Disciples

¹⁹ On the evening of that day, the first day of the week, the doors being locked where the disciples were for fear of the Jews, Jesus came and stood among them and said to them, "Peace be with you." ²⁰ When he had said this, he showed them his hands and his side. Then the disciples were glad when they saw the Lord. ²¹ Jesus said to them again, "Peace be with you. As the Father has sent me, even so I am sending you." ²² And when he had said this, he breathed on them and said to them, "Receive the Holy Spirit. ²³ If you forgive the sins of any, they are forgiven them; if you withhold forgiveness from any, it is withheld."

Jesus and Thomas

²⁴ Now Thomas, one of the twelve, called the Twin, was not with them when Jesus came. ²⁵ So the other disciples told him, "We have seen the Lord." But he said to them, "Unless I see in his hands the mark of the nails, and place my finger into the mark of the nails, and place my hand into his side, I will never believe."

²⁶ Eight days later, his disciples were inside again, and Thomas was with them. Although the doors were locked, Jesus came and stood among them and said, "Peace be with you." ²⁷ Then he said to Thomas, "Put your finger here, and see my hands; and put out your hand, and place it in my side. Do not disbelieve, but believe." ²⁸ Thomas answered him, "My Lord and my God!" ²⁹ Jesus said to him, "Have you believed because you have seen me? Blessed are those who have not seen and yet have believed."

The Purpose of This Book

³⁰ Now Jesus did many other signs in the presence of the disciples, which are not written in this book; ³¹ but these are written so that you may believe that Jesus is the Christ, the Son of God, and that by believing you may have life in his name.

JESUS SAID TO HER, "DO NOT CLING TO ME, FOR I HAVE NOT YET ASCENDED TO THE FATHER; BUT GO TO MY BROTHERS AND SAY TO THEM, 'I AM ASCENDING TO MY FATHER AND YOUR FATHER, TO MY GOD AND YOUR GOD.'" MARY MAGDALENE WENT AND ANNOUNCED TO THE DISCIPLES, "I HAVE SEEN THE LORD"—AND THAT HE HAD SAID THESE THINGS TO HER.

John 20:17-18

Chapter Twenty-One
Jesus Appears to Seven Disciples

After this Jesus revealed himself again to the disciples by the Sea of Tiberias, and he revealed himself in this way. ² Simon Peter, Thomas (called the Twin), Nathanael of Cana in Galilee, the sons of Zebedee, and two others of his disciples were together. ³ Simon Peter said to them, "I am going fishing." They said to him, "We will go with you." They went out and got into the boat, but that night they caught nothing.

⁴ Just as day was breaking, Jesus stood on the shore; yet the disciples did not know that it was Jesus. ⁵ Jesus said to them, "Children, do you have any fish?" They answered him, "No." ⁶ He said to them, "Cast the net on the right side of the boat, and you will find some." So they cast it, and now they were not able to haul it in, because of the quantity of fish. ⁷ That disciple whom Jesus loved therefore said to Peter, "It is the Lord!" When Simon Peter heard that it was the Lord, he put on his outer garment, for he was stripped for work, and

threw himself into the sea. ⁸ The other disciples came in the boat, dragging the net full of fish, for they were not far from the land, but about a hundred yards off.

⁹ When they got out on land, they saw a charcoal fire in place, with fish laid out on it, and bread. ¹⁰ Jesus said to them, "Bring some of the fish that you have just caught." ¹¹ So Simon Peter went aboard and hauled the net ashore, full of large fish, 153 of them. And although there were so many, the net was not torn. ¹² Jesus said to them, "Come and have breakfast." Now none of the disciples dared ask him, "Who are you?" They knew it was the Lord. ¹³ Jesus came and took the bread and gave it to them, and so with the fish. ¹⁴ This was now the third time that Jesus was revealed to the disciples after he was raised from the dead.

Jesus and Peter
¹⁵ When they had finished breakfast, Jesus said to Simon Peter, "Simon,

THIS IS THE DISCIPLE WHO IS
BEARING WITNESS ABOUT THESE
THINGS, AND WHO HAS WRITTEN
THESE THINGS, AND WE KNOW
THAT HIS TESTIMONY IS TRUE.

John 21:24

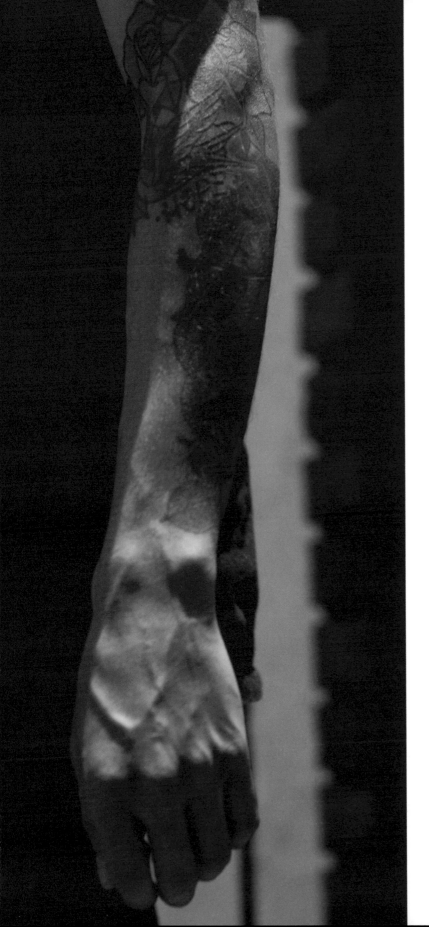

son of John, do you love me more than these?" He said to him, "Yes, Lord; you know that I love you." He said to him, "Feed my lambs." [16] He said to him a second time, "Simon, son of John, do you love me?" He said to him, "Yes, Lord; you know that I love you." He said to him, "Tend my sheep." [17] He said to him the third time, "Simon, son of John, do you love me?" Peter was grieved because he said to him the third time, "Do you love me?" and he said to him, "Lord, you know everything; you know that I love you." Jesus said to him, "Feed my sheep. [18] Truly, truly, I say to you, when you were young, you used to dress yourself and walk wherever you wanted, but when you are old, you will stretch out your hands, and another will dress you and carry you where you do not want to go." [19] (This he said to show by what kind of death he was to glorify God.) And after saying this he said to him, "Follow me."

Jesus and the Beloved Apostle

[20] Peter turned and saw the disciple whom Jesus loved following them, the one who also had leaned back against him during the supper and had said, "Lord, who is it that is going to betray you?" [21] When Peter saw him, he said to Jesus, "Lord, what about this man?" [22] Jesus said to him, "If it is my will that he remain until I come, what is that to you? You follow me!" [23] So the saying spread abroad among the brothers that this disciple was not to die; yet Jesus did not say to him that he was not to die, but, "If it is my will that he remain until I come, what is that to you?"

[24] This is the disciple who is bearing witness about these things, and who has written these things, and we know that his testimony is true.

[25] Now there are also many other things that Jesus did. Were every one of them to be written, I suppose that the world itself could not contain the books that would be written.

Inspired by the Holy Spirit

EXPERIENCE
JOHN

JESUS IS FULLY GOD AND FULLY HUMAN

"I GLORIFIED YOU ON EARTH, HAVING ACCOMPLISHED THE WORK THAT YOU GAVE ME TO DO. AND NOW, FATHER, GLORIFY ME IN YOUR OWN PRESENCE WITH THE GLORY THAT I HAD WITH YOU BEFORE THE WORLD EXISTED."
John 17:4-5

HOW JOHN FITS INTO GOD'S STORY AND MY STORY

God is not a distant force, but a personal Being. Jesus intervenes in the world's problems John 3:16

I can connect with God by connecting with Jesus.

KEY CHARACTERS

Jesus, John the Baptist, Satan, Peter, Mary Magdalene, the Beloved Disciple

NO OTHER GOSPEL HIGHLIGHTS
THE IMPORTANCE OF BELIEF LIKE JOHN'S.
BELIEF IN CHRIST IS ACTIVE BUT
IT ALSO REQUIRES ACTION.

KEY WORD IN JOHN: BELIEVE
Greek: πιστεύω, *pisteuō*, to believe

The Greek verb, *pisteuō*, is found 98 times in John's gospel and often means "to believe". It is no coincidence that the author uses this word so often. From the very beginning of the Gospel, all are called to believe (1:7) and John finishes his Gospel by stating his purpose in writing: that his readers would believe (20:31). No other Gospel highlights the importance of belief like John's. Belief in Christ is active but it also requires action. John uses the term to reiterate to his readers that belief does not remain stagnant. It is alive and dynamic, bearing fruit that helps all to abide in Christ (John 15:1-11).

KEY THEME: TESTIMONY - THE "SEVEN WITNESSES" OF JOHN

1. John the Baptist—"This is the Son of God " (John 1:34) 2. Nathanael—"Rabbi, you are the Son of God" (John 1:49) 3. Peter—"You are the Holy One of God!" (John 6:69) 4. Jesus—"I am the Son of God" (John 10:36; see also 4:25-26; 8:58) 5. Martha—"You are the Christ, the Son of God" (John 11:27) 6. Thomas—"My Lord and my God!" (John 20:28) 7. John—"Jesus is the Christ, the Son of God" (John 20:31)

THE WOMAN SAID TO HIM, "I KNOW THAT MESSIAH IS
COMING (HE WHO IS CALLED CHRIST). WHEN HE COMES,
HE WILL TELL US ALL THINGS." JESUS SAID TO HER,
"I WHO SPEAK TO YOU AM HE."

John 4:25-26

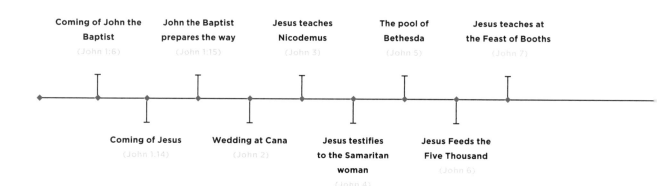

Coming of John the Baptist (John 1:6)

John the Baptist prepares the way (John 1:15)

Jesus teaches Nicodemus (John 3)

The pool of Bethesda (John 5)

Jesus teaches at the Feast of Booths (John 7)

Coming of Jesus (John 1:14)

Wedding at Cana (John 2)

Jesus testifies to the Samaritan woman (John 4)

Jesus Feeds the Five Thousand (John 6)

UNIQUE LITERARY MOTIF: "I AM" STATEMENTS

Jesus frequently makes "I am" statements in John's Gospel. This repetition of the phrase recalls texts like Exodus 3:14 where God tells Moses his name, which is "I Am that I Am" or "I will be what I will be" (which is almost like God telling Moses to mind his own business). The significance in John is that the name "I am" subtly connects Jesus with Yahweh, the God of the Old Testament. Jesus is not merely a man doing good works but also God bringing both miracles and signs. 1. "I am the bread of life" (John 6:35) 2. "I am the light of the world" (John 8:12; 9:5) 3. "I am the door of the sheep" (John 10:7, 9) 4. "I am the good shepherd" (John 10:11, 14) 5. "I am the resurrection and the life" (John 11:25) 6. "I am the way, and the truth, and the life" (John 14:6) 7. "I am the true vine" (John 15:1)

JOHN: QUICK FACTS

• Was written, in part, to Christians who misunderstood Jesus' identity. • "John" was most likely the disciple "whom Jesus loved", the son of Zebedee and Salome, a Galilean fisherman from Bethsaida. • In Mark 3:17, Jesus nicknamed John and his brother James, "Sons of Thunder". • He was the disciple to whom Jesus Christ entrusted the care of his mother, Mary (John 19:26). • Many scholars believe the purpose of the Gospel is found in John 20:31 — "But these are written that you may believe that Jesus is the Messiah, the Son of God, and that by believing you may have life in his name." • John is the only Gospel account that does not share most of the same stories found in Matthew, Mark and Luke. • The narrative timeline of John's Gospel is different from the other Gospels. This shows that chronology is second to story in the Gospel narratives. • The Holy Spirit is most explicit in John's Gospel. • The Gospel of John was constructed based on the eyewitness accounts of John, son of Zebedee. • There are twenty-one chapters in John's Gospel, and it can be divided into four parts: The Prologue (1:1-18); The Book of Signs (1:19-12:50); The Book of Glory (13:1-20:31) — these eight chapters cover the week of Jesus' death and resurrection; The Epilogue (21:1-25)

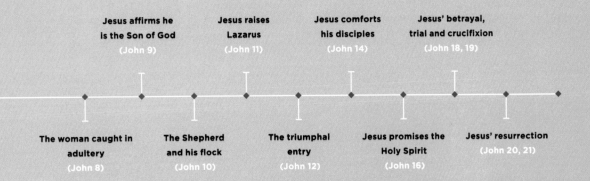

Jesus affirms he is the Son of God (John 9)

Jesus raises Lazarus (John 11)

Jesus comforts his disciples (John 14)

Jesus' betrayal, trial and crucifixion (John 18, 19)

The woman caught in adultery (John 8)

The Shepherd and his flock (John 10)

The triumphal entry (John 12)

Jesus promises the Holy Spirit (John 16)

Jesus' resurrection (John 20, 21)

KEY PATTERN: SIGNS AND MIRACLES

Miracles in the Gospel of John are referred to as "signs". They point to the identity of the Christ as the one sent by God. 1. Jesus turns water into wine in Cana (John 2:1-11) 2. Jesus heals an official's son in Capernaum (John 4:46-54) 3. Jesus heals at the pool of Bethesda in Jerusalem (John 5:1-18) 4. Jesus feeds the five thousand near the sea of Galilee (John 6:5-14) 5. Jesus walks on the water of the sea of Galilee (John 6:16-21) 6. Jesus heals a blind man in Jerusalem (John 9:1-7) 7. Jesus raises Lazarus from the dead in Bethany (John 11:1-45)

THEY SAW JESUS WALKING ON THE LAKE AND
COMING NEAR THE BOAT, AND THEY WERE
FRIGHTENED. BUT HE SAID TO THEM,
"IT IS I; DO NOT BE AFRAID."

John 6:19-20

Jesus Is

In the beginning was the Word, the Word was with God and the Word was God. He is the Messiah, the anointed One. His name is Emmanuel — God with us. He took on the position of a slave and appeared in human form. His name is the name above all names. His is the visible image of the invisible God. He existed before God made anything at all and is supreme over all creation. He is the One through whom God created everything in heaven and earth. He made the things we can see and the things we can't see — such as thrones, kingdoms, rulers and authorities in the unseen world. Everything has been created through him and for him. He existed before everything else began, and he holds all creation together. He is the head of the church, which is his body. He was raised from the dead as the first of all who will rise from the dead. He is the first in everything. In him lives all the fullness of God in human form. Through him God reconciled everything to himself. He made peace with everything in heaven and on earth by means of his blood on the cross. His act of righteousness brings right relationship with God and new life for everyone. He made us pure and holy, and he freed us from sin. He came as a servant to the Jews to show them that God is true to the promises he made to their ancestors. And he came so the Gentiles might also give glory to God for his mercy towards them. And so it is: all who put their faith in him share the same blessing Abraham received because of his faith. He cancelled the record of the charge against humanity and took it away by nailing it to the cross. He is the One who decided to shape the lives of all who love him from the beginning. He, Jesus, stands first in the line of humanity he restored. We see the original and intended shape of our lives in him. All who put their faith in His finished work on their behalf are healed, forgiven, and free — born anew.

"WHILE I WAS WITH

them, I kept them in your name, which you have given me. I have guarded them, and not one of them has been lost except the son of destruction, that the Scripture might be fulfilled. But now I am coming to you, and these things I speak in the world, that they may have my joy fulfilled in themselves. I have given them your word, and the world has hated them because they are not of the world, just as I am not of the world. I do not ask that you take them out of the world, but that you keep them from the evil one. They are not of the world, just as I am not of the world. Sanctify them in the truth; your word is truth. As you sent me into the world, so I have sent them into the world. And for their sake I consecrate myself, that they also may be sanctified in truth."

John 17:12-19

CONTRIBUTORS

FRONT
Unsplash
Rob Bye, Sam Wermut, Dey Mendoza, Colin Rex, Alex Iby, Joel Filipe, Tomas Anton Escobar

MATTHEW
Lead Photographer: Luke Williams
Satan shoot: Daniel Bastidas; Styling: Jose-Luis Alvarez [www.jlalvarez.com]
Models: Rob Thomas, Caitie Curwall, Charlotte Gower, Louis Darby, Shaq Taylor, Toni-Marie Hope
Prayer photography: Velizar Ivanov

Unsplash
Amanda Jordan, Nico Frey, Anton Tevajarvi, Xandtor, Timothy Paul Smith, Brunel Johnson, Efe Kurnaz,
David East, Jaime Street, Tom Sodoge, Henry Be, Monty A, Matthew Macquarrie, Max De Rohan Willner,
Verne Ho, Jaanus Jagomagi, Joshua K. Jackson, Benjamin Davies

MARK
Lead Photographer: Evan Rummel [www.allstreets.nyc]
Lead Location Photographer: Leonardo Garzón
Models: Clara Luthas, Criseli Saenz, Gabriel Wright, Keith Newton, Lizandri Almanzar,
Ronny Sujuko, Selani Thomas

Unsplash
Zac Ong, Luca Bravo, Felix Russell Saw, Jesse Williams, Alex Jodoin, Chris Barbalis, Jon Tyson,
Dean Rose, Andre Benz, The Vantage Point, Bobby Ghoshal

Editorial
The Life of Jesus: Phil Barnard
Gospel Information pages: Isaac Soon
Katie Newton-Darby, Ray Newton, Kathy Dyke

The Church, The Holy Spirit, The Bible
Art Direction: Judith Achumba-Wöllenstein @judithwoellenstein
Post-Production: Timothy Achumba @timothyachumba
Photographer: Sierra Pruitt @sierrapruitt
Models: Daniela Figueroa, Madara Stankus
Assistants: Isabella Figueroa, Andrea Afolabi

ABRUPT MEDIA
CREATING DYNAMIC RESOURCES TO INSPIRE A VISUAL GENERATION
WWW.ABRUPT-MEDIA.COM + @ABRUPTMEDIA

LUKE
Lead Photographer: River Bennett
Models: Sarah Moore, Sharon Christina Rørvik, TJ Stretten, Zion Bennett
The Gospel photography: Oleg Laptev

Unsplash
Sergee Bee, Ryan Loughlin, Mikael Kristenson, Juskteez Vu, Alan Lapisch,
Ana Pavlyuk, Milada Vigerova, Laura Cros, Annie Spratt, Ethan Ou, Ichsan, Jeremy Bishop,
Greyson Joralemon, Yatharth Vibhakar, Anna Popovic, Atlas Green, Velizar Ivanov,
Bulkan Evcimen, Diego Hernandez, Elti Meshua

JOHN
Lead Photographer: Leonardo Garzón @leogarzonph,
Sebastián Pérez @jsebastianpaezq, Oscar Ramirez @ramirezosc
Team: Ana Peralta Mejía, Laura Pantoja
Models: Paola Andrea Alonso R., Ana Peralta Mejía, Laura Peñuela,
Miguel Ángel Balcázar Camacho, Diego Alejandro Restrepo Villate, Julián Ramírez,
Laura Pantoja, Paola Vera, Sebastián Pérez, Leonardo Garzón
Grace photography: Imani Clovis

Unsplash
Cassi Josh, Jeremy Thomas, Aster Patagonia Glacier Irg, A Neqelaogm Jay Dantinne,
Ian Dooley, Art by Lonfeldt, Dan Gold, Ivana Cajina, Laura Vinck,
Christopher Burns, Laura Cros

Jesus Is photography: Nick Dunlap
Salvation Prayer photography: Thomas Charters

Creative Director
Carlos Darby

Graphic Design
Mark and Susanna Hickling
Mark Robertson, Julian Humphries

Artwork: Jonny Hutton @jonnyhuttonart
Icons: Noel Shiveley @noeltheartist

Thank you to the Unsplash photography
community for their generosity.

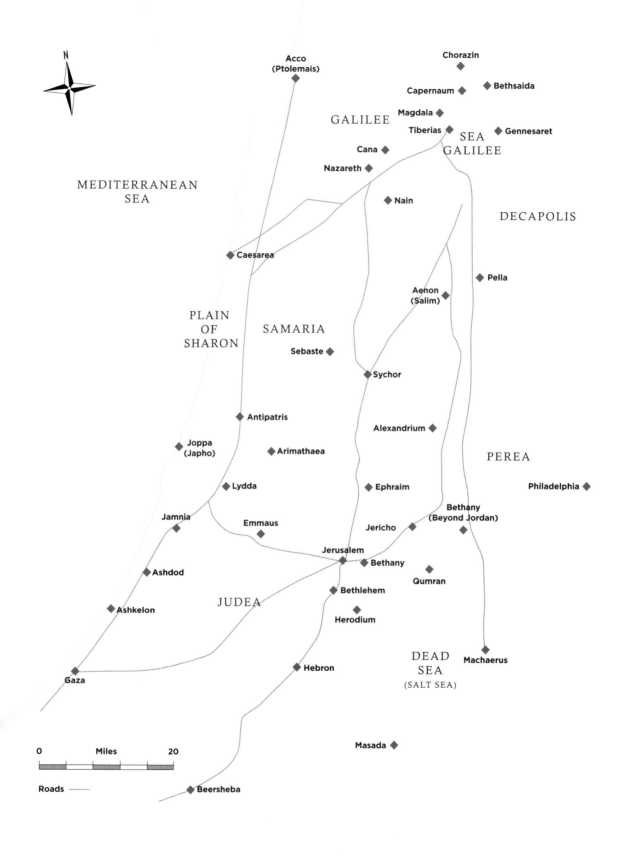

SALVATION PRAYER

There will be many people picking up this Bible who don't believe in God, or who are searching for answers and exploring the Christian perspective of life. Well, if that's you, and you have got to this point and want to make a decision to follow Jesus, we'd love to help you do that. Giving your life to God really is the most powerful decision you could ever make.

The Bible says that God "desires all people to be saved and to come to the knowledge of the truth" (1 Timothy 2:4). God desires for you to accept the finished work of Jesus and give your life to him. The Bible is his love letter to you, to show you how much he cares for you and desires to be in relationship with you.

So, if you'd like to make Jesus the Lord and Saviour of your life, simply pray this prayer, wherever you are:

Heavenly Father, thank you for your love for me and for sending Jesus to die on the cross for my sins. As I put my trust in Jesus, I am washed clean and made righteous. All my sins are forgiven. I accept your love and grace for me and ask you to be my Lord, I know that your goodness and mercy will follow me all the days of my life from this moment on. In Jesus' name. Amen.

That decision to follow Jesus is the best you could ever make, because it has brought you into a relationship with God. By dying on a cross and rising from the dead 2000 years ago, Jesus took upon himself all the sin, shame and condemnation of humanity, giving us true freedom and eternal life.

"IF YOU CONFESS WITH YOUR MOUTH THAT JESUS IS LORD AND BELIEVE IN YOUR HEART THAT GOD RAISED HIM FROM THE DEAD, YOU WILL BE SAVED. FOR WITH THE HEART ONE BELIEVES AND IS JUSTIFIED, AND WITH THE MOUTH ONE CONFESSES AND IS SAVED."

Romans 10:9-10